Atheism in Five Minutes

Religion in 5 Minutes

Series Editors
Russell T. McCutcheon
University of Alabama
Aaron W. Hughes
University of Rochester

Volumes in the Religion in 5 Minutes book series are each an opportunity for novice readers to benefit from the expertise of scholars, all addressing common questions about everything from Hinduism and Buddhism to paganism and Indigenous religion. Students and general readers will find here questions that they might ask—What is the oldest religion? Do all religions have scriptures?—all answered in a readable manner. Because each chapter can be read in about five minutes, the books offer ideal supplementary resources in classrooms or an engaging read for those curious about the world around them. And sooner or later, the assumptions entailed in the questions themselves take center stage for the contributors. With recommended readings in each chapter, the Religion in 5 Minutes book series meets readers where they are and invites them to entertain just how fascinating the world might be.

Published

Religion in Five Minutes
Edited by Aaron W. Hughes and Russell T. McCutcheon

Buddhism in Five Minutes
Edited by Elizabeth J. Harris

Hinduism in Five Minutes
Edited by Steven W. Ramey

Indigenous Religious Traditions in Five Minutes
Edited by Molly Bassett and Natalie Avalos

Forthcoming

African Diaspora Religions in Five Minutes
Edited by Emily D. Crews and Curtis J. Evans

Ancient Religion in Five Minutes
Edited by Andrew Durdin

Christianity in Five Minutes
Edited by Robyn Faith Walsh

Islam in Five Minutes
Edited by Edith Szanto

Judaism in Five Minutes
Edited by Tim Langille

Pagan Religions in Five Minutes
Edited by Suzanne Owen and Angela Puca

Atheism in Five Minutes

Edited by
Teemu Taira

eⓠuinox

SHEFFIELD UK   BRISTOL CT

Published by Equinox Publishing Ltd.

UK: Office 415, The Workstation, 15 Paternoster Row, Sheffield, South Yorkshire S1 2BX

USA: ISD, 70 Enterprise Drive, Bristol, CT 06010

www.equinoxpub.com

First published 2022

British Library Cataloguing-in-Publication Data

A catalogue record for this book is available from the British Library.

ISBN-13   978 1 80050 236 9   (hardback)
          978 1 80050 237 6   (paperback)
          978 1 80050 238 3   (ePDF)
          978 1 80050 259 8   (ePub)

Library of Congress Cataloging-in-Publication Data

Names: Taira, Teemu, editor.
Title: Atheism in five minutes / edited by Teemu Taira.
Description: Sheffield, South Yorkshire ; Bristol, CT : Equinox Publishing Ltd, 2022. | Series: Religion in 5 minutes | Includes bibliographical references and index. | Summary: "Atheism in Five Minutes offers insights into a number of commonly held questions about the ideas, practices and attitudes concerning atheism and atheists. The volume highlights approaches based on the study of religion, sociology, history, anthropology, politics and psychology. It also examines the implications and assumptions in common questions about atheism. Each essay is based on the latest research written by a leading scholar in the field. They offer concise and thoughtful answers along with suggestions for further reading. This book is Ideal for both classroom use and personal study"-- Provided by publisher.
Identifiers: LCCN 2022009839 (print) | LCCN 2022009840 (ebook) | ISBN 9781800502369 (hardback) | ISBN 9781800502376 (paperback) | ISBN 9781800502383 (epdf) | ISBN 9781800502598 (epub)
Subjects: LCSH: Atheism.
Classification: LCC BL2747.3 .A798 2022 (print) | LCC BL2747.3 (ebook) | DDC 211/.8--dc23/eng20220831
LC record available at https://lccn.loc.gov/2022009839
LC ebook record available at https://lccn.loc.gov/2022009840

Typeset by Scribe Inc.

Contents

Beliefs, values, and practices

Future

Preface

Teemu Taira

The study of atheism—including attendant phenomena and categories such as nonreligion and the secular—has been one of the emerging academic trends in the twenty-first century. Atheism is not only the subject of academic research; the topic has also enjoyed wider interest among media professionals and the general public. It has been one of my interests as well, both in research and in teaching, for more than fifteen years and increasingly so in the years that followed the initial conference of the Nonreligion and Secularity Research Network at Oxford University in 2009. In the beginning of summer 2020, when exchanging emails with one of the editors of the Religion in 5 Minutes series, Russell T. McCutcheon, I asked whether anyone had proposed editing a volume on atheism for the series. After some more emails involving another editor of the series, Aaron W. Hughes, and the publisher, I agreed to take the lead in the task of editing *Atheism in Five Minutes*.

This volume has sixty-four short chapters. Each chapter title poses a question, and the chapter contents then provide an answer that one should be able to read in "five minutes." The chapters consist of expert answers to the questions, on many occasions including reflections on the questions themselves. Each chapter has a short list of suggested articles and books that readers and course instructors may consult for further information.

The title indicates that atheism is the focus of the volume, but two issues should be kept in mind. First, there is no single definition of atheism that all authors agree upon. Atheism is usually defined in relation to belief—broadly as an absence of the belief in God, gods, or other supernatural beings or more narrowly as a denial of the existence of God—or understood as a term people use to identify themselves, sometimes situationally. It is left to the individual authors to use the definition they see fit, given the question they are dealing with, and several authors actually discuss this very matter, since the data they refer to may include more than one definition. It is one of the pedagogical tasks of this volume to demonstrate the heterogeneity of the field by letting the conceptual discussion flow. Second, atheism has not been understood as a limiting term. Related categories are also present, as certain entries attend to people who have been conceptualized as "nonreligious," "secular," or "unaffiliated." The starting point has been to include such discussion but specify when the author is referring to, for example, unaffiliated or "nones" rather than atheists. This may sound confusing to some—an alternative would have been to define atheism strictly and exclude everything else—but I believe that the more inclusive approach hones the skills of readers to pay attention to these often overlapping but slightly different terms.

The chapters in this volume follow the idea of *Religion in Five Minutes* (2017, edited by Aaron W. Hughes and Russell T. McCutcheon) in utilizing actual student questions when deciding what the volume should look like. With the help of my colleagues Alexandra Bergholm and Heikki Pesonen, I received more than two hundred questions from students who participated in the introductory course to the study of religion at the University of Helsinki, Finland, in 2020. The majority of the participants were first-year students in the Faculty of Theology's bachelor's program in theology and religious studies, but there were also students of the BA program in cultural studies (Faculty of Arts and Humanities), where the study of religion is also represented. A portion of the questions in this volume are taken directly from the students, but I have taken the liberty to divide some into two or three separate entries, and in certain cases, I have combined several questions into one. Some questions are also chosen from elsewhere because Finnish students may ask very different things than students in the United States, for example.

In choosing the chapter topics outside the actual student questions, I browsed several textbooks and handbooks dealing with atheism, secularism, and nonreligion and collected frequently recurring themes and topics that could serve as resources for good questions to raise in this volume. I also compiled a list of common stereotypes concerning atheism, reflecting on whether those should be answered here. I tried to remember typical questions that students and laypeople have had when I have been teaching about atheism and nonreligion or when I have been a speaker or discussant at nonacademic events. On this basis, I made a tentative list of questions. Due to my work schedule, this was done before I received the student questions from the introductory course. The students' questions provided me with a "reality check" as to whether the tentative list was useful as well as guidance on what should be added to the list. I decided which questions to include by reflecting on which ones might translate well for an international readership and what would be relevant for an international audience but had not been asked by Finnish students. The end result is an amalgam that combines student questions and my own deliberations regarding an international audience. In some cases, the individual authors have slightly refined a question. In other cases, the question has remained as is, and authors have then discussed why they found it problematic and explained why an alternative formulation could be more fruitful.

It should also be noted that the selection of questions does not determine the answers and their "situatedness." My aim was to have authors from multiple countries and research areas. Accordingly, there is great variation among the contributors, although the end result is quite Euro-American. One could argue that it accurately reflects the study of atheism, and I decided not to use variation as a forced criterion in seeking contributors for the individual questions. Instead, the first criterion was always to consider who might know enough about this particular topic and also be willing to contribute and then see during the process whether enough variation emerged "naturally."

The overall combination of questions, answers, and authors reflects the multidisciplinary nature of the research of the topic itself. My own background in the study of religion and my interests in sociological approaches and media are perhaps visible to the reader, but the contributors include scholars from a variety of fields, such as history, psychology, philosophy, anthropology, theology, and politics. While the questions asked in this volume by no means represent the whole of multidisciplinary studies of atheism, I see no need to apologize if the selection reflects my own deliberate choices. However, I have attempted to be inclusive enough that the selection tells us about both real novice questions and academic scholarship on atheism.

The questions have been divided into four main sections. The first section, "Conceptual and Historical Issues," introduces atheism and related categories, including some entries about the study of atheism. The second section, "Society, Politics, and Media," addresses how atheism is related to various socially significant issues, thus emphasizing sociological approaches, politics, and media studies. The third, "Beliefs, Values, and Practices," highlights atheism more on the individual level and combines views based on psychology, philosophy, and sociology. The final section, "Future," consists of the editor's concluding chapter, which speculates about the future of atheism.

I would like to thank the series editors for their overall support, which covers much more than this project. I would also like to thank Janet Joyce and Valerie Hall at Equinox for their encouragement. Finally, it is my pleasure to say thank you to all the contributors and note my gratitude to those who have helped me with their suggestions for potential authors.

Teemu Taira, senior lecturer in the study of religion,
University of Helsinki.

Conceptual and historical issues

1
What does the term "atheism" mean?

Nathan G. Alexander

On its face, trying to understand the meaning of the word "atheism" should be simple. One just needs to look at the ancient Greek roots of the word *atheos*, which combines *theos*, or "God," and the prefix *a-*, which means an absence or negation of the thing the prefix is attached to. In ancient Greece, therefore, the word referred to a lack of belief in or denial of God or gods. But the meaning was not so simple, even then, since the term could also mean someone who was abandoned or forsaken by the gods or someone who dishonored the gods.

Further questions can be raised about both parts of the word: *a-* and *theos*. As we will see, a crucial problem is whether the *a-* means a direct rejection of a thing or merely an indication of an absence or lack of belief in it. Likewise, some have argued that the *theos* part of the equation refers only to the God of monotheism in Abrahamic religions, like Judaism, Christianity, and Islam. Others have suggested it should apply to the entire range of gods and similar beings in polytheistic religions and even to broader categories like the divine or the supernatural. Some—like the nineteenth-century British atheist Charles Bradlaugh—have suggested that the term "God" is itself so fuzzy and impossible to define that to talk about denying "God" is nonsensical. Knowing the Greek roots of the word, therefore, does not necessarily offer a straightforward way to understand the meaning of the word.

The word "atheism" first jumped into European vernacular languages, including English, in the 1500s and 1600s, a time when a range of new vocabulary emerged to describe the diversity of religious (and irreligious) viewpoints during the upheaval of the Protestant Reformation. During the early modern period (roughly 1500 to 1800), there were few, if any, professed atheists. This meant the word was used almost always as a description of *someone else* rather than *oneself*, since "atheism" was seen as a scandalous thing, and to call oneself an atheist was to risk serious punishment.

For much of the term's history, since those doing the defining were opposed to atheism, atheism was seen as an active denial of God's existence. Because of this, sometimes early modern people even claimed there were no atheists, since it would be too illogical to deny God's existence! This definition of active denial was preferred because, in some ways, it made it more difficult to be an atheist. It was not enough, under this definition, for one to say there was no evidence for God's existence; one needed to present positive evidence that God did not exist.

However, by the 1800s, when atheists first began to make their arguments openly and use the label for themselves, some atheists rejected this formulation. They suggested that, actually, they simply did not believe in God. In this way, they suggested, the onus was not on them to prove God didn't exist; it was rather on Christians and other believers to offer proof that God *did* exist.

This distinction has since been called strong (or positive/hard) atheism versus weak (or negative/soft) atheism. The strong atheists are those who make a positive claim that God (or gods or the divine) definitely does not exist, whereas the weak atheists insist they simply lack a belief in God.

An added wrinkle is "agnosticism," a term coined in the late nineteenth century by the British scientist T. H. Huxley. For Huxley, to be agnostic was to admit a lack of knowledge. On the question of God's existence, to be agnostic was to suggest that the question was ultimately unknowable. In this way, there is considerable overlap between weak atheism and agnosticism, with the difference being that weak atheists suggest it could in theory be possible for new evidence to emerge for God's existence, while agnostics say this question is forever unknowable.

This distinction between strong and weak atheists raises a further question: Is atheism merely the absence of a world view, or is it a world view itself? In other words, are there positive propositions that atheists also espouse, such as a belief in materialism (the idea that the only thing that exists is matter)? Some authors even suggest it might be better to talk about "atheisms"—plural—rather than a singular "atheism." This allows for an ever-greater range of categories of world views, like scientific atheism, humanistic atheism, and so on.

How should we decide which definition to choose? Partly this depends on our goals. The way most dictionaries define a word is to examine how other people have used it. But even then, one must make a decision, since people may use the term in slightly different ways.

Scholars might want to choose a particular definition that they see as useful. For example, the definition given by the academic Stephen Bullivant for "atheism" is "an absence of belief in the existence of a God or gods," a definition that he says is based on "scholarly utility." In other words, this definition captures a certain range of viewpoints that would allow for effective scholarly study. Other scholars instead want to focus on those people who self-identify as "atheists," without forcing a rigid definition upon them.

Another reason might be political. An atheist activist, for example, might wish to define "atheism" in the broadest way possible in order to show that the number of atheists in the world is high, while supporters of theism might define it in such a way as to claim—as many Christians did in the early modern period—that there were actually no atheists at all. Theological or philosophical considerations might also weigh on the choice of definition. As we saw, opponents of atheism might stress a definition that makes it more difficult to be an atheist—for example, by demanding someone offer positive proof that God does not exist. Many atheists in turn might wish to reject this definition and offer one of their own.

But what is the *true, correct* definition of "atheism"? Though this chapter has offered lots of questions but few definitive answers, I hope that it has shown that there are different ways people might define the term and that it has revealed some of the major fault lines of these disagreements. Ultimately, words only have the definitions human beings give them. There are no objective definitions that somehow float above the messy world of human affairs. This means that definitions are something that people with different interests and viewpoints fight over. Which definitions become established tells us something about which groups have power in a certain society, if not necessarily anything about "truth."

About the author

Nathan G. Alexander is a writer and historian from Canada. He is the author of *Race in a Godless World: Atheism, Race, and Civilization, 1850–1914* (New York University Press / Manchester University Press, 2019).

Suggestions for further reading

In this book
See also chapters 2 (difference between the terms) and 7 (identity).

Elsewhere
Alexander, Nathan G. "Defining and Redefining Atheism: Dictionary and Encyclopedia Entries for 'Atheism' and Their Critics from the Early Modern Period to the Present." *Intellectual History Review* 30(2) (2020): 253–271.

Bullivant, Stephen. "Defining 'Atheism.'" In *The Oxford Handbook of Atheism*, edited by Stephen Bullivant and Michael Ruse, 11–21. Oxford: Oxford University Press, 2013.

Durkin, Philip. "Linguistic History of the Terms 'Atheism' and 'Atheist.'" In *The Cambridge History of Atheism*, edited by Stephen Bullivant and Michael Ruse, 11–13. Cambridge: Cambridge University Press, 2021.

Vainio, Olli-Pekka, and Aku Visala. "Varieties of Unbelief: A Taxonomy of Atheistic Positions." *Neue Zeitschrift für Systematische Theologie und Religionsphilosophie* 57(4) (2015): 483–500.

2

What is the difference between "atheism," "agnosticism," "nonreligion," and "secular"?

Christopher R. Cotter

The key term "atheism," around which this volume is organized, is discursively entangled with a wide range of related terms in popular and academic discourse in English. These include, but are not limited to, "agnosticism," "antireligion," "disbelief," "irreligion," "nonbelief," "nonreligion," "secular," "secularism," "secularity," "secularization," and "unbelief." This chapter introduces three of these entangled terms—"agnosticism," "nonreligion," and "secular"—in some detail before mapping the similarities and differences in different contexts. I shall dispense with an explicit discussion of the meaning of "atheism," as this has been addressed in the previous chapter. The take-home message throughout should be that difference is in the eye of the beholder and depends on who is utilizing the terms and for what purpose.

"Agnosticism" was coined in 1869 by English biologist and anthropologist Thomas Henry Huxley. The term is derived from the classical Greek *a-* ("without") and *gnosis* ("knowledge or insight concerning the divine, transcendent, and so on"). In Huxley's model, agnosticism was a method, not a creed, and involved an attitude of following reason to its limits but not presuming to make conclusions that are not sufficiently demonstrated or demonstrable. Thus, one might remain "agnostic" regarding various truth claims—religion related or otherwise. In contemporary usage, the term has been taken up as an identification, signaling a variety of positions relating to the world beyond empirical experience. An agnostic might "not know" or think that "we cannot know" the truth of various assertions, they might withhold judgment on the same assertions, or they might simply not care.

The term "secular" has its roots in the medieval period in Christian Europe, where a distinction developed between religious and secular space and time, with the former referring to monastic life and the latter taking on an "ordinary" or "worldly" quality. During the Enlightenment, buoyed by the associated colonial activities of European powers, the notion of plural "religions" developed alongside the idea of a secular public space from which these religions could be differentiated. "Secular" as we know it today can be applied to a broad range of phenomena where religion is seen as of secondary or no concern. Paradoxically, then, while the term describes a state of being that is unrelated to religion, the term itself is inextricably linked to religion. Individuals might identify themselves as secular in various contexts to indicate that they are unconcerned with matters relating to religion or that they are, in Max Weber's phrasing, "religiously unmusical." Or they might indicate a "secularist" stance: advocating that religion should be kept private and particularly that it should not interfere with the machinations of the political state.

While the previous two terms are utilized relatively frequently in nonacademic contexts, "nonreligion" is a much more recent addition to the academic lexicon. In everyday speech, people might use the phrase "I'm nonreligious" or "I'm not religious" to indicate something similar to "I'm secular." Academically, the word has emerged in the past decade or so to serve as a broad umbrella term for indicating a "meaningful" difference in contextual notions of religion. Lois Lee has used the example of "nonviolence" to capture this sense of meaningfulness—the term is relational to things that are typically considered violent. Therefore, nonreligion is not simply "everything that is not religious" (which is one potential interpretation of "secular") but includes a whole host of phenomena—or aspects of them—that are in relationships of difference to the category of religion. This would include atheism-in-practice (which tends to be antireligious) as well as atheism-by-definition (because theism is generally considered an aspect of religion-related traditions).

With these brief discussions, you should already be getting a sense of the similarities and differences these terms have with atheism and that making these distinctions is not necessarily a simple matter. In some senses, "atheism" and "agnosticism" are clearly related in that they concern the domain of "belief" and both might be considered forms of "nonreligion" or "secular" outlooks. Functionally, one might ask what the difference is between stances of atheism and agnosticism when both ostensibly involve not believing in deities (and, potentially, a host of other things as well). Indeed, even the prominent "New Atheist" Richard Dawkins attests to technically being an agnostic (leaning toward atheism) in matters relating to the existence of gods, since fully committing to atheism requires (in his view) a level of conviction that is unwarranted based on the (lack of) evidence. This has led some to dub agnosticism a milder form of "negative atheism" (the supposedly milder "lack" of belief, contrasted with an explicit "positive" rejection). But others would argue that agnosticism indicates a clear philosophical outlook, distinct from (a)theistic alternatives, that can be appealing to postmodern relativists and rational materialists alike (but for quite different reasons).

When considering the relationship of atheism to nonreligion and the secular, it is perhaps useful to consider these latter words in terms of theoretical distance from the category of religion, with nonreligion being in a position of meaningful difference and secular covering phenomena that are further removed. Although the term "atheism" designates a relationship to a particular form of "theism" and is, thus, not inherently antagonistic to the concept of "religion," in practice, the term tends to be a placeholder for a particular antireligious and antisupernaturalist attitude that places into a meaningful relationship of difference to religion—making it a form of nonreligion. This begs the question, Is atheism secular? Also, the level of engagement required in many contexts to identify as an atheist implies a level of engagement with theism and related concepts that might mean that "devout" theists and atheists have more in common than the more "nominal" (secular?) of their fellow theists and atheists. Furthermore, some "religious" traditions—forms of Buddhism being the prime example—can be described as "atheist," meaning that in some contexts, atheism might be neither secular nor a form of nonreligion. And if we define religion in terms of ritual, ultimate concern, or some other aspect, we might similarly struggle to fit many atheists into these boxes.

Finally, if we move beyond the realm of academic theorizing, we might well find some "religious" adherents for whom the distinction between the antagonistic forces of atheism, agnosticism, nonreligion, and the secular is functionally meaningless, as well as, of course, those who do meaningfully differentiate between these categories or even apply some (or all) of them to themselves. How one differentiates between these terms depends on one's motivations and one's position in the field of relations between them in a given context.

About the author

Christopher R. Cotter is a staff tutor and lecturer in religious studies and sociology at the Open University in the United Kingdom.

Suggestions for further reading

In this book
See also chapters 1 (term) and 11 (New Atheism).

Elsewhere
Blankholm, Joseph. "The Political Advantages of a Polysemous Secular." *Journal for the Scientific Study of Religion* 53(4) (2014): 775–790.

Cotter, Christopher R. *The Critical Study of Non-religion: Discourse, Identification and Locality.* London: Bloomsbury, 2020.

Lee, Lois. *Recognizing the Non-religious: Reimagining the Secular.* Oxford: Oxford University Press, 2015.

Lee, Lois, and Stephen Bullivant. *The Oxford Dictionary of Atheism.* Oxford: Oxford University Press, 2016.

3

Why have researchers become interested in atheism?

Stephen Bullivant

Atheism is, as readers will surely agree, an important, interesting, and intricate subject. Historically, philosophically, sociologically, politically, psychologically—you name it—there's a lot there worth digging into. This book is proof enough of this. And there's nothing terribly new about it. Atheism has been around a long time, certainly as an idea but also as a belief, or lack of one, held by significant numbers of people.

It is not true to say that the academic study of atheism only really began, say, fifteen years ago: its status as a "hot topic" has waxed and waned in different places and for different reasons. But it *is* the case that recent years have seen a significant, sustained, and "disciplinary widespread" upswing in interest, especially in the fields of history and several of the social sciences. (To give a personal example, when I first got seriously interested in the subject in the mid-2000s, it didn't take me long to catch up on roughly 80–90 percent of everything published in English in history, sociology, or psychology over the past hundred years. Now I struggle to keep up with what's published month by month in one of those disciplines, let alone all three.) Even in the one scholarly field where atheism has arguably been a constant topic of concern—that is, the philosophy of religion—one can certainly note increasingly direct attention on atheism and related subjects (e.g., agnosticism) in their own right.

But why? Academic fad, fashion, and sheer bloody-mindedness cannot—indeed, must not ever—be discounted as an explanation. But there's more to it as well. Two main factors, I think, have contributed to the sudden surge of interest, and these two, along with a third factor, have united to keep it going and growing.

The first is perhaps the most obvious. The new interest in atheism can be dated, roughly, to the mid-2000s: the time when a good number of today's "old-timers" (myself included) began getting interested in the topic.

This was also the time that atheism-with-a-capital-*A* gained a huge amount of attention thanks to a slew of surprise best sellers, with Sam Harris's *The End of Faith* (2004) the first and Richard Dawkins's millions-selling *The God Delusion* (2006) the best known. This so-called New Atheism, coupled with growing media attention given to "the rise of the nones" (i.e., the percentage of people identifying as having "no religion" on surveys—not all of whom, of course, are atheists), meant that atheism, nonreligion, and allied topics were hard to ignore, *even* for so myopic and culturally off-trend a group of people as academics. Fortuitously, these topics were also becoming much easier to study. In the past, it was difficult to find groups of atheists: unlike religious folks, they tend not to congregate together at a specific time and place each week. However, the internet, which since its earliest days has long had a thriving atheist presence, opened up both new means of finding and recruiting atheist participants and exciting, original, and easily accessible online field sites; blogs, LISTSERVs, forums, and social media platforms (which also began taking off in a big way around this time), such as Twitter, Facebook, and YouTube, have all served atheism researchers well.

Second and relatedly, the emphasis on *identity* among atheists and fellow travelers (as among many other groups) is another key consideration. This "atheist pride," with its emphasis on the importance of "coming out," already prominent in the New Atheists, has in turn been fueled by research into antiatheist stigma and prejudice. Academic researchers have traditionally been attracted to minority groups, especially ones perceived to be objects of marginalization and discrimination. Add to this the fact that atheists, agnostics, and "nones" have long been well represented among social science faculty—not least among those whose job it is to study religion—and it is no surprise that growing numbers of (especially) American and European sociologists, psychologists, anthropologists, and political scientists might feel "nudged" to turn their professional attentions to these topics. By no means are *all* of those studying atheism themselves atheists or something similar (indeed, I am not one myself), but a good proportion are.

In themselves, these two factors are not enough to explain the sustained and seemingly ever-growing interest in atheism among researchers. Academic trends come and go. A sudden upsurge of interest and excitement in a topic is not enough to create a solid, self-sustaining tradition of study: academia's no-man's-land is littered with the corpses of failed subfields. This is where our third factor, building upon and cementing the first two, comes in.

As a nucleus of isolated scholars, many of them doctoral students actively looking for an underresearched field to make their own, began working on these topics, they started seeking one another out (another catalytic effect of the internet). They soon started putting together small events, one-day conferences, email mailing lists, online bibliographies—as much to find and encourage other kindred spirits as to publicize their own work. The fact that atheism was a topic of wide popular and media interest further helped them: magazines, newspapers, book and journal editors, and publishers were actively looking for "experts" in the area—*not* the kind of interest that doctoral or other early career researchers are used to receiving. It also helped, of course, that a great deal of this emerging research was excellently done: empirically rigorous, methodologically innovative, theoretically insightful. In short, all of this contributed to "nonreligion studies" rapidly becoming *a thing*, in turn attracting more and more people (and not incidentally, grant funding!) into the fold: the field is so large, varied, and relatively unstudied that there's plenty to go around.

Of course, there's rather more detail that could be added to this story—there always is. But insofar as the social-scientific study of atheism is itself amenable to a kind of social-scientific "origins story," these are, I think, the most important plot points.

About the author

Stephen Bullivant is a professor of theology and the sociology of religion at St Mary's University, United Kingdom. His books include *The Oxford Dictionary of Atheism* (coauthored with Lois Lee; Oxford University Press, 2016), *The Oxford Handbook of Atheism* (Oxford University Press, 2013), and *The Cambridge History of Atheism* (Cambridge University Press, 2021) (both coedited with Michael Ruse).

Suggestions for further reading

In this book
See also chapters 4 (promoting), 7 (identity), and 11 (New Atheism).

Elsewhere
Bullivant, Stephen. "Explaining the Rise of 'Nonreligion Studies': Subfield Formation and Institutionalization within the Sociology of Religion." *Social Compass* 67(1) (2020): 86–102.

Cimino, Richard, and Christopher Smith. *Atheist Awakening: Secular Activism and Community in America.* New York: Oxford University Press, 2014.

Stark, Rodney. "Atheism, Faith, and the Social Scientific Study of Religion." *Journal of Contemporary Religion* 14(1) (1999): 41–62.

Taira, Teemu. "New Atheism as Identity Politics." In *Religion and Knowledge: Sociological Perspectives*, edited by Mathew Guest and Elisabeth Arweck, 97–113. Farnham: Ashgate, 2012.

4

Are researchers of atheism promoting atheism?

Lois Lee

Researchers of atheism are often drawn into debates about whether their work has an atheist or nonreligious agenda. And they are just as often accused of having a theist or religious agenda. Both can be true, but regardless of that, the fact that these accusations are being made at all tells us something interesting about the strength of feeling that both religious and nonreligious attitudes and world views excite. It also hints at how the dominant way of thinking about the relationship between religious believers and nonbelievers, past and present, focuses on competition, hostility, and antagonism, when in fact these relationships are and have been far more diverse and far more complex than this simple story suggests.

All of this is interesting, but what marks the study of atheism much more than the theist or atheist views of its researchers is those same researchers' commitment to a standard of neutrality in their work. This means that, generally, the answer to this question is no: by and large, researchers of atheism are not promoting atheism. This is especially true of researchers in the social sciences and humanities. Exceptions may be found in theology or philosophy, disciplines that have significant branches that are explicitly normative—that is, branches that seek to say not only how things are or could be but how they *ought* to be. These disciplines are, however, explicit about this aspect of their work, and scholars within them are seeking to promote atheism or theism not as an end in itself but as an outcome of their inquiries. They are also the exceptions that prove the rule.

Focusing on those disciplines in which objectivity and neutrality are crucial scholarly standards, the study of atheism within them attempts to be free of any judgment about atheism, positive or negative. Indeed, researchers in these disciplines acknowledge that personal biases always exist, and it is therefore a central activity of their research to find ways to prevent these biases from undermining the validity of their findings.

Researchers have developed various strategies for this. One approach is to adopt "methodological atheism" in their research designs. The *Oxford Dictionary of Atheism* (*ODA*) describes this as "a device used by empirical researchers, especially in sociology and other human sciences, to bracket metaphysical questions for the purposes of research and focus exclusively on naturalist explanations for religious phenomena." That is, because these researchers are interested in the natural and social world, they use methodological atheism to focus on "this-worldly" questions (e.g., How many people in the world describe themselves as "atheist"? What impact does being an atheist have on a person's well-being?). And because they strive to be neutral toward any metaphysical or supernatural claims—including the denial of these claims—they design their studies to come to this-worldly answers to these questions.

And they do not stop there. Methodological atheism—and related approaches like methodological agnosticism—are constantly being debated. Do these approaches, for example, actually marginalize or ignore elements of religious experience by "bracketing" them from research? Do they in fact privilege naturalist over supernatural explanations for phenomena? Scholars debate these issues in order to make sure that strategies to manage the impact of their own theistic or atheistic outlooks do not end up creating new misdirections or blind spots in research. It is never possible to achieve perfect objectivity—that is a truism in any kind of research, in every field, in every discipline. But these ongoing debates show how seriously researchers take the standard of objectivity: acknowledging that these attempts fall short and need to be constantly reviewed is one of the most important ways of upholding that standard.

These strategies were initially developed by researchers of religion, but the same ideas are used by researchers of atheism. And it means that they are as applicable to the partner question to whether researchers of atheism promote atheism: Are researchers of atheism promoting *theism*? For example, in the twenty-first century, the study of atheism has sometimes been provoked by controversial public atheists such as Richard Dawkins and Sam Harris, whose outlooks have strongly antireligious aspects and have been accused of problematic, even racist attitudes toward some religions. Some research has been motivated by critical and/or proreligious responses to this material, and these motivations have therefore shaped research agendas, be it through the questions that scholars prioritize or how they present their findings.

Certainly, it is as possible that theistic interests might shape—or undermine—the study of atheism as atheistic ones. The study of atheism has been led by religious organizations: it was the Vatican that held the first major social science conference on the topic in 1969. Even the concepts we use—"atheism," "unbelief," "nonbeliever," "secularity"—arise out of religious traditions and religious ways of thinking about what it means to be atheistic or nonreligious. And some research that has been criticized for displaying proatheist attitudes is responding to antiatheist research that preceded it. For example, some scholars are emphatic about the moral capacity of atheists in a way that responds to a long tradition of research shaped by a religious concern that atheists do *not* have the same moral capacity as theists.

Nevertheless, the idea that researchers who are interested in atheism are promoting atheism is widespread. Researchers of atheism are frequently assumed to be themselves atheists, while organizations like the Nonreligion and Secularity Research Network, the leading international scholarly organization for the study of atheism (among other things), are sometimes mistaken for campaigning rather than researching groups.

One important factor may be simply that the empirical study of atheism is a relatively new field, and, for now, the history of academic and popular engagement with atheism is massively weighted toward arguments for and against atheism, which have a much longer lineage. The study of atheism has a way to go to come out of that shadow. Another factor is that, like politics, theism and atheism do provoke strong feelings in many people, researchers included, and that means research in these areas is always at particular risk of promoting or demoting those feelings and attitudes.

For all these reasons, it is important that researchers think carefully and explicitly about how their own work may be promoting their personal viewpoints, even when they do not intend that to be the case. For these reasons too, we as readers also need to approach research findings—in these fields of research as in others—with a vigilant and critical eye.

About the author

Lois Lee is a senior lecturer in religious studies at the University of Kent and the founder of the Nonreligion and Secularity Research Network. Her books include *Recognizing the Non-religious: Reimagining the Secular* (Oxford University Press, 2015) and *Negotiating Religion: Cross-Disciplinary Perspectives* (Routledge, 2017).

Suggestions for further reading

In this book
See also chapters 3 (researchers), 5 (study of atheism), and 11 (New Atheism).

Elsewhere
Bullivant, Stephen. "Explaining the Rise of 'Nonreligion Studies': Subfield Formation and Institutionalization within the Sociology of Religion." *Social Compass* 67(1) (2020): 86–102.

Lee, Lois, and Stephen Bullivant. *The Oxford Dictionary of Atheism*. Oxford: Oxford University Press, 2016.

5

What are the most common ways to study atheism?

Lois Lee

The study of atheism underwent a major change a little over a decade ago. Before then, atheists had mostly been of interest to social scientists merely as a way of assessing how far *religion* had declined as a result of secularization. There is nothing wrong with this, and underlying this apparently simple goal is a complicated area of research with much to study: as well as noticing the number of people who have atheist beliefs or atheist identities, researchers might be interested, for example, in how committed atheists are to their atheism or whether religion still plays a role in their lives—or even in their atheism!—despite their atheistic beliefs or identities.

Nevertheless, all of these inquiries—and the secularization theory itself—are religion-centric. Even though they are concerned with the declining role of religion in mental and social life, secularization-focused approaches adopt an exclusive understanding of religion as a sole example of a type of human experience, thought, and action—one that has no meaningful equivalents. In this outlook, atheists are just that: people without theism. Even though much is possible in the study of atheism in relation to religious decline, this way of thinking also discourages more expansive approaches to the study of atheism. For many years, the typical way to study atheism was to head-count atheists and not much else besides.

In the last decade, that has all changed. Researchers have become much more interested in people who describe themselves or are described as atheists in their own right and for their own sake. What does being an atheist actually entail? What are the nature and diversity of belief, identity, and practice underlying this deceptively simple category? If atheists are one of the world's largest "religious" populations, what kind of discrete traditions are associated with atheism, and what are the similarities and differences between them? Do atheists of different "traditions" come to their atheism for different reasons, and if so, where does that leave secularization as the main way of understanding the shift from theistic to nontheistic world views seen in many parts of the world over recent centuries?

These are big questions, and the shift toward atheist-centered research has massively expanded not only what we want to know about atheism but how we study it too.

One of the major changes of the twenty-first century is a much larger and more developed place for "qualitative" ways of studying atheism: research methods that are designed to understand the detail and texture of atheist experience. The method of participant observation, which has its roots in anthropology, has become increasingly important as atheism is recognized as a cultural phenomenon and not merely the absence of one. This means researchers can embed themselves in a community or social network that has significant atheistic elements and observe the nature of that atheism and how it shapes the interactions of the people involved.

This method of study is familiar from the study of religion, and transferring it to the study of atheism has often seen a focus on "congregational" forms of atheism. Researchers have worked, for example, with those who gather at the in-person meetings of community humanist organizations or with new movements like the Sunday Assembly, dubbed "the atheist church" by the media. They have also explored social interactions that take place online, though in general the study of atheism and media is one of the areas most ripe for expansion and development in the field. Participant observation also has the potential to better understand atheism outside of these organizational settings.

But atheism frequently lacks the kind of institutional history associated with theistic traditions, and the way it emerges in individual and social lives is therefore often diffuse and hard to predict. In many places in the world, atheists do not tend to congregate together as atheists. They do not necessarily even think of themselves as atheists, even when atheism is something that impacts their lives. Atheistic outlooks are, for example, discussed within friendship groups, but perhaps only occasionally and without obvious triggers. For this reason, in-depth interviews have played a central role in the new study of atheism. Interviews allow researchers to access aspects of atheist life and experience that they may only be dimly conscious of or that may only come to the fore at particular moments.

Prominent atheistic and nonreligious movements have increased scholarly interest in the cultural manifestations of atheism—in politics, media, and the arts. The diversity of these cultures has only recently been emphasized in research, with scholars beginning to broaden their focus from the small number of largely British and US white men most associated with the New Atheist movement that came to prominence in the first decade of the twenty-first century. As well as considering the diversity of atheist culture today, this means reconsidering conventional and colonial histories of atheism that focus on the development of (some) Western philosophy and science to the exclusion of all else.

None of this means that head counts don't matter. In fact, they matter more and have become much more sophisticated as our understanding of atheism has improved. They are no longer merely concerned with who is not theistic: they want to understand this population in much more detail. Surveys are increasingly used, for example, to provide much more complicated profiles of who atheists are, to map atheist populations across countries and demographic groups, and to understand differences within them. The need to expand from a research base in the West and especially the United States has become a major concern, as has the diversification of the study of atheism from the white men who once dominated atheist populations within those contexts but have ceased to do so as atheist populations grow.

This brief summary ignores some important areas of activity and innovation. Cognitive scientists, for example, are also working to explore atheism by investigating similarities and differences between the cognitive structures and pathways associated with theism and atheism. But across the board, the study of atheism bears the mark of this shift from the idea that atheists are not very interesting in and of themselves to the new idea that atheism—or the populations we describe as atheist—involves a diversity of psychological, social, and cultural phenomena that have the power to shape how individuals experience the world around them and the societies they live in.

About the author

Lois Lee is a senior lecturer in religious studies at the University of Kent and the founder of the Nonreligion and Secularity Research Network. Her books include *Recognizing the Non-religious: Reimagining the Secular* (Oxford University Press, 2015) and *Negotiating Religion: Cross-Disciplinary Perspectives* (Routledge, 2017).

Suggestions for further reading

In this book
See also chapters 3 (researchers), 4 (promoting), and 6 (measuring).

Elsewhere

Bullivant, Stephen. "Explaining the Rise of 'Nonreligion Studies': Subfield Formation and Institutionalization within the Sociology of Religion." *Social Compass* 67(1) (2020): 86–102. https://doi.org/10.1177/0037768619894815.

Bullivant, Stephen, Miguel Farias, Jonathan Lanman, and Lois Lee. *Understanding Unbelief: Atheists and Agnostics around the World*. London: St Mary's University, Twickenham, 2019. https://kar.kent.ac.uk/78815/.

Bullivant, Stephen, and Michael Ruse, eds. *The Oxford Handbook of Atheism*. Oxford: Oxford University Press, 2013.

6

How should atheism be measured?

Ryan T. Cragun

Measuring atheism is somewhat tricky because atheism is the absence of something—the absence of the belief in a god, gods, or a higher power. A common way of thinking about atheism in comparison to belief in a god, gods, or higher powers is to compare it to hair colors. If belief in the Christian God is like having red hair, belief in Zeus and the Greek pantheon is like having brown hair, and belief in the Japanese kami is like having blond hair, then atheism is like being bald. Atheism is not a type of belief in the supernatural; it's the absence of such belief.

Of course, it is possible to measure *how* bald someone is. Someone could be completely bald or just beginning to lose their hair. In that sense, it is possible to measure *how* atheistic someone is. Does someone reject the existence of just one of the gods (e.g., Mercury, the Roman god of financial gain) out of the many gods that have been postulated? Do they reject most of the gods (e.g., they believe in the Norse gods but reject all the others)? Do they reject all the gods but one, which is the position of most monotheists (i.e., Christians, Muslims, and Jews)? Or do they reject all the gods, which is typically what is meant by atheism?

Likewise, it is possible to measure how confident or certain someone is in their atheism. Confidence or certainty in the nonexistence of a god or gods can range from extremely confident to not confident at all. An atheist may be extremely confident that Osiris, the Egyptian god of fertility and the afterlife, does not exist but may be less confident that the creator deity postulated by deism—a deity that does not intervene in the natural world—does not exist.

This is often when agnosticism is introduced into discussions about the supernatural, but it shouldn't be. Agnosticism refers to the absence (*a-*) of knowledge (*-gnosis*) and has nothing to do with confidence or certainty about the existence of gods. To return to the baldness analogy, agnosticism would be the position of someone who had never seen, felt, touched, or otherwise sensed or measured hair and had no way of ever measuring hair—they cannot know if hair exists because they have no knowledge of hair and no way of gaining such knowledge. In this sense, agnosticism isn't a measure of one's confidence in the belief or absence of the belief in gods but rather a position on whether gods are knowable. Thus, someone can be both an atheist (lack belief in a god) and an agnostic (not believe that knowledge of a god is possible).

What atheism is not is a religious affiliation or religious identity. As noted, atheism is a position vis-à-vis the existence of a god, gods, or higher powers. Religious affiliation is a self-stated alignment with a religious organization, like the Catholic Church, Shinto, or Islam. It is possible for someone to be both a Catholic and an atheist. Identifying as Catholic simply means that one claims to affiliate with a religious organization; it does not indicate that such an individual adheres to all the tenets and beliefs of that organization. There are atheist Muslims, atheist Buddhists, atheist Mormons, and so on. Some surveys include atheism in their list of religious affiliations when they ask people to identify their religion. This reflects a lack of understanding of atheism on the part of the people who designed the survey. If someone is an atheist *and* has no religious affiliation, that individual should be given the option of "no religious affiliation" or "none" when asked about their religious affiliation and then should be asked about their belief in a god, gods, or higher powers in a separate question.

It is the case that some people, when asked about their religion, respond that they are atheists. This, too, is a misrepresentation of atheism. The individuals who do this may be aware that atheism is not a religion but may intend to convey a specific message to those asking the question—that they both do not have a religious affiliation and do not believe in a god, gods, or higher powers. In this sense, atheism can be an identity someone holds—an identity that conveys their rejection of both religious affiliation and god belief. But atheism is not a religious affiliation.

Finally, there are multiple ways to be an atheist. One can learn about a specific god, such as Mlondolozi, the creator deity in a number of African cultures, and reject the existence of that god. This is often referred to as "positive" atheism—a positive assertion about the nonexistence of a deity is being made. In contrast, someone may have never heard of the apu—the mountain spirits of the Quechua people of Peru—and, as a result, not believe in the apu. This is often referred to as "negative" atheism—someone lacks belief in a god not because they are asserting that god's nonexistence but because they have never heard of the god. Given the many gods that have been postulated—estimates vary from tens of thousands to tens of millions—most people are negative atheists toward countless gods simply because they have never heard of those gods.

To summarize, atheism is not a religion; it is the absence of belief in a god, gods, or higher powers. To measure atheism, people should be asked their views toward a specific god, all gods, or supernatural/higher powers. As a follow-up, people could be asked how confident they are in their belief or nonbelief in a god, gods, or higher powers. Additionally, people could be asked whether they believe someone can know whether gods exist, which would capture agnosticism. Finally, people could be asked whether they have heard of specific gods as a measure of positive or negative atheism. Such a battery of questions would provide a comprehensive measure of someone's atheism.

About the author

Ryan T. Cragun is a professor of sociology at the University of Tampa. His research focuses on Mormonism and the nonreligious and has been published in various scholarly journals. He is also the author of several books.

Suggestions for further reading

In this book
See also chapters 1 (term), 5 (study of atheism), and 12 (atheistic religions).

Elsewhere
Cragun, Ryan T. "Questions You Should Never Ask an Atheist: Towards Better Measures of Nonreligion and Secularity." *Secularism and Nonreligion* 8 (2019). https://secularismandnonreligion.org/articles/10.5334/snr .122/.

Schnell, Tatjana. "Dimensions of Secularity (DoS): An Open Inventory to Measure Facets of Secular Identities." *International Journal for the Psychology of Religion* 25(4) (2015): 272–292.

Smith, George H. *Atheism: The Case against God*. Amherst, NY: Prometheus, 1980.

7

When did it become possible to identify as an atheist?

Gavin Hyman

The most straightforward answer to this question is that it first became possible to identify as an atheist in the eighteenth century. It is widely thought that the French philosopher Denis Diderot (1713–1784) was one of the first intellectuals to describe himself as an atheist and that he was one of the first to develop a systematic atheistic philosophy. He had not always been an atheist and, at various points in his life, would be more accurately characterized as a theist, a deist, or a pantheist. His thought evolved, and only gradually did it emerge as being explicitly atheistic. But ultimately, he did deny the existence of God and sought to develop a philosophy that had no need for, and made no reference to, God. As a self-proclaimed atheist, Diderot therefore paved a way for others to follow.

This answer must, however, be qualified on a number of fronts. For one thing, even if not explicitly described as "atheistic," various forms of doubt, skepticism, and unbelief may be found much earlier than this. Indeed, they became increasingly widespread in Europe from the early seventeenth century onward, coinciding with the birth of modernity. Skeptics, doubters, and "libertines" may be found in various parts of Europe from around the 1630s onward. Furthermore, as the historian Alec Ryrie has recently shown, evidence has even been found of various forms of doubt, skepticism, and unbelief in Europe in the medieval period, but these instances were always underground and unofficial, being found in isolated pockets among the general populace and rarely being given explicit or official intellectual expression. Going back further still to the ancient Greek and Roman world, one may find instances of thinkers questioning the existence or nature of the gods. They were rare individuals, and they rarely put their theories into practice or developed them systematically, but they nonetheless existed. In all of these cases, it is important to note that such individuals would not have described themselves as "atheists."

Second, the term "atheism" itself also predates Diderot, although its meaning in these times was somewhat different. The term was being used in the sixteenth century to denote various forms of religious heresy, such as the denial of divine providence, rather than an outright denial of the existence of God. Again as Ryrie has noted, the term "atheism" began to be used around this time to refer to those who *live as if* there were no God rather than those who outright deny, in an intellectual or rational sense, the existence of God. By the early seventeenth century, it was beginning to be used to denote skeptics as well as heretics, and by the late seventeenth century, it had become the accepted term to refer to those who outright denied the existence of God. But it is generally acknowledged that what all these early usages have in common is that the word was being used as an accusation or as a pejorative term of abuse. It had not yet become a positive term for self-identification, and it was in this respect that Diderot was innovative. Although by the time he was writing, the word's meaning had changed to denote an outright denial of the existence of God, he sought to claim what had previously been a term of abuse and turn it into a positive and respectable badge of self-identification.

But old ways of thinking are slow to die, and for many years, the term "atheism" carried negative connotations, not only because of its denial of a still dominant theism, but also because it continued to be associated with subversion, revolution, and violence. These associations had been planted in people's minds by the French Revolution, an atheistic revolution marked by violence and terror. The association was perhaps reinforced by the philosophy of Karl Marx in the nineteenth century, whose revolutionary political philosophy was explicitly atheistic in character. It is perhaps not surprising, therefore, that nineteenth-century thinkers who wanted to signal their rejection of theism sought to develop terms other than atheism. In 1869, Thomas Huxley coined the term "agnosticism." He was motivated to stake out a philosophical ground that was distinct from atheism, feeling that what had become known as "atheism" made too bold a metaphysical claim. He instead sought to develop a position that was perhaps closer to the skepticism of David Hume, which insisted on the metaphysical impossibility of either asserting or denying the existence of God. But he was also motivated by a concern to coin a more "respectable" term of self-identification that was distanced from the still morally and politically disreputable "atheism."

In the nineteenth century, there was much concern, particularly in England and France, at the extent to which atheism was to be found among the general populace and especially among the working classes. There was a general consensus that "irreligion" was particularly widespread among these classes at this time and that they were much less religiously observant than the middle classes. But census takers and worker priests were careful to distinguish this "irreligion" from what had then become the meaning of the term "atheism." The nineteenth-century working classes of Western Europe could perhaps be described as "atheist" only in the older sixteenth-century sense of those who *live as if* there is no God, living their everyday life with no regard to considerations of God or religion. In other words, they displayed apathy or indifference toward religion rather than active hostility, and they did not espouse a well-formulated theoretical stance. We might therefore say that two different forms of atheism coexisted in Western European society. Among the uneducated working classes could be found the older sixteenth-century form of *practical* atheism—an atheism of indifference—while among (some) of the educated middle classes could be found the post-seventeenth-century form of *theoretical* atheism, or an intellectual or rational form of antitheism.

In the twentieth century, as social hierarchies became more blurred, this division began to break down. Furthermore, the older negative and pejorative connotations of atheism began to dissolve. From the mid-twentieth century, "atheist" as a term of self-identification became widespread in Europe—and it encompassed *both* the practical and theoretical senses. In the early twenty-first century, "atheist" was proclaimed as a proud badge of self-identification by the so-called New Atheists—Richard Dawkins, Daniel Dennett, Sam Harris, and Christopher Hitchens. It is doubtful, however, whether this movement represented a new meaning or definition of atheism. While the vociferous character of their proclamations was perhaps new, many have pointed out that their understanding of atheism is very much in line with the mainstream intellectual definitions of the nineteenth and twentieth centuries.

About the author

Gavin Hyman is a senior lecturer in the Department of Politics, Philosophy and Religion, University of Lancaster, United Kingdom. He has written widely on atheism and on the philosophy of religion more generally, including *A Short History of Atheism* (I. B. Tauris, 2010).

Suggestions for further reading

In this book
See also chapters 1 (term), 8 (famous atheists), and 11 (New Atheism).

Elsewhere

Buckley, Michael J. *At the Origins of Modern Atheism*. New Haven, CT: Yale University Press, 1987.

Erdozain, Dominic. *The Soul of Doubt: The Religious Roots of Unbelief from Luther to Marx*. Oxford: Oxford University Press, 2015.

Hyman, Gavin. *A Short History of Atheism*. London: I. B. Tauris, 2010.

Ryrie, Alec. *Unbelievers: An Emotional History of Doubt*. Cambridge, MA: Belknap, 2019.

8
Who are the most famous atheists?

Christopher R. Cotter

Any short essay addressing questions of fame is bound by necessity to be subjective. The definition of "famous" in the *Cambridge Dictionary*— "known and recognized by many people"—immediately raises issues surrounding which people in which sociohistorical context are the arbiters of this fame and how we are to assess the degree to which they are known and recognized. And even if we set aside the difficulties in defining "atheism," these issues are exacerbated further by the identifier "atheist." Do we mean people who are famous for being atheists? People who are famous for other reasons but who are also atheists? Or those who are important to the history of atheism but who might not have (been) identified as atheists? Are we interested in fame among atheists or among general populations? And do we legitimize the power dynamics inherent in fame/infamy or attempt an emancipatory account foregrounding famous atheists among the marginalized or in contexts less tied to Euro-American history? This chapter will highlight some "famous atheists" from a variety of sociohistorical contexts while attempting to address some of these questions.

"Atheism" is as tied to a certain narrative of "Western" history as "theism," and it therefore makes sense for me to begin in the same place: ancient Greece. In Plato's account of Socrates's trial in 399 BCE, we find the first occurrence of a word for atheist—*atheos*—which implied "godlessness," yet Socrates's crime was denying the gods of Athens, not gods in general. While Socrates and others around this time might be considered influential in the history of "atheism," they can hardly be considered "atheists" in the modern sense of the word. Moving into the Roman period, charges of atheism were regularly leveled by Romans at Christians and Jews, and vice versa, where the central issue seems to have been practical refusal to worship specific deities rather than explicit denial of *any* deity.

Steamrolling through to the "modern" period (although as chapters in *The Cambridge History of Atheism* demonstrate, the intervening centuries were far from wall-to-wall theistic piety), we meet the relentless skepticism of David Hume (1711–1776), the evolutionary theory of Charles Darwin (1809–1882)—himself not an "atheist" but recognizing the implications of his theory for the argument from design—and the surprisingly robust agnosticism of "Darwin's bulldog," Thomas Henry Huxley (1825–1895). Other notable individuals in this "coming-of-age" moment for atheism include Jean Meslier (1664–1729), a Catholic priest whose repudiation of the God of Christianity and of deism was discovered after his death; Ludwig Feuerbach (1804–1872), with his projectionist argument that theological claims reveal anthropological truths; Karl Marx (1818–1883), who advanced a thoroughly economic critique of religious systems as numbing distractions from the suffering of the masses; Friedrich Nietzsche (1844–1900), with his thoroughgoing critique of European moral commitments; Sigmund Freud (1856–1939), who developed a psychoanalytic critique of religion as a universal obsessional neurosis; and Jean-Paul Sartre (1905–1980), who was particularly influential in the development of an atheistic—though theologically engaged—strand of existentialism. And of course, one could also look to prominent women in the suffrage movement at this time, such as Ernestine Rose (1810–1892), Elizabeth Cady Stanton (1815–1902), or Matilda Joslyn Gage (1826–1898), who contributed much to advance feminist, antichurch, and atheist thought.

As I proceed to the twentieth century and beyond, I am duty bound to mention the "Four Horsemen" of "New Atheism": Richard Dawkins, Daniel Dennett, Sam Harris, and Christopher Hitchens. But I might also mention Ayaan Hirsi Ali, the Somali-born Dutch American activist, author, and former politician who infuses her atheistic writings with her lived experience as a former Muslim woman. If I take a broader look at atheistic writers, names like A. C. Grayling, Bertrand Russell, Ayn Rand, Julian Baggini, Michel Onfray, and Alain de Botton spring to mind. I could also highlight scores of influential skeptical writers, speakers, and activists, from Madalyn Murray O'Hair, who founded American Atheists in the 1960s, into the present day, with Greta Christina, Jennifer Michael Hecht, and Rebecca Watson (who are well known in atheist/skeptic circles but less among the wider public). Or I might look to popularizers of science who are associated with atheism, such as Carl Sagan, David Attenborough, Alice Roberts, Stephen Hawking, and Neil deGrasse Tyson—although the latter is quite emphatic that due to his commitment to the scientific method, he remains an agnostic (and even Dawkins occasionally admits as much). Or I could begin an interminable list of celebrities who are, to varying degrees, outspoken about their atheism, such as actors Jodie Foster, Ian McKellan, Daniel Radcliffe, and Emma Thompson. But now we are getting further and further from highlighting individuals who are primarily known for their alleged atheism.

At this point, readers can hardly have escaped noticing that the voices that have been highlighted have been primarily white, male, and European or (latterly) North American. To a large extent, this reflects my own positionality as a white, male European, and you might well be able to think of many more examples from your own or other contexts. On the other hand, it reflects the nature of discourse on explicit atheism, which is very much a "Western" phenomenon. Mention could be made of Communist leaders such as Vladimir Ilyich Ulyanov (a.k.a. Lenin, 1870–1924), Joseph Vissarionovich Stalin (1878–1953), and Mao Zedong (1893–1976) for their roles in instantiating atheistic political regimes in the USSR and PRC, respectively. Or I could point to the skeptical and anti-Christian rhetoric of influential Japanese educators Fukuzawa Yukichi (1835–1901) and Inoue Tetsujiro (1855–1944), but then we are straying into regions where it perhaps makes little sense to refer to "atheism" as a dominant feature—historically or contemporarily—due to the contextual dominance of other religious formations with their own histories of dissent. That is not to diminish the presence of atheism or atheistic thought in "non-Western" contexts—see many of the chapters in the *Cambridge History*, for example. But it is important to acknowledge that the selection processes involved in constructing a tradition of famous atheists will highlight some voices and exclude others and will somewhat inevitably be bound to the demographics of explicit atheism, which remains a predominantly (although by no means exclusively) white, male, Euro-American preserve. Which tells us a lot more about the power and privilege of this global minority than many might like to admit . . .

About the author

Christopher R. Cotter is a staff tutor and lecturer in religious studies and sociology at the Open University in the United Kingdom.

Suggestions for further reading

In this book
See also chapters 7 (identity), 9 (Darwin), and 11 (New Atheism).

Elsewhere

Bullivant, Stephen, and Michael Ruse, eds. *The Cambridge History of Atheism* (2 volumes). Cambridge: Cambridge University Press, 2021.

Cameron, Christopher. *Black Freethinkers: A History of African American Secularism.* Evanston, IL: Northwestern University Press, 2019.

Hitchens, Christopher, ed. *The Portable Atheist: Essential Readings for the Nonbeliever.* Philadelphia: Da Capo, 2007.

Schwartz, Laura. *Infidel Feminism Secularism, Religion and Women's Emancipation, England 1830–1914.* Manchester: Manchester University Press, 2013.

9

Was Darwin an atheist?

Bernard Lightman

Contemporary atheists like to claim Darwin as one of their own. One of the so-called New Atheists, popularizer of science Richard Dawkins, recruited Darwin into the atheist cause in his book *The God Delusion* (2006). Dawkins argued that Darwin's theory of evolution by natural selection was the ultimate scientific consciousness raiser, as it shattered the illusion of design within the domain of biology and teaches us to be suspicious of any kind of design hypothesis in physics and cosmology as well. Darwin, according to Dawkins, demolished natural theology, which attempts to prove the existence of a divine being by pointing to the evidences of divine design in the natural world. The only proper conclusion to draw from the current state of scientific knowledge is that atheism is the most enlightened position to embrace. Darwin was also accused of atheism by nineteenth-century contemporaries. His *On the Origin of Species* (1859) was greeted with fury and anger when it was first published. The American botanist Asa Gray, one of Darwin's allies, wrote to Darwin in 1860 that the eminent Swiss American biologist and geologist Louis Agassiz publicly denounced it as atheism. In 1872, Darwin told the Catholic biologist St. George Jackson Mivart that he had grown accustomed to accusations of atheism from Christian opponents. But seven years later, in a letter to John Fordyce, a Scottish-born congregationalist minister and author, Darwin claimed that he had never been an atheist in the sense of denying the existence of a God. Since this was just three years before Darwin's death, this can be taken as a fairly definitive statement of his mature views. The story of the evolution of Darwin's religious views confirms that he was never an atheist, even when he raised the most difficult questions about how humans can know that a God exists.

Ironically, Darwin went to Cambridge in 1828 as the first step to becoming an Anglican country parson. He was still a believer when he went on the five-year HMS *Beagle* voyage from December 1831 to October 1836. It wasn't until after the trip, as he analyzed the specimens that he had collected while on the *Beagle*, that he began to entertain doubts about both current scientific views on the fixity of species and the contemporary religious beliefs based on them. In his private notebooks, Darwin played with the radical idea of transmutation and the materialism associated with it. He realized that evolutionary theory challenged some of the basic principles behind Christian notions of God and nature. This is one of the reasons why Darwin did not publicize his "conversion" to evolution for many years. In fact, he concealed his dangerous ideas from all but a handful of close friends until just before the publication of *On the Origin of Species*. Evolution was associated with working-class radicals who defended atheism and materialism. Darwin wanted to be seen as a respected scientist by his contemporaries. He feared that his reputation would be destroyed and that his scientific discoveries would not receive a fair hearing if word got out that he was a dangerous, radical evolutionist.

Although Darwin did not become an atheist as a result of his work on evolutionary theory from the time of the *Beagle* voyage to the publication of *Origin*, his religious beliefs were undermined by personal tragedy. His eldest daughter, Annie, died at the age of ten in 1851 after a painful illness. Annie was Darwin's favorite, and her death hit him hard. It led him to lose faith in the Christian ideal of a personal, caring God. But in *The Autobiography of Charles Darwin*, written in 1876, Darwin claimed that when he wrote *Origin*, he was still a theist. There are traces of Darwin's theism in *Origin*, especially in the closing paragraph of the book. Darwin actually altered the final sentence in later editions to give it a more theistic resonance. Here he discussed the grandeur of the evolutionary process, pointing specifically to how "the Creator" had originally breathed life into a few forms or into one. Darwin conceived of evolution as a law impressed on nature by a divine being at the time of creation, who then stepped back and watched it operate. This was deism, which is still a form of theism. Although in *Origin*, Darwin rejected the notion that a personal, intervening God had created a perfectly designed world composed of fixed species at the beginning of time, and although he used his notion of evolutionary adaptation to undermine the design argument, he nevertheless accepted evolution as divine law.

However, Darwin's views changed after he wrote *Origin*. In both his autobiography and his letters, he claims that he oscillated between agnosticism and theism from 1859 on. The term "agnosticism" was invented in 1869 by Darwin's friend and defender, the biologist T. H. Huxley, a.k.a. "Darwin's bulldog." To Huxley, agnosticism was the position that knowledge is limited due to the very nature of the human mind. Huxley often used the agnostic position to deflate the pretensions of Christian theologians claiming to know things about the transcendental world. It had the added advantage of protecting Huxley, to some extent, from charges of being an atheist. Like Darwin, many Victorians who lost their faith in traditional Christianity found the term "agnosticism" useful as a description of their religious uncertainty. Darwin once wrote that he could not trust the human mind, keeping in mind its bestial origins, when it drew "grand conclusions" about the existence of God. So even in the period after he wrote *Origin*, Darwin did not embrace atheism.

About the author

Bernard Lightman is a distinguished research professor of humanities at York University, Toronto, Canada, and a fellow of the Royal Society of Canada.

Suggestions for further reading

In this book
See also chapters 2 (difference between the terms), 10 (scientists), and 31 (racism).

Elsewhere
Brooke, John Hedley. "Darwin and Victorian Christianity." In *The Cambridge Companion to Darwin*, edited by Gregory Radick and Jonathan Hodge, 192–213. Cambridge: Cambridge University Press, 2003.

Lightman, Bernard. *The Origins of Agnosticism: Victorian Unbelief and the Limits of Knowledge*. Baltimore: Johns Hopkins University Press, 1987.

Moore, James R. "Of Love and Death: Why Darwin 'Gave Up Christianity.'" In *History, Humanity and Evolution: Essays for John C. Greene*, edited by James R. Moore, 195–230. Cambridge: Cambridge University Press, 1989.

10
Have all great scientists been atheists?

Aku Visala

Let us take the sciences to refer to something like modern natural sciences, such as physics, biology, and chemistry. Let us further assume that a great scientist is a person who has made groundbreaking contributions to their respective field of science and enjoys a well-earned good reputation in their field. Finally, let us understand atheism broadly as including nonbelief in God or gods or the denial of everything supernatural. Given these definitions, the answer to the question is negative. Not all great scientists have been atheists. In fact, up until the twentieth century, most great scientists have held standard religious beliefs, mostly Christian, or some nonstandard religious beliefs. Many great scientists of the twentieth and twenty-first centuries have been atheists, but roughly half of all scientists hold some kind of religious belief.

Many of the founders of modern science were religious people who held rather orthodox Christian beliefs. Nicolaus Copernicus (1473–1543), who developed the sun-centered model of the solar system, was a Catholic believer. Similarly, most early astronomers, like Galileo Galilei (1564–1642) and Johannes Kepler (1571–1630), were devout Christians, who understood the whole project of science (or natural philosophy, as it was called then) as "uncovering God's mind in nature." Devout Christians also had a significant role in ushering in the scientific revolution in domains other than physics and astronomy. Robert Boyle (1627–1691) in England is widely considered as one of the first modern chemists while also being an ardent Christian apologist. The English philosopher Francis Bacon (1561–1626), who laid the philosophical foundations of the new inductive and empiricist scientific method, was also a Christian. Later in the eighteenth century, many Christians found their way into the sciences, including Antoine Lavoisier (1743–1794) in chemistry and Carl Linnaeus (1707–1778) in biology.

The fact that great scientists of the seventeenth and eighteenth centuries were, for the most part, Christians should not strike us as surprising. The whole project of the natural sciences and the subsequent scientific revolution had their roots in medieval and ancient mathematics, natural philosophy, and logic. These were practiced in a religious context and were often intertwined with theistic, especially Christian, notions of God as the rational source of the created order. Furthermore, as we have seen, many Christians built their personal pursuit of science as well as the whole project of natural science on a theological basis. Because humans were created in the image of God, they could understand the rational nature of God's creation. By doing natural philosophy—namely, the experimental and mathematical study of nature—they were engaging in a spiritual enterprise of understanding the mind of God. Such a way of seeing the meaning of science was rather typical until the end of the nineteenth century, especially in the English-speaking world. Contemporary historians of science have convincingly argued that our categories of "science" and "religion" have very little purchase before the nineteenth century. Not only were the sciences often motivated by theological concerns and supported by theological concepts, but they were also linked to religious denominations and institutions as well.

All this is not to say that atheists or nonstandard religious believers had been absent from early modern natural sciences. Most famously, the English physicist Isaac Newton (1642–1727) wrote extensively on esoteric themes and rejected many standard Christian beliefs, such as the doctrine of the Trinity. Especially during the Enlightenment period of the late eighteenth century, various forms of nonstandard religious belief became popular among scientists. Deism, for instance, could be neatly combined with the emerging rationalist and mechanist world view. Deists, like the French mathematician Pierre-Simon Laplace (1749–1827), thought that God created the world according to rational principles but does not intervene in the world. Deists defended a form of rational or natural religion that rejected the possibility of revelation and were, thus, critical of religious institutions, especially the Roman Catholic Church.

The Enlightenment period, especially in France and Germany, produced the first explicitly atheist scientists and philosophers, called materialists at their time. These included the physician Julien Offray de la Mettrie (1709–1751) and Denise Diderot (1713–1784) in France and Karl Marx (1818–1883) a bit later in Germany (and England). While many great scientists were agnostics at this time, they nevertheless upheld an amicable relationship with their respective churches and authorities, like Charles Darwin (1809–1882) in England. Despite the emergence and dominance of materialism and naturalism toward the end of the nineteenth century among scientists, many explicitly religious great scientists can still be found. These include the English physicists James Clerk Maxwell (1831–1879) and Michael Faraday (1791–1867).

The last century has seen the overall secularization of university institutions and the sciences. Many great scientists have been and are atheists. Most famously, the physicist Albert Einstein (1879–1955) was critical of established religions, like Judaism and Christianity, but apparently considered himself more of an agnostic rather than an atheist. By the end of the twentieth century, some atheist scientists became public celebrities via the media. Scientists like biologist Richard Dawkins (1941–) and physicists Carl Sagan (1934–1996) and Stephen Hawking (1942–2018) had a significant impact on the public's understanding of science and religion.

Despite this overall secularization of the sciences, a significant amount of scientists of the twentieth and twenty-first centuries have held religious beliefs and identified with some religion, most often Christianity. Of all the Nobel Prize laureates between 1901 and 2000, approximately 65 percent identified as Christian. Contrary to Einstein and Hawking, some twentieth-century pioneers of physics held strong religious beliefs, like Werner Heisenberg (1901–1976) in Germany and Arthur Eddington in England (1882–1944). Some influential scientists of today also profess religious beliefs. These include the American geneticist Francis Collins (1950–), English evolutionary biologist Simon Conway Morris (1951–), and recently departed English physicist Freeman Dyson (1923–2020).

According to a Pew Research Center study from 2009, the number of scientists that hold religious views is much lower than those of the general public. More than eight out of ten Americans, for instance, say they believe in God, whereas only 33 percent of scientists report the same. Eighteen percent admit to believing in some universal spirit or higher power, while roughly one-third of scientists explicitly deny the existence of God. So the amount of atheists among scientists is much higher than among the general public (in the United States, roughly 5 percent identify as atheists that believe in the nonexistence of God). Surprisingly, the balance of religious and nonreligious scientists has remained essentially constant since the early twentieth century up until today. The year 1914 saw the first survey of this kind reporting the religious views of American scientists. That study showed that out of one thousand scientists, approximately 40 percent believed in God and another 40 percent denied the existence of God. Apart from the slight decrease in theism among the scientists (33 percent), the situation today has not changed that much.

About the author

Aku Visala is a research fellow at the University of Helsinki, Finland. He has held postdoctoral positions at the University of Oxford (United Kingdom), Princeton University (United States), and the University of Notre Dame (United States). His work is located at the crossroads of analytic philosophy, theology, and the cognitive sciences.

Suggestions for further reading

In this book
See also chapters 4 (promoting), 7 (identity), and 9 (Darwin).

Elsewhere
Giberson, Karl, and Mariano Artigas. *Oracles of Science: Celebrity Scientists against God and Religion*. New York: Oxford University Press, 2007.

Harrison, Peter. *Territories of Science and Religion*. Chicago: University of Chicago Press, 2015.

Maski, David. "Religion and Science in the United States." Pew Research Center. https://www.pewforum.org/2009/11/05/an-overview-of-religion-and-science-in-the-united-states/.

11
What is New Atheism?

Christopher R. Cotter

All of us will be familiar with the time-bound nature of describing some-thing as "new." That once "new" coat we proudly wore about town quickly became just our "coat" before eventually, through falling out of favor or into disrepair, being supplanted by another "new" coat. Or that state-of-the-art MiniDisc player that we bought in the late '90s that never quite caught on in the way we predicted and, unlike the resurgent LP or the obstinate compact disc, has disappeared into the sands of time, such that the labels "retro" or "old" don't even seem to apply. With this in mind, and nearly two decades on, what can we say about New Atheism?

For a start, we can state that the term "New Atheism" emerged pri-marily as a journalistic rather than scholarly term—commonly traced to a *Wired* magazine article from 2006. At that point, it referred narrowly to a trio of white men—Richard Dawkins (author of *The God Delusion*), Daniel Dennett (*Breaking the Spell*), and Sam Harris (*The End of Faith* and *Letter to a Christian Nation*)—who had recently published popular science-laden, antireligious texts. Although these were not significant departures from the general output of the former two (Harris was then relatively unknown), they were noteworthy for their specific focus on "religion" (Christianity and Islam, in the main) and riding a wave of post-9/11 antireligious sentiment that led to inordinately high sales figures and airtime for the "faithless" that was heretofore unknown. Add into the mix another publication from the late journalist Christopher Hitchens (*God Is Not Great*), and within the year, the appellation "New Atheism" was gaining traction, with these four authors rallying under the moniker the "Four Horsemen" in a specially filmed dialogue-and-drinks session, with other potential candidates willingly or unwillingly circling the bandwagon yet never quite breaking into that inner foursome. In its most narrow sense, then, "New Atheism" refers to the atheism propounded by these four authors. More broadly, it might be understood to refer to a broader discursive movement within recent atheistic history that emerged in the aftermath of the 9/11 terrorist attacks. However, both interpretations have issues if we grant them too much fixity.

To be sure, there is much that is similar in the publicly available work of these authors. Their critiques of religion engage with some traditional philosophical arguments surrounding the existence of a deity and condemning religion for inspiring violence; having questionable, vague, or ineffectual moral codes; and opposing or limiting (scientific) knowledge and progress. As well as criticizing religion, they also coalesce in promoting free speech, free inquiry, critical thinking, secularism, a valorization of science, a reverential attitude toward nature, and a celebration of atheist identity politics through deliberately drawing on minority rights discourses. However, these similarities contrast with some very real differences. Harris maintains a much more positive attitude toward "Buddhism" and notions of "spirituality" than the others, and Dennett's engagement with "religion" is somewhat less vitriolic than his fellows' and reads much more like a beginner's attempt at genuine social science of religion in places. At times, each author seems to advocate for the complete eradication of religion, yet both Dawkins and Hitchens acknowledge a latent affection for the Church of England and lament its present insipidity. Thus, we must always be careful of uncritically assuming that a coherent "New Atheism" or "New Atheist approach" is being advanced by these four authors. We have good reason—historical, discursive, political, circumstantial, journalistic, and so on—to consider their works alongside one another, as we have done. But just like "religion," New Atheism—even in this narrow interpretation—should not be used as a shorthand uncritically.

If we broaden our conception of New Atheism, we similarly broaden these issues of uncritical oversimplification while also problematically constructing a monolithic "old" atheism against which this "new" variety can be contrasted. First, one need only glance at the dozens of chapters in the recently published *The Cambridge History of Atheism* to ascertain that it is highly anachronistic to speak of a singular "old" atheism. Further, Stephen LeDrew does an excellent job of demonstrating a clear line of evolution of a post-Enlightenment "scientific" strand of atheism—exemplified by thinkers such as Hume, Huxley, and Nietzsche—into the "New Atheism" of today, suggesting that "new" is not the most appropriate descriptor. On the other hand, there are several identifiable features of early twenty-first-century atheistic discourse that arguably mark it out as unique. The explanations for religion that are popular in this milieu make extensive use of contemporary developments in evolutionary biology and cognitive science that were not available in previous decades. The tone of the discourse is another factor, with New Atheists frequently utilizing satire and parody with a confident and rambunctious tone that has led to charges of militancy or disrespect. While this is all in the realm of discursive politics—one side's "militant" is another's "passionate" and so on—there is some truth to the observation of a tonal shift. Finally, although some would contest whether the rhetoric translates into practice, New Atheist discourse is heavily influenced by, and supportive of, historically recent struggles for gender, racial, and sexual equality. Thus, depending on where one positions oneself in relation to New Atheism, it is possible to argue that it is a distinctive and new phenomenon, that it is merely a continuation of older forms of atheism and offers nothing new, or some combination of both.

Whether New Atheism, whatever it is, will continue to develop or remain a historical moment of more or less significance remains to be seen. But one thing that we can say for certain is that "it" achieved a level of popularity rarely enjoyed by religion-related discourse, set the terms of the atheism-theism debate for a hot minute, and, perhaps, widened the discursive pool, enabling "less controversial" and "more nuanced" positions to gain greater social acceptance. Whether that is seen as a "good" thing or not depends on who is answering the question.

About the author

Christopher R. Cotter is a staff tutor and lecturer in religious studies and sociology at the Open University in the United Kingdom.

Suggestions for further reading

In this book
See also chapters 3 (researchers) and 8 (famous atheists).

Elsewhere
Cotter, Christopher R. "New Atheism." In *The Cambridge History of Atheism*, edited by Stephen Bullivant and Michael Ruse, 1007–1023. Cambridge: Cambridge University Press, 2021.

Cotter, Christopher R., Philip Quadrio, and Jonathan Tuckett, eds. *New Atheism: Critical Perspectives and Contemporary Debates*. Dordrecht: Springer, 2017.

LeDrew, Stephen. *The Evolution of Atheism: The Politics of a Modern Movement*. Oxford: Oxford University Press, 2016.

McAnulla, Stuart, Steven Kettell, and Marcus Schulzke. *The Politics of New Atheism*. London: Routledge, 2018.

12
Are there atheistic religions?

Teemu Taira

A straightforward answer to the question of whether there are atheistic religions can be provided only if one is clear about how the terms "atheism" and "religion" are defined. If one defines atheism as a lack of belief in God, gods, or supreme beings and religion as something that requires belief in such beings, the answer is negative. However, if one defines religion as a unified system of beliefs and practices relative to sacred things, as Émile Durkheim did, or as the state of being grasped by an ultimate concern, as Paul Tillich did, then there may well be atheistic religions.

Although the answer depends on definitions and on the assumption that something really interesting is revealed about the particular object ("religion") if one knows whether the object is or is not atheistic, these aspects are often taken for granted. Therefore, it is common to find examinations of some religions and whether they count as atheistic.

The most typical example of a "religion" that might count as atheistic is Buddhism. There is not a supreme being in Buddhism that would be equivalent to how the Christian God, for example, is conceived. This has led some to suggest that Buddhism is an atheistic religion, meaning that it fulfills other relevant criteria of what "religion" consists (such as community, ethical teachings, myths, rituals, and so on) but not the belief in God. This view assumes that "religion" consists of several aspects and the belief in God is not a necessary criterion for something to count as religion. However, even if the existence of a supreme being is rejected, the Buddhist tradition includes "counterintuitive" agents, concepts, and ideas that are considered typical of religions.

The most typical examples of "religions" that are not atheistic are Christianity and Islam, which are classified as monotheistic. Polytheistic religions are also—by definition—examples of nonatheistic religions. Hinduism is often presented as a textbook example of a polytheistic world religion, although there are scholars and practitioners who suggest that it could be understood as monotheistic (i.e., that the Hindu pantheon is just a manifestation of one supreme being). However, the different participants in such a debate share the premise that Hinduism is not atheistic. There are Hindu schools and Jain teachings that deny the existence of a creator god, but why would that be enough to label Hinduism or Jainism as atheistic?

Judaism is a complicated case. While it is typically considered a monotheistic religion, many scholars suggest that believing in the existence of God is not very relevant to the practice of Judaism. A joke credited to the great rabbi of Strasbourg by André Comte-Sponville in his *The Little Book of Atheist Spirituality* highlights how the belief in God is not essential to Judaism. Two rabbis dining together have a long discussion about the existence of God in which they come to the conclusion that God does not exist. The next morning, one of the rabbis looks for his friend and unexpectedly finds him in the garden doing his ritual morning prayers. He says, "Hey! What are you doing?" His friend replies, "I'm saying my ritual morning prayers." "That's just what surprises me! Last night we decided that God does not exist, and here you are saying your ritual morning prayers?" His friend says, "What does God have to do with it?"

This joke suggests that one can be a practicing Jew while not paying much attention to the existence of God. Thus, it could be suggested that Judaism is an atheistic religion from the point of view of some practicing Jews but certainly not for everyone. Similarly, people in general can be atheists and still be affiliated with a religion.

The question of whether some religions might be atheistic is even trickier when examples such as paganism and Satanism are considered. Both traditions include references to magic and invisible forces, and as such, they cannot be said to be completely atheistic, but many practitioners deny the existence of God and identify as "atheistic pagans" or "nontheistic Satanists." Many pagans acknowledge the existence of multiple spirits, gods, and goddesses, and some Satanists classify themselves as theistic Satanists. It seems that "atheism" is not something that is key to understanding such "religions" (if they are considered religions in the first place), but it can be one of the dividing lines in terms of how practitioners within such traditions group themselves.

Despite the fact that Christianity has provided a prototype of what religion is—including the assumption that belief in the existence of God or similar supernatural beings is the main defining trait of religion—there are also self-identifying Christians who deny the existence of God or at least diminish the importance of the role of God for living one's life as a good Christian. Although these "Christian atheists" are often educated theologians, it is not uncommon for ordinary people to consider themselves

Christian and atheists. Similarly, there are plenty of Quakers who classify themselves as nontheist or atheist Quakers. They do not accept theistic beliefs but affirm Quaker practices. Some regard their practices as religious, but, again, that is a matter of how one defines religion.

In addition to these examples, where the possibly "atheistic" nature of a particular tradition is examined, there are cases in which the atheistic aspect is taken for granted but the possible religiosity is negotiated. For instance, some suggest that humanism could be understood as a religion, as in Auguste Comte's Religion of Humanity (*la religion de l'Humanité*). In such cases, "religion" is not defined on the basis of beliefs in the existence of gods or supernatural forces. Those who think that the definition of religion has to contain such beliefs will object to the classification.

These musings over atheistic religions can be helpful in learning how heterogeneous and complex most traditions are, but they still assume that both terms—"atheism" and "religion"—can be defined in a meaningful manner and that they are typically not overlapping. The overlap reflects a deviation from the norm that most religious people are not atheists, and therefore, it represents a curiosity that merits our attention. However, if one thinks that both "atheism" and "religion" are contestable terms that one should define and use in a heuristic manner for particular research purposes or if one takes the use of such concepts as relevant objects of study, then the whole question about atheistic religions raises another, perhaps more interesting question: "What is at stake when people make claims about some religion being atheistic?" Does this make a religion inauthentic or less valuable? Does it make the tradition more rational or compatible with a scientific world view? Whose interests are served by labeling particular objects "atheistic religions," and what are the consequences of such classificatory acts?

About the author
Teemu Taira is a senior lecturer in the study of religion at the University of Helsinki.

Suggestions for further reading
In this book
See also chapters 15 (Buddhism), 16 (Christian atheism), and 21 (world view).

Elsewhere
Pyysiäinen, Ilkka. "Buddhism, Religion, and the Concept of God." *Numen* 50(2) (2003): 147–171.

Wernick, Andrew. *Auguste Comte and the Religion of Humanity: The Post-theistic Program of French Social Theory.* Cambridge: Cambridge University Press, 2001.

13

Were there atheists in ancient Greece and Rome?

Ramón Soneira Martínez

The first thing we need to clarify is what we mean by "atheist." If we understand the term in a modern sense as a person who criticizes religion in a belligerent way and who thinks that religion is evil and only for ignorant people, then we should answer this question negatively: there were no atheists in ancient Greece and Rome. However, if we reduce the meaning of atheism to an individual who questions the nature or existence of the gods, the answer is rather different. The term "atheist" has Greek roots. Etymologically, "atheist" is the evolution of the Greek term *atheos*, compounded by the privative alpha (*a-*) to express negation and the word *theos*, which means "god." Unlike neologisms that use ancient Greek to refer to irreligious positions such as "agnostic," the term *atheos* is not a modern invention. The word appears in different Greek texts. The problem with the term is the variety of its meanings in the Greek context. Sometimes *atheos* means "god-forsaken"; other times, it refers to a person who denies the existence of the gods but also to a person who claims that the gods exist but do not care about human beings. The multiple meanings of the term *atheos* make it difficult to answer this chapter's question easily.

It is undeniable that atheistic positions were developed in ancient Greece. The gods of Greek mythology were questioned from very early on. The first Greek philosophers, known as pre-Socratics, began to explain the natural world by putting aside the traditional myths of the epic poets such as Homer and Hesiod. In the sixth century BCE, one of these pre-Socratics, called Xenophanes, claimed that "both Homer and Hesiod have ascribed to the gods all deeds which among men are matters of reproach and blame," such as "thieving, adultery, and deceiving one another." His critique of the anthropomorphism of the divinities initiated a critique of the traditional image of the gods that had its greatest peak in classical Athens. During the fifth century BCE in Athens, different intellectuals questioned the nature of the gods and their role in the world, especially the so-called Sophists. They were professional educators hired by young aristocrats to improve their skills in rhetoric and their philosophical knowledge. One of these Sophists was Protagoras. In the introduction to his lost book *On the Gods*, Protagoras claimed that, concerning the gods, he had "no means of knowing either that they exist or that they do not exist." His statement is a clear example of the debate developed in Athens on the gods, their nature, and their existence.

Protagoras was not the only one who discussed the gods. Other Sophists such as Prodicus or Critias theorized about the origin and nature of the gods. For Prodicus, the gods had arisen through the divinization of natural elements such as wine or wheat, whereas for Critias, the notion of a god was introduced by a "wise" man to ensure that people respected the laws not only in the public spaces but also in their homes where no one saw them. In the theater, these reflections on the gods were also present, especially in Euripides's tragedies. In the play *Bellerophon*, a character questions the existence of the gods, claiming that there are no gods in heaven. A different example is found in *The Bacchae*. In this tragedy, Pentheus is called *atheos* for denying the divinity of Dionysus.

However, the most relevant *atheos* in this context was Socrates. The philosopher was prosecuted in 399 BCE for not believing in the gods of Athens. The accuser Meletus labels Socrates *atheos*, blaming him for corrupting the young with his "impious" teachings. Socrates denies the label *atheos*. Remarkably, he acknowledges his criticism of traditional mythology but denies his unbelief in any god. Socrates's reaction allows us to observe not only that the critique of the traditional idea of the gods was common within Athenian intellectual circles but also that the term *atheos* acquired negative connotations in classical Athens. The word was used to discredit another person as an insult. This negativity of the term explains why none of these authors called themselves *atheos*, although some of them, such as Diagoras of Melos, were labeled *atheos* in the *index atheorum* of latter sources.

This negative view of the term can be observed in the Platonic dialogue *Laws*, written in the fourth century BCE. In this work, Plato lists the arguments defended by the *atheoi*: (1) they do not believe in the existence of the gods, (2) they believe that the gods exist but argue that they are not interested in mortals, and (3) they believe in the gods but argue that the deities can be bribed with offerings. Therefore, the term *atheos* included not only those who denied the existence of the gods but also those who had a "misconception" of the divine. These arguments associated with the *atheoi* remained during the Hellenistic period. At the end of the fourth century BCE, figures such as Theodorus "the Atheist" or Euhemerus continued questioning the traditional gods. Euhemerus claimed that the gods were truly ancient kings divinized. We can easily add here Epicurus. He was also considered *atheos*, although he did not deny the existence of the gods. However, Epicurus stated that the gods, as perfect beings, had no need to worry about human beings.

All these ideas about the gods were collected by Roman authors. In *De natura deorum*, Cicero describes a dialogue between an Epicurean, a Stoic, and an academic skeptic. In the dialogue, we can observe the influence of the atheistic positions developed by Carneades in the Academy of Athens during the second century BCE. However, there is no evidence of a Roman figure who called himself *atheos* or, in the Latin version, *atheus*. Indeed, *atheus* was derived from the Greek word *atheos* only in the early modern period. In ancient Rome, atheistic positions were irrelevant or even rare compared to the classical Greek period. It was not until the arrival of Christianity that the word *atheos* and the accusations of denying the divine reappeared. During the two first centuries of the Common Era, the accusations of being "atheist" were used to discredit philosophers who defended Christianity and vice versa. Christian thinkers called polytheists *atheoi*, while polytheists called Christians *atheoi*. The consequent hegemony of Christianity gradually limited the meaning of the term. From that moment on, being an "atheist" was perceived as contrary to Christian dogma and, therefore, associated with heresies. The modern notion of the term was constructed within this context. In the early modern period, the term *atheus/atheos* evolved linguistically into the vernacular languages being used as a label to define those who rejected the nature or the existence of the Christian God.

In sum, the criticism of the gods is not alien to ancient Greece and Rome. Different philosophers introduced debates about the nature of the gods and even about their existence. Although these philosophers did not criticize religion as such, and they never used the term to label themselves, they did question the idea of the divine by developing atheistic arguments.

About the author

Ramón Soneira Martínez is a doctoral researcher in religious studies at the Max Weber Centre for Advanced Cultural and Social Studies of the University of Erfurt (Germany). His research interests lie in the study of atheism and unbelief in different historical contexts, particularly in classical Athens.

Suggestions for further reading
In this book
See also chapters 1 (term), 7 (identity), and 8 (famous atheists).

Elsewhere

Bremmer, Jan N. "Atheism in Antiquity." In *The Cambridge Companion to Atheism*, edited by Michael Martin, 11–26. Cambridge: Cambridge University Press, 2007.

Edelmann-Singer, Babett, Tobias Nicklas, Janet E. Spittler, and Luigi Walt, eds. *Sceptic and Believer in Ancient Mediterranean Religions*. Tübingen: Mohr Siebeck, 2020.

Sedley, David. "From the Pre-Socratics to the Hellenistic Age." In *The Oxford Handbook of Atheism*, edited by Stephen Bullivant and Michael Ruse, 139–151. Oxford: Oxford University Press, 2013.

Whitmarsh, Tim. *Battling the Gods: Atheism in the Ancient World*. New York: Alfred A. Knopf, 2015.

14

What is the relationship between Judaism and atheism?

Daniel Langton

Attitudes toward atheism and atheistic tendencies in Judaism are complicated and have shifted over time just as the meaning of atheism has shifted over time.

One might begin with the ancient world and with practical atheism—that is, living one's life as though God does not exist. The Hebrew Bible hints at the idea with the word *nabal*, or fool: "The fool says in his heart, 'There is no God'" (Psalm 14:1). In the first-century BCE, Philo condemned those for whom nothing exists but the visible universe, which was eternal, without a pilot, guardian, or protector (*On Dreams* 2.43). And likewise, Josephus, writing soon after, condemned those epicureans who denied providence and believed that the universe governed itself without a divine ruler, as a threat to the social order—for without a pilot, how could any ship navigate safely (*Antiquities* 10.11.7)? Ironically, in the ancient Greco-Roman world, Jews were regarded as atheists for refusing to recognize the official pantheon of the Greco-Roman gods and for insisting instead on their invisible God.

In the Talmud and later rabbinic literature, the phrase *kofer be'ikkar* is often translated as "one who denies God" in the sense that denying the fundamental principle or truth of God's existence and unity is effectively denying God. Another important term is *min*, usually translated as "heretic" or "apostate," and among the heresies of the *min* is atheism, at least according to later commentaries. The Talmud also includes the mysterious figure of Elisha ben Abuya, who, according to tradition, was a gifted legal scholar in the first century who came to doubt God's existence as a result of observing the death of a religiously observant child (or the humiliating death of a Jewish sage, depending on the source)—that is, as a result of the problem of evil and suffering. The Talmud went on to refer to him as *acher*, or "other," and condemned him for turning others away from the Torah (Jewish teaching).

Throughout the medieval period, Jewish philosophical writings that listed the rational weaknesses of disbelief proliferated. The towering figure of Maimonides (1135–1205) condemned in his *Guide for the Perplexed* those who denied God's existence and explained the universe in terms of chance. And elsewhere he defined faith in terms of theological beliefs in such a way that one could lose one's place in the world to come for disbelief in the existence of God and related ideas such as divine inspiration or providence, so that atheistic beliefs were seen to have existential consequences (*Mishneh Torah* 3:6–8). Despite this, Maimonides also appears to have taught ideas that could be regarded today as undermining belief in theism. Quite apart from insisting upon naturalistic explanations for prophecy and miracles and privileging scientific knowledge over superstitious traditions, his concern to present the case against anthropomorphism led famously to his negative theology concerning the nature of God. This was the argument that we cannot know anything about God other than that He exists, so one can only speak about what God isn't—that is, in the negative. A God who is defined in terms of what one cannot say about Him sounds rather like a God whose existence is irrelevant to humankind. Such ideas were repeated by the fourteenth-century Gersonides (1288–1344), who came to believe that God has no knowledge of earthly life and is distant and unknowable/undefinable (*Ein Sof*). Many would have taken issues of such a conception of God as one unworthy of pious belief.

As Jews were emerging from the ghettos, many were embracing the *Haskalah* or Enlightenment, and for many, this meant leaving their religious beliefs behind and becoming "non-Jewish Jews." Naphtali Herz Wessely (1725–1805), a *maskil* or enlightened Jew living in Denmark who was concerned about skeptical tendencies among his fellow Jews, complained in the 1760s of those who denied God, explained existence in terms of accidents, and denied the superiority of man over animals. The late eighteenth-century anti-Hasidic Lithuanian rabbi Israel Loebel distinguished between different atheists, including deists (who rejected the biblical conception of God) and the "new epicureans" (who denied providence and the divine origins of the Torah). With Baruch Spinoza (1632–1677), we reach a point when the critics could put a face to the accusations. For example, Samuel David Luzzatto (1800–1865) famously attacked Spinoza as an atheist in the 1820s for honoring God in the open while denying his existence in his heart, and he attacked Spinoza's book *Ethics* for implying that to the extent that there is any place for religion, it is on account of the ignorance of the multitude and its intellectual decrepitude.

A pastiche of medieval and early modern Jewish discussions and imaginings of the atheist suggests that disbelievers in God were regarded as, among other things, deniers of divine creation; of providence and His knowledge of men; of the divine origins of the Torah; of God's Unity, incorporeality, independence of time, and perfection, who threatened the foundations of society by undermining religious authority itself and the morality it taught. Each of these was identified by one pious authority or another at one time or another as admitting to atheism or the denial of the existence of God.

With the arrival of modernity, the charge of atheism has become commonplace and, in many ways, simpler. Whereas before the Enlightenment, accusations tended to be made against individuals or philosophies, afterward, it was possible to think of atheistic movements and social groups of unashamed disbelievers. The nineteenth-century emergence of Reform Judaism, which had a tendency to deprioritize Jewish tradition wherever it was perceived to conflict with modern thought and science, was frequently denounced as atheistic by the Orthodox. And in fact, atheistic Jewish groups did spring up. One example in the United States was led by Felix Adler (1851–1933), a former Reform rabbi who instigated the Jewish Ethical Culture movement in 1876—which espoused postdenominational, postreligious, Jewish ethics, and social justice—and whose highly knowledgeable attacks on traditional Judaism made him a very serious threat to that community. And from the 1920s onward, a new movement called Reconstructionism started to influence North American Jewry; led by Mordecai Kaplan (1881–1983), author of *Judaism as Civilization* (1934), it offered a nonsupernatural conception of the Jewish religion with no need for the God of the Bible, which provoked charges of heresy and atheism.

One of the most important events in recent Jewish history has been the establishment of the State of Israel in 1948. Many Jewish Zionists before and modern Israelis later regarded themselves as *chiloni'im*, or "secularists," derived from *chol*, or "profane." Such a term does not equate precisely with "atheist," but it does suggest how Jews familiar with traditional texts and the Hebrew language might regard the English term "atheism" as having negative connotations. Furthermore, the world's only Jewish state makes concrete and unavoidable certain questions that have emerged since the Enlightenment—namely, how to think about the phenomenon of secular Jews, who do not define themselves religiously but rather culturally or nationally and who are practical if not philosophical atheists. After all, historically speaking, Jews have never defined themselves as adherents of a particular religion.

About the author

Daniel Langton is a professor of Jewish history at the University of Manchester.

Suggestions for further reading

In this book
See also chapters 12 (atheistic religions), 15 (Buddhism), and 16 (Christian atheism).

Elsewhere
Berlinerblau, Jacques. "Jewish Atheism." In *The Oxford Handbook of Atheism*, edited by Stephen Bullivant and Michael Ruse, 320–336. Oxford: Oxford University Press, 2013.

Feiner, Shmuel. *The Origins of Jewish Secularization in Eighteenth-Century Europe*. Philadelphia: University of Pennsylvania Press, 2010.

Langton, Daniel R. "Discourses of Doubt: The Place of Atheism, Scepticism and Infidelity in Nineteenth-Century North American Reform Jewish Thought." *Hebrew Union College Annual* 88 (2018): 203–253.

15

Why has Buddhism been perceived as atheistic?

Jens Schlieter

The historical Buddha? Sure, he was an ordinary human being. No, he was not a god, nor did he believe in any gods, and neither do his followers. Buddhism is atheistic—end of story? Indeed, many Christian missionaries, Islamic scholars, and prominent Western philosophers have stated that Buddhism is atheistic throughout. Variants of the view that Buddhism is a religion without speculative views and may therefore be regarded as a moderate, tolerant atheism—or at least as fully compatible with atheism—have also been defended by influential Buddhist converts with a Christian or Jewish background. Living in a post-Enlightenment world and trained in empirical sciences, they declared that Buddhism is predominantly a philosophy and a way of life and not a religion. This argument allowed Buddhist modernists to claim that Buddhism builds on experience and evidence and, once it is freed from the baggage of traditional Asian culture, will overcome certain dogmatist views on gods and practices of their vain veneration. According to some Western Buddhists, Buddhism could even embrace a strict scientific naturalism. As a consequence, Buddhism, purified from theistic references, can be completely, explicitly, and intentionally transformed into a secular therapy to overcome existential anxieties, a belief-free cultivation practice of mindfulness, or a mystical experience of "oneness."

In contrast to these latest Western endeavors, scholars of religion could demonstrate that Buddhism, from early on, is certainly not devoid of the belief in gods and other supernatural beings. In Asian countries and among Asian migrants in the West, many "cradle Buddhists"—Buddhists by birth—actually believe in gods, even if they regard them as endowed with limited powers. Moreover, certain Buddhist traditions include the veneration of transcendent Bodhisattvas—that is, of spiritual beings who have taken the vow to guide ordinary sentient beings in their quest to overcome the world of suffering. Over time, the historical Buddha himself was deified, and some traditions transformed Buddhas into transcendent entities. In Buddhist temples or other sacred sites, one can see large and richly decorated statues of the Buddha and Bodhisattvas. Buddhist practitioners assemble in front of these, pray and pose offerings, and venerate non-Buddhist (local) gods for various worldly reasons and purposes. Finally, famous contemporary Buddhist teachers, such as the Vietnamese monk Thich Nhat Hanh, usually do not describe themselves as atheists. On the contrary, many of them emphasize, for example, that Buddhist mindfulness may even help Christians get in touch with God (the latter, however, understood in a Buddhist way—i.e., as a manifestation of everything or of emptiness). Examples like this one are quoted as evidence by those who argue that Buddhism cannot be atheistic at its core.

So how can we deal with the fact that Buddhism is perceived by some as atheistic while others emphasize its acceptance of gods and, although in rare instances, of God? Certainly, it is not the task of scholars of religion to decide whether or not a Buddhist can believe in a Christian or Jewish God or be a Buddhist and a Jew at the same time—nor if a secular Buddhism without the belief in karma and reincarnation is still Buddhism. All of these normative questions must be left for the practitioners to decide.

What scholars can discuss, though, are Buddhist practices and textual sources and the views expressed therein. In doing so, they should also aim to become aware of their own preconceptions and biases. Therefore, we may follow a well-trodden path in the study of religion and, starting with some definitions, take a closer look at the history and genealogy of conflicting views. Although there is no direct equivalent of "atheism" in premodern Asian languages, early and medieval Indian sources of the Hindu traditions declare Buddhism as "nontheistic." Various important early Buddhist scriptures state that a highest, all-knowing "God" (*īśvara*) does not exist. Buddhism is conceived as a "system/way without a Supreme God" (*anīśvaravāda*). Thus, if atheism is defined as the explicit denial that a monotheistic God—a personal, all-powerful, all-knowing, and all-good God who has created the universe—exists, most schools of Buddhism could be considered atheistic.

But what if the definition of atheism encompasses "any form of disbelief in God or gods"—that is, if we disentangle the concept of atheism from its Abrahamic monotheist complement? In fact, atheism, in its modern meaning, builds on a strong monotheism that was absent in early India, when Buddhism emerged. Actually, early scriptures do not dispute the existence of lower "gods" (*deva*), and many Buddhist traditions concede a certain limited usefulness to worshipping supernatural beings—gods but also transcendent Buddhas and Bodhisattvas. With this second definition in mind, Buddhism should not be defined as atheistic.

In other words, it is not the existence of gods that Buddhists usually deny. They only dispute that gods may help in securing one's liberation—to overcome the world of suffering. The latter must be reached through insight, wisdom, ethics, and self-cultivation practices. Gods do not entertain any personal relationship with humans, nor do they offer concrete help in the spiritual quest. Gods, and even the Buddhas, cannot change the order of the world: a world that was not created but evolved on its own. Gods and the Buddhas cannot prevent that humans die or change the fact that everything is impermanent, nor do they have nirvana on offer, simply because they do not possess the power to manipulate the quality of karma. According to mainstream Buddhism, it is only one's own thoughts, words, and actions that will determine how and as what life-form one will be reborn. These aspects discussed so far are of soteriological significance and therefore are considered to surpass any supernatural power.

So if there is such abundant evidence for not defining Buddhism as outright atheistic, why is it that Buddhism is still often described in that way? This brings us to a final aspect: the long Christian apologetic story behind the notion of Buddhism as an "atheistic religion." Indeed, already in the sixteenth century, Spanish Jesuit missionaries saw in Japanese Zen Buddhism the specter of atheism. Zen Buddhists seemingly rejected the idea of a creator god that can be distinguished from creation. Unlike early modern Christians who saw in Buddhism the heresy of "pantheism" and pagan idolatry, for later thinkers, it morphed into a cult of emptiness, an empty longing for final dissolution. Colonial Orientalists, Christian missionaries, and Western philosophers such as Leibniz, Kant, Hegel, and even Nietzsche collaborated to portray Buddhism as nihilism. In the nineteenth century, only a few thinkers, such as Arthur Schopenhauer, meant something positive when speaking of Buddhism as an "atheist religion." To define Buddhism as atheistic in a strong sense would mean either to declare certain views and practices pertaining to gods as random cultural particularities or—equally problematic—to define "atheism" merely against the backdrop of Abrahamic preconceptions: not as the "absence of beliefs in god/s" per se but as a hideous *presence* of the *wrong* gods and of a heretical conception of the absolute.

About the author

Jens Schlieter is a professor at the Institute for the Science of Religion, University of Bern.

Suggestions for further reading

In this book
See also chapters 12 (atheistic religions), 14 (Judaism), and 16 (Christian atheism).

Elsewhere

Batchelor, Steven. *Buddhism without Beliefs: A Contemporary Guide to Awakening.* New York: Riverhead Books, 1997.

Droit, Roger-Pol. *The Cult of Nothingness: The Philosophers and the Buddha.* Chapel Hill: University of North Carolina Press, 2003.

Skilton, Andrew. "Buddhism." In *The Oxford Handbook of Atheism,* edited by Stephen Bullivant and Michael Ruse, 337–350. Oxford: Oxford University Press, 2013.

von Glasenapp, Helmuth. *Buddhism: A Non-theistic Religion.* New York: George Braziller, 1966.

16
What is Christian atheism?

Gavin Hyman

Christian atheism most commonly refers to the work of a group of thinkers who argued that atheism should be combined with—rather than opposed to—Christianity. It originated in the United States in the 1960s and is usually associated with thinkers such as Paul van Buren, William Hamilton, and Thomas J. J. Altizer. Their work came to particular prominence when it was featured in the American popular news magazine *Time*. The infamous issue of the magazine published during Easter in 1966 featured a plain black cover with the three words "Is God Dead?" emblazoned in red lettering. Inside the magazine, the feature article reported on the work of Altizer, van Buren, and Hamilton and reported their argument that even theology must now accept the fact of God's death.

Thomas J. J. Altizer (1927–2018) emerged as the leader of this group of thinkers, and his book *The Gospel of Christian Atheism* (1966) was widely discussed. Altizer's work was deeply influenced by Hegel, Nietzsche, and Blake, and Hegel was the preeminent philosophical presence. Drawing on Hegel's philosophy and reading of Christianity, Altizer argues that atheism is not the negation but rather the fulfillment of Christianity. In the doctrines of the Trinity, incarnation, and crucifixion, a progressive death of the transcendent God is enacted, as God empties himself of his alienating transcendent otherness and enters ever more fully into the immanent created world. In the incarnation, God the Father empties himself of his transcendent otherness in order to enter creation as God the Son, Jesus Christ. In the crucifixion, God dies for a second time, as God the Son dies and gives way to the God the Holy Spirit, an entirely immanent and nontranscendent epiphany of the divine. For Altizer, therefore, atheism is not to be rejected as a negation of Christianity but rather to be welcomed as Christianity's apocalyptic fulfillment.

For Altizer, Christianity is the only religion that enacts the death of God and, in anticipating the apocalyptic union of heaven and earth, sees the death of God as something to be joyfully embraced. This apocalypse has arrived here and now, and this is the "good news" of Christian atheism. Consequently, Altizer believes Christianity to be the harbinger of a truly radical message, but it was a message that the early Christians could not see or could not countenance. They therefore reversed this radical message into a retrospective and backward-looking restoration of transcendence. In developing the doctrine of the ascension, whereby the risen Christ ascends into heaven, the early Christians reversed the radical content of their own message. Nonetheless, such a reversal could only be temporary, and in the ensuing centuries, the radical message of Christianity was enacted as the death of God was actually realized in human history. It is also worth noting that, for Altizer, secular atheists are unable to see the true meaning and significance of the atheistic condition. For him, only Christianity is able to see the death of God as a fulfillment of their religion, as the overcoming of alienation, and as a joyful liberation—the true and final union of God and humanity.

In the United Kingdom, "Christian atheism" has been associated with a different train of thought. In the 1980s, the radical theologian and Anglican priest Don Cupitt (1934–) developed what he described as a "Christian nonrealism," which has sometimes also been described as a "Christian atheism" and a "Christian Buddhism." Cupitt is much less influenced by Hegel and was far more influenced by Kant, Kierkegaard, and the Buddha. Drawing on and developing the work of Kant, Cupitt argued that God should be understood as a "regulative ideal" rather than an objectively existing being. God is a symbol who represents our highest ideals and values. Cupitt has been quite happy to admit that this God does not exist objectively and independently of humanity but is instead an ideal or symbol that has been created by human beings. But for Cupitt, this need not mean the end of Christianity or of religion. Drawing on and developing the work of Kierkegaard, Cupitt argued that the essence of religion lies not in intellectual assent to objective metaphysical doctrines but rather in the spiritual enactment of religious ideals and values—in particular, religious lives. For Cupitt, Christianity can continue to be practiced (and, indeed, can be purified) without objective metaphysics or belief in an objective God. In this respect, the example of Buddhism is instructive in that it is a religion that is in no way dependent on an objective God and does not give priority to metaphysical speculation. Cupitt believed that Christianity could and should transform itself so as to operate along similar lines. The result would be a more mature, more credible, and purer form of religious practice.

Cupitt, therefore, would have no philosophical or metaphysical argument with atheists. He would be happy to agree with them that an objective

God does not exist. But for Cupitt, an atheistic life without a religious shape and practice would be impoverished. For life to be meaningful and fulfilled, we need a structure and framework for life, with ideals to cherish, goals to pursue, and categories to live by. Religion can provide all of these things. While great artists find expression and meaning through their artworks and great composers find meaning and significance through their compositions, so too do we all need a medium through which to express ourselves and give our lives meaning. For those who are not gifted artists or composers, religion can play a similar kind of role, giving meaning, significance, and structure to our lives. And to play this role, religion need not depend on an objectively existing God. Instead, God becomes our highest ideal, our "pearl of great price," which is a symbol of everything that we cherish and hold dear in our religious lives.

In 1984, Cupitt presented a BBC television series, *The Sea of Faith*, which promoted his views, and put them in a philosophical and historical context. This, in turn, inspired the Sea of Faith movement, which comprised radical Christians who were inspired by Cupitt's work and who sought to put his "Christian nonrealism" into practice. It organizes meetings, conferences, and newsletters and is particularly prominent in the United Kingdom, Australia, and New Zealand.

More recently, Brian Mountford has used the term "Christian atheism" to refer to those who "belong without believing"—those who are drawn to, inspired by, and live according to Christian narratives, liturgy, doctrine, and ethics, but without actually believing in God. This group of people is closely related to Christian nonrealism, although Mountford says that this is "a wider and more miscellaneous phenomenon," as many of these people do not overtly identify with Christian nonrealism or with the Sea of Faith movement. But he says there has been a "paradigm shift," and such people are to be found in increasing numbers in Britain and perhaps also in other parts of Europe.

About the author

Gavin Hyman is a senior lecturer in the Department of Politics, Philosophy and Religion, University of Lancaster, United Kingdom. He has written widely on atheism and on the philosophy of religion more generally, including *A Short History of Atheism* (I. B. Tauris, 2010).

Suggestions for further reading

In this book
See also chapters 12 (atheistic religions), 14 (Judaism), and 15 (Buddhism).

Elsewhere

Altizer, Thomas J. J. *The Gospel of Christian Atheism.* Philadelphia: Westminster, 1966.

Cupitt, Don. *Taking Leave of God.* London: SCM, 1980.

Hyman, Gavin, ed. *New Directions in Philosophical Theology: Essays in Honour of Don Cupitt.* Aldershot: Ashgate, 2004.

McCullough, Lissa, and Brian Schroeder. *Thinking through the Death of God: A Critical Companion to Thomas J. J. Altizer.* Albany: SUNY, 2004.

Mountford, Brian. *Christian Atheist: Belonging without Believing.* Alresford: O Books, 2011.

17

What does Islam teach about atheism?

Ilkka Lindstedt

Does the scripture of Islam, the Qur'an, address atheism? Does it condemn it? How about the commentators of the Qur'an and Muslim theologians more generally? The conventional answer would be "Yes, absolutely, Islam condemns atheism," but things are in fact somewhat more complicated than that.

There are no clear Qur'anic equivalents for the words "atheism" and "atheists." Two concepts, *kufr* and *shirk*, are often adduced in this context, but their usage is rather different from the modern-day understanding of the word "atheism." In the Qur'an, *kufr* means a plethora of things—for instance, ingratitude; rejecting, denying, or hiding the truth; insolence; and finally, disbelief (a person entertaining *kufr* is called a *kafir* in the Qur'an). The concept is connected not only with disbelief in God, the Prophets, and revelations (e.g., Qur'an 3:21) but also with oppressing the weak (Qur'an 4:168), amassing wealth (Qur'an 19:77), and fighting for the sake of evil beings (Qur'an 4:76). Clearly, atheism, as we understand it nowadays, cannot be equated with the Qur'anic *kufr*. A *kafir* is not merely, or primarily, an atheist or a disbeliever. Rather, the Qur'an distinguishes a *kafir* also for the fact that she/he acts in a deeply immoral way, hurting her/his fellow human beings.

As for *shirk*, it is a more restricted concept that denotes "joining partners with God" (a person engaging in *shirk* is called a *mushrik*). It is a cardinal sin according to the Qur'an (4:48): "God does not forgive the joining of partners with Him: anything less than that He forgives to whoever He will, but anyone who joins partners with God has concocted a tremendous sin" (translated by Muhammad Abdel Haleem). The word *shirk* is often translated as "polytheism" or "idolatry," but this, too, is simplistic. Like *kufr*, *shirk* is sometimes connected with more generally immoral and spiteful deeds. The *mushriks*, for example, torment believers (Qur'an 3:186). Moreover, recent historical research makes one doubt whether there were many polytheists or idolaters around anymore when the Prophet Muhammad lived: most Arabians appear to have been Jews or Christians. The Qur'anic insistence to avoid *kufr* and *shirk* can be read in the context of theological discourse about the divine *as well as* ethical reasoning about evil.

Premodern Muslim exegetes and theologians very rarely engaged in the question of atheism (in the sense of rejecting the existence of God). For the most part, they did not conceive of it as a common phenomenon or problem and, accordingly, did not censure it. The theologians were more often interested in engaging in polemics with other religious communities (Jews, Christians, Zoroastrians, and others) as well as intra-Islamic delineation (condemning "heretics") rather than discussing and denouncing those who did not believe in God. There are only single instances of atheism addressed in medieval Islamic theology. The famous Iraqi scholar Abu Hanifa (died 767 CE) reported that there were some people who did not believe in the afterlife or in God, since He cannot be observed with the senses. Naturally, Abu Hanifa endeavored to refute their views. The rarity of this discourse, however, is noteworthy and points toward the fact that there were, in the medieval Middle East, probably very few people that we would classify as atheists.

The case of Ibn al-Rawandi is important in this connection. He lived in the ninth century CE, though his exact dates are not known. He hailed from Khurasan and lived most of his life in Baghdad. He began his career as an "orthodox" Muslim theologian, but he started writing against Islam at some point in his life. In particular, Ibn al-Rawandi took issue with what he perceived as problems in the Qur'anic presentation of theodicy (the problem of evil). He goes so far as to call such a deity "stupid" (*safih*) that would castigate disbelief or sin with eternal punishment. For Ibn al-Rawandi, God's mercy is the dominant attribute. He also rejected the importance of prophecy and scripture, claiming that reason alone is sufficient for arriving at a system of ethics. There are also some rare and difficult-to-interpret passages in which Ibn al-Rawandi appears to deny God's active role, relegating Him to the role of a distant Creator instead. What is important to note is that, based on the sources available to us, Ibn al-Rawandi did not face persecution (or worse) during his life. He was free to voice his views, and his works were copied, read, and engaged with throughout the Middle Ages (only some fragments are extant today). True, Ibn al-Rawandi was often condemned as a *zindiq* (heretic), but some scholars viewed him more neutrally.

In modern times, there have been quite a few attempts to interpret the Qur'an and Islamic tradition in a way that would allow for pluralism and freedom of religion, including atheism. For instance, the South African Muslim scholar Farid Esack (born in 1955) has presented an Islamic liberation theology. In his interpretation, the word *kufr* is to be understood primarily through the context of oppression and violence, citing, for example, Qur'an 3:21–22, which criticizes "those who reject (*yakfurun*) God's revelations, who unjustifiably kill prophets, who kill those who command that justice is done: the deeds of such people will come to nothing in this world and in the next and no one will help them." According to Esack, the Qur'an discusses the relationship not only between the human being and the divine but also between the human and another. The Qur'an can be read in the context of emancipation, liberation, and equality, with an emphasis on helping the poor (Qur'an 2:83, 271) and the disempowered (Qur'an 34:31), who are oppressed by the ruling aristocracy (Qur'an 11:27). The religious and ethical fault lines are re-envisaged by Esack. In his reading, Islam does not simply call for monotheism and belief but (perhaps more importantly) for solidarity toward different subaltern groups and individuals against those who oppress and amass wealth at the expense of other human beings.

About the author

Ilkka Lindstedt is a lecturer in Islamic theology at the University of Helsinki. He has worked on early Islamic history and classical Arabic literature. Recent publications include the article "Who Is In, Who Is Out? Early Muslim Identity through Epigraphy and Theory" in *Jerusalem Studies in Arabic and Islam* (2019) and the chapter "The Islamic World" in *The Cambridge History of Atheism*.

Suggestions for further reading

In this book
See also chapters 14 (Judaism) and 18 (Muslim countries).

Elsewhere
Esack, Farid. *Qur'an, Liberation and Pluralism: An Islamic Perspective of Interreligious Solidarity against Oppression.* Oxford: Oneworld, 1997.

Saeed, Abdullah, and Hassan Saeed. *Freedom of Religion, Apostasy and Islam.* Aldershot: Ashgate, 2004.

Stroumsa, Sarah. *Freethinkers of Medieval Islam: Ibn al-Rāwandī, Abū Bakr al-Rāzī, and Their Impact on Islamic Thought.* Leiden: Brill, 1999.

18

Is it difficult to be an atheist in Muslim countries?

Karin van Nieuwkerk

You want a short answer? Yes, it is difficult! But not in all countries, not for everyone to the same extent, and also depending on whether, how, and where you disclose your nonbelief. Yet despite it being difficult, there appears to be a growing number of people who identify as atheists in many Muslim countries. So for the longer answer, we will need to unpack the question. I will do so in reverse order:

- What is meant by *Muslim countries*? And what is the number of nonbelievers in different countries?
- What is meant by *atheism* in the context of Muslim countries?
- Is it difficult *to be* a nonbeliever or to show nonbelief? Who is coming out?
- What kind of *difficulties* and consequences might atheists experience?

"Muslim countries" connotes not only that the majority of the population is Muslim but also that Islam plays a major role in law and public order. Yet in what we perhaps better label as "Muslim-majority countries," there is a huge variation in the role religion plays in the rule of the country. Whereas in some countries such as Saudi Arabia or Pakistan, religious law or sharia plays a large role in the judicial system, other Muslim countries' judicial systems are based on secular laws or a mixture of both. Accordingly, "apostasy" cases are dealt with differently by states.

In Saudi Arabia in 2012, activist and blogger Raif Badawi, who never renounced religion, was accused of apostasy and sentenced to ten years in prison, a public flogging, and a fine. In Sudan, twenty-five Muslims have been threatened with the death penalty on charges of apostasy. The *Guardian* reported that the accused belong to the Hausa minority, many of whom follow a different interpretation of Islam than the one sanctioned by the regime. In other countries where apostasy is not illegal, blasphemy laws are used to silence atheists. Although there is "freedom of belief" in these countries, there is no "freedom of expressing nonbelief." These examples demonstrate the ambiguity of what exactly apostasy is and how it is difficult to distinguish from heresy or blasphemy. This lack of clarity opens up space for the political use of accusations of apostasy and blasphemy to sentence political opponents or silence deviant opinions.

Yet despite the danger involved, according to research by the Arab Barometer, the number of people in, for example, the Middle East identifying as "not religious" has risen from 8 percent in 2011 to 11.6 percent in 2018, and in the age category under thirty, 15.5 percent identify as not religious.

Defining atheism in Muslim-majority countries is not easy because there are several notions connected to nonbelief, and most labels are highly negatively charged: a *kafir* is a non-Muslim, a *murtadd* is born Muslim or entered Islam and then leaves it for another religion but is still a believer, and a *rububi* is a deist who believes in God but not in religion. *La adri*, literally "I don't know," translates as "agnostic" and neither affirms nor denies the existence of God, whereas a *mulhid* believes neither in religion nor in God. *Mulhid* is the term closest to atheist, but it actually derives from the Arabic word for "deviance." And as we saw above, states often accuse "deviant" people—whether religiously or politically—as "atheist." Finally,

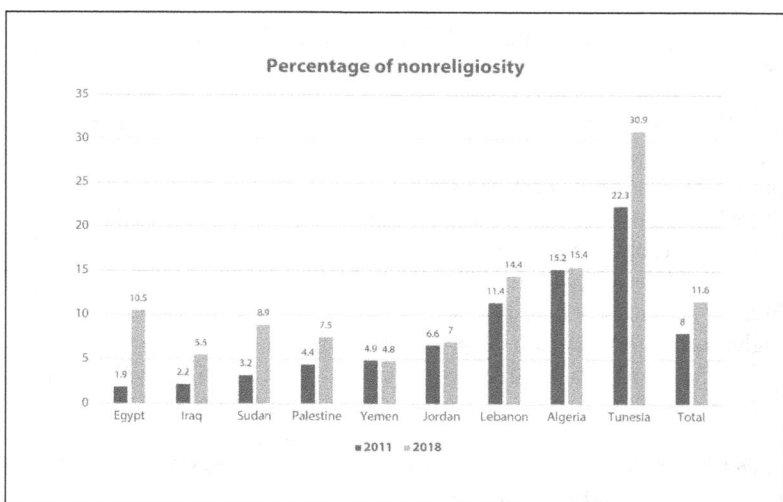

Percentage of nonreligiosity

Egypt: 1.9, 10.5
Iraq: 2.2, 5.5
Sudan: 3.2, 8.9
Palestine: 4.4, 7.5
Yemen: 4.9, 4.8
Jordan: 6.6, 7
Lebanon: 11.4, 14.4
Algeria: 15.2, 15.4
Tunesia: 22.3, 30.9
Total: 8, 11.6

■2011   ■2018

the notion of *la dini*, which literally translates as "nonreligious," is often used as an overarching label and is less stigmatizing. Most nonbelievers I have interviewed feel comfortable with being categorized as "nonreligious" because it includes the various shades of unbelief, doubt, and even nonreligious spirituality. The problem is that all these terminological subtleties are lost on most people, and all "religious deviants"—even "secularists"—can be accused of being "atheists."

Many people in Muslim-majority countries—as elsewhere—lead "secret lives." Regarding taboo issues—such as religion, sexuality, and politics—people can have their private convictions, but they better not express them. As mentioned above, in several Muslim-majority countries, there is "freedom of belief" but not "freedom of expression." Since atheism is perceived as deviance and blasphemy as a disturbance of the public and moral order, most nonbelievers hide their atheism or only disclose it to people they trust, such as like-minded friends. When they do not speak out and hide their atheism, it is not necessarily difficult to be an atheist. But keeping what most nonbelievers often consider an important part of their identity concealed at all times is stressful.

Yet in the age of social media, some platforms provide relatively safe and anonymous spaces to discuss atheism—to find information about "New Atheism," for instance, or to share experiences. After the Arab uprisings, several atheists—particularly young male activists—felt emboldened to start YouTube channels in which they reveal their identities. Yet most of them are harassed by political and religious authorities and have hard times. Although there is no indication that nonbelief is limited to this group, it is particularly the well-educated, young male urban professionals with a middle-class background who publicly speak out. Young women also come out but more often prefer to remain anonymous, hiding their faces while speaking out. Women face different challenges when they are accused of "deviance" and "atheism."

The potential consequences of coming out for or being accused of atheism are manifold, not the least being the legal consequences: this pertains to the possibility of not only being sentenced to death, imprisonment, or fines—depending on the state laws—but also being disinherited, forced to divorce, or refused as a marriage partner by the family (since a Muslim is not allowed to be married to a nonbeliever). In addition to the potential legal consequences, the social rejection can be harsh as well. Relatives and friends can cut ties with nonbelievers, and they can lose their job. Atheists are often perceived as abnormal, mentally ill, and immoral. The accusation of immorality makes nonbelief even more sensitive for women. Atheists can become social outcasts, and therefore it is no wonder that most prefer to keep silent.

About the author

Karin van Nieuwkerk is a professor in Islam studies at Radboud University, the Netherlands.

Suggestions for further reading

In this book

See also chapters 17 (Islam), 22 (most atheistic societies), and 38 (discrimination).

Elsewhere

Cottee, Simon. *The Apostates: When Muslims Leave Islam*. London: Hurst, 2015.

Van Nieuwkerk, Karin, ed. *Moving In and Out of Islam*. Austin: University of Texas Press, 2018.

Whitaker, Brian. *Arabs without God: Atheism and Freedom of Belief in the Middle East*. Self-published, CreateSpace, 2014.

19

Are pagans and Satanists really atheists?

Jesper Aagaard Petersen

> For years I have said vaguely that I could not hope to begin to do anything with a man until he had become an Atheist. (I don't mean a born Atheist, I mean one who has won to that Eminence through frightful struggles.) Expand this slightly. You can't expect to get Thelemites . . . without disintegrating the corpse of the Dying God by T.N.T.
>
> —Letter from A. Crowley to N. Mudd, April 20, 1924
> (Yorke Collection, Warburg Institute)

This may seem like a straightforward question, but to answer it, we must unpack the categories and assumptions within it. Pagans and Satanists come in many shapes and sizes, and we should be careful of lumping together heterogeneous currents under wider umbrella terms. We should also be attentive to judgments implicitly reducing one type of belief to another.

First, "pagans and Satanists" are not one kind—they are not even the same thing. The two religious currents might share some history, especially as broad new religious movements gained traction from the 1960s onward. They also share the practice of borrowing heavily from religious and artistic expressions from earlier periods, and many pagans and Satanists are deeply engaged with occult and esoteric beliefs and practices. That said, purists on either side frequently disown each other as airheaded nature lovers on the one hand and radical devil worshippers on the other, while some freely mix and choose from both. So while modern paganism and Satanism might be examined as neighboring traditions coming of age during the occult explosion of the countercultural West, alongside the New Age and Human Potential movements, for example, they should not be conflated.

Further, each individual category of pagan or Satanist is an umbrella term subsuming many interpretations and practices exhibited by a number of groups and individuals within it. In other words, even though we can talk about "pagans" or "Satanists" just like we use "Christians" or "atheists," they are not very precise concepts outside daily speech. Within each of these terms hides a multitude of differences, and even their similarities might be shared by some but not all elements within the category. To ask if pagans or Satanists are atheists, you have to follow the history, beliefs, and practices of significant spokespersons and groups within these two broad movements.

Now we arrive at the first answer to the question. Simply put, some are atheists, and some are not. Almost all pagans and Satanists share an antitheist stance in terms of refusing the monopoly of the Christian god, but they do not necessarily reject gods, forces, or powers per se. Some are vibrantly polytheist, animist, or pantheist, believing the world to be suffused with spirits, gods, or spiritual energies. Others reject a spiritual world view for a more psychologized one, even though magic as such still works as a potent tool. They also commonly express a material, this-worldly position, engaging with a good life here and now and not in some distant future (although the world-rejecting or even ascetic position is perhaps rarer than we think, as religions and ideologies always give us blueprints from which to live our life).

Take the brutal antitheism of the quote from British occultist Aleister Crowley (1875–1947) that prefaces this chapter. Strictly speaking, as a mystic and ceremonial magician, Crowley was neither pagan nor Satanist, but he can be understood as a strong influence on both writings and eclectic practices throughout his life. Blowing up "the Dying God" with explosives might not be a definition of atheism that we see very often. What he seems to imply is that we can come to a rejection of God or gods as almighty beings through "frightful struggles." Only then have we won the freedom to do and think as we please—in Crowley's terms, to become "Thelemites," or adherents of his new religion, Thelema. Theism, then, is the obstacle we need to overcome to live a full life. In this sense, many new religions, paganism and Satanism included, can be seen as a-theist.

We now arrive at the second unpacking, that of atheism in the modern sense. The antitheism examined above is a weaker form of atheism, the "absence of the belief in the existence of a God or gods," to use a popular definition. On the other hand, the active rejection of a specific set of beliefs while retaining others makes the absence of belief both stronger than the merely "nonreligious" and weaker than the strongly secular. They also combine the rejection with an active adoption of other beliefs that are not atheist in the above sense, depending on which pagans or Satanists you ask. As such, if used at all, they consider atheism a starting point, not the end point.

For example, the Church of Satan, founded in 1966 in San Francisco by Anton S. LaVey, considers atheism a foundation on which to build a material and naturalistic world view, but they also use the term "I-theism" to explain how Satanists move beyond the mere absence of belief or rejection of God to the carnal self-worshipping of modern Satanism. This includes unexplained phenomena and ritual activities, although the interpretation and specifics are up to each individual. Going further, the Satanic Temple, bursting onto the national stage in the United States in 2013, posits Satanism as a secular religion aligned with liberal, atheist, and progressive values to fight for the continued separation of church and state. Both positions can be found within pagan groups as well. For example, Zsuzsanna Budapest (1940–) and Starhawk (1951–) both promoted a feminist spirituality loosely aligned with the broader Goddess movement of the 1970s. Although neither is recognizably atheist, they both reject God and the patriarchy in the return to Mother Earth and communal faith-based activism.

So where does this leave us? I want to conclude with a final unpacking closely related to the first one on umbrella concepts. This relates to the identity implied in the word "really"—that is, the cutting through insignificant noise and complications that is frequently inherent in that word. If pagans and Satanists are *really* something else, the surface differences important to the people using these terms for themselves are not really that important. We see through the form to the postulated essence behind it. Here I can give a clearer answer: neither pagans nor Satanists are merely (or really) atheists. All three currents are movements with distinct histories, sometimes competing, sometimes allied, but all based on a rejection of traditional Christian beliefs and values. It is what they fill this absence with that makes them interesting.

About the author

Jesper Aagaard Petersen is an associate professor and the head of research at the Department of Teacher Education, Norwegian University of Science and Technology, Norway. In the past two decades, he has done extensive work on identity and discourse within modern Satanism and the Satanic milieu. His current research areas include critical religious education, the democratic effects of conspiracy thinking, and the representation of and interaction between religion and science in the classroom.

Suggestions for further reading

In this book
See also chapters 2 (difference between the terms), 12 (atheistic religions), and 21 (world view).

Elsewhere

Adler, Margot. *Drawing Down the Moon*. 1979. Reprint, London: Penguin Arkana, 1986.

Asprem, Egil. "Magic Naturalized? Negotiating Science and Occult Experience in Aleister Crowley's Scientific Illuminism." *Aries* 8(2) (2008): 139–165.

Dyrendal, Asbjørn, James R. Lewis, and Jesper Aa. Petersen. *The Invention of Satanism*. Oxford: Oxford University Press, 2015.

Laycock, Joseph P. *Speak of the Devil: How the Satanic Temple Is Changing the Way We Talk about Religion*. Oxford: Oxford University Press, 2020.

20
What kind of dialogue is there between atheists and religious people?

Paul Hedges

This question itself poses a number of further questions, including the following:

1. Is there actually any dialogue between atheists and religious people?
2. What do we mean by "atheists" and "religious people"?
3. What is meant by "dialogue"?

Here are some simple answers, starting in reverse:

3. We are discussing interreligious dialogue, by which we mean meaningful exchanges across world views and the potential role of atheists in this.
2. Some explicitly deny the claims of those things we call religions, and some accept them (especially, perhaps, claims about the existence of a deity).
1. Many topics come up when such people meet, from polemics about the question of evil and God's existence to agreements about shared social action.

But things are not so simple, so let's break down some of the problems with our questions and answers. We'll begin with the second, the distinction between "atheists" and "religious people." Much popular debate presupposes these as clearly demarcated categories, but this is far from so. What we typically call atheism arose within a Western European context, and so often we mean that an atheist is an "a-theist," one who opposes the "theism," or belief in the deity, of Christianity (also Judaism and Islam). But such an all-powerful creator deity is exactly what Buddhism traditionally opposed, which, along with its denial of a "soul," earned it the title of an "unorthodox" (*nastika*) tradition in South Asia. But today, we typically class Buddhists as "religious people," although some Buddhists self-identify as atheists. Again, those often termed the "nones" (those who adhere to no religious tradition), although often thought of as atheists, typically accept a range of things we may typically term "religious" or "spiritual" (i.e., reincarnation, horoscopes, "psychic" phenomena such as ghosts, etc.). Even some atheists will assert they have some form of "spirituality" (itself a dodgy term, especially when distinguished from "religion"). "Religious people" are no more a common "type" than "atheists" or "nonreligious people," and both groups overlap.

Regarding dialogue, our focus is interreligious dialogue. Some argue for including atheists, agnostics, and others in this, perhaps renamed as "inter-world-view" dialogue. But some may ask why atheists would, or even should, be interested. When we hear "interreligious dialogue," we may envisage a bunch of elderly male leaders discussing doctrines and metaphysics. But interreligious dialogue can describe a wide range of activities, including

- joint social action around areas of common concern (dialogue of action),
- exchange of prayer or meditational practices (dialogue of religious experience),
- theological discussion (dialogue of theological exchange), and
- mundane encounters in day-to-day interaction (dialogue of life).

Furthermore, by dialogue, what we will discuss here is meaningful engagement across world views that aims at understanding rather than the polemical debates between (often) Christian or Muslim apologists and "New Atheist" rhetoricians (such as Richard Dawkins or Sam Harris), in which each seeks to prove or disprove the existence of God or whether religion is a boon or bane in human life. Even some more positive learning encounters may not involve meaningful engagement across world views (i.e., it may be less like dialogue). For instance, the atheist popular philosopher Alain de Botton has written on what atheists may learn from religion, arguing that such things as ritual, aesthetic admiration, and communal gatherings are beneficial, but he takes a hectoring tone when he suggests that "religion" is woefully inadequate.

Atheists are included in a number of interreligious (or inter-world-view) dialogue events, which range from the local and informal to international and formal. At the second Assisi Day of Prayer ("Day of Reflection,

Dialogue and Prayer for Peace and Justice in the World," October 27, 2011), Pope Benedict XVI invited Julia Kristeva to speak on humanism. Humanism has long been represented at the Parliament of World Religions. At the 2018 parliament in Toronto, over a dozen of the workshops discussed atheism, humanism, or other nonreligious sectors of society. Meanwhile, the first International Conference on Cohesive Societies hosted by the Singapore government in 2019 explicitly included nonreligious voices alongside the voices of "faith," something planned to be repeated at the second conference in 2022. But it is not only at such high-profile events that we see atheists in dialogue with representatives of religions; it also happens globally in grassroots initiatives.

In terms of the four types of dialogue, atheists are engaged in all. Kristeva's talk typifies the dialogue of theological exchange or attempts to understand the meaning of life, attitudes toward the world, and the values expounded by various traditions. Such dialogue may seek common ground or points of difference, with the latter sometimes being seen as a potential learning experience. It is not simply restricted to elites, with a series of "Ask Me Anything" events in Singapore, letting Hindu, Sikh, Buddhist, Muslim, humanist, and other speakers engage an audience eager to find out about the people who live around them in society.

The dialogue of action has seen those identifying as "religious" and "nonreligious" actively engaged in such diverse projects as cleaning up the local park or advocating for action on climate change. Groups such as the Interfaith Youth Core in the United States arrange events that bring young people (often high school or university students) together on common projects. In families, we see the dialogue of life when partners, if one of them is atheist and one religiously affiliated, seek to negotiate the celebration of festivals, bring up children with respect for others and their heritage, and fit in with wider family customs and traditions. Such dialogue occurs globally in multicultural societies, with atheist-religious marriages also sometimes crossing ethnic as well as religious borders. Finally, the dialogue of religious experience is arguably seen when atheists seek out religious teachers for meditation to help calm their minds. We arguably also see an implicit dialogue between "religion" and "nonreligion" in the practice of "mindfulness," which draws from Buddhist meditation but is typically framed as a "secular" technique of awareness or breathing for relaxation.

About the author

Paul Hedges is an associate professor in the Studies in Interreligious Relations in Plural Societies Programme, RSIS (S. Rajaratnam School of

International Studies), Nanyang Technological University, Singapore. He
has published fourteen books, the most recent being *Religious Hatred:
Prejudice, Islamophobia, and Antisemitism in Global Context* (Bloomsbury,
2021) and *Understanding Religion: Theories and Methods for Studying
Religiously Diverse Societies* (University of California Press, 2021).

Suggestions for further reading

In this book
See also chapters 11 (New Atheism), 37 (converting), and 62 (value in
religion).

Elsewhere
Fiala, Andrew, and Peter Admirand. *Seeking Common Ground: A Theist/
Atheist Dialogue*. Eugene, OR: Cascade Books, 2021.

Hedges, Paul. *Towards Better Disagreement: Religion and Atheism in Dialogue*. London: Jessica Kingsley, 2017.

Mohamed Taib, Mohamed Imran. "'Nones' in Inter-faith Dialogue: The
Case for Inclusion." IPS Commons, November 1, 2016. https://ipscommons
.sg/nones-in-inter-faith-dialogue-the-case-for-inclusion/.

Stedman, Chris. *Faitheist: How an Atheist Found Common Ground with the
Religious*. Boston: Beacon, 2012.

21

Is atheism a religion, a belief system, or a world view?

Paul-François Tremlett

This question appears inviting, but it is prudent to proceed cautiously. Perhaps a definitive answer depends on the precise delineation of the question's key terms as a means of establishing whether atheism *is* or *is not* a religion, a belief system, or a world view. But pausing to reflect on the impulse to delineate, define, and circumscribe the meanings of terms, it might be altogether more productive to treat the terms in question and their meaning(s) as mutable and dynamic. For example, atheism is derived from the Greek *a-*, meaning "without," and *theos*, meaning "God." The word is commonly associated with an absence of the belief in God or gods. Must it, then, refer to a fixed or constant mental state corresponding to an absence of belief?

In Europe and North America in the twentieth century, atheism has been associated with a range of apparently antireligious political and cultural figures, ideas, and movements, including anarchists, Marxists, and nihilists, as well as Dadaism, punk, and Ayn Rand's Objectivism. However, such associations may be misleading given the fact that fairly cursory research turns up Christian anarchists (Leo Tolstoy), Christian punks (the 77s), and religious atheists (Thomas J. J. Altizer). More recent decades have seen the emergence of self-styled "New Atheists," among them Richard Dawkins, as well as a plethora of online groups, including the Brights, notable for their vocal critiques of religion but also for their cultural and political distance from radical subcultures. It seems unlikely that, across these different political, cultural, and religious formations, "atheism" has maintained a singular meaning or referred to just one kind of psychological state. Moreover, it would seem plausible that atheism is about not only the absence of certain beliefs but the presence of others.

Is East Asia, where Confucian cultures privilege protocols that make no reference to God or gods but do discipline subjects in embodied interactions with ancestors, elders, and juniors, the home of atheism? If so, would atheism there refer to a psychological state or to an embodied one? Some, notably Auguste Comte, sought to create public spaces where certain bodily affects and dispositions might be amplified and others inhibited through the spatial materialization of a deliberately atheist habitus. So is atheism about the body or about the mind?

If "atheism" has proved to be a somewhat slippery word that may well mean different things in different contexts, it might be helpful to think of the initial question as a thought experiment that invites critical reflection upon the word "atheism" by demanding its juxtaposition with other words—in this case, "religion," "belief system," and "world view." Lois Lee has written provocatively of the "atheist worshipper" and nonreligious (or secular) experiences of the transcendental, inviting juxtaposition with the term "religion." Historically, religion has been defined in terms of beliefs (E. B. Tylor), in terms of rituals (Émile Durkheim), and in terms of functions (Bronislaw Malinowski). No one seems able to say, definitively, what religion is, yet everyone remains confident that they know what religion is when they see it. Worse, the term is saturated with white, gendered, Protestant assumptions that have, for complex economic and political reasons, become hegemonic. Juxtaposing "atheism" and "religion," then, can invite straightforward comparisons between religious and nonreligious worshippers but also strategic reflections on atheism as a possible marker of certain beliefs, ritual practices, and functions and critical analysis of atheism as a term that carries ordinarily concealed or ideological assumptions.

Beliefs are typically taken to be propositional or representational mental states. That is, beliefs are held to say something about the way the world is and, as such, guide action. If action is to be rational and purposeful, then perhaps the beliefs people hold form coherent systems. A "belief system" is such a web of mutually interlocking concepts, notions, and ideas that provides an account of reality. But do beliefs really form coherent systems, or do they rather coalesce in ad hoc assemblages of social, cultural, historical, and religious experience and knowledge? Tanya Luhrmann's ethnographic account of ritual magic in London in the 1980s is notable for what Luhrmann called "interpretive drift," which she used to make sense of people who programmed computers by day and participated in ritual magic by night. It turned out to be rather easy to participate in two seemingly contradictory belief systems at the same time.

"World view" is a phrase derived from the German, *Weltanschauung*. The term is somewhat a la mode today in religious studies, but if something is described as "a world view," is the implicit suggestion that it is one view among others? If so, is a world view a view that one might try out for a while before discarding it or exchanging it for another? What consequences follow from thinking in this way? The privileging of the optical that accompanies the term "world view"—and, by extension, the cognitive and psychological—denies the role of the body and of the emotions. As Monique Scheer, Nadia Fadil, and Birgitte Schepelern Johansen suggest, the material and affective turn that productively transformed the study of religions in the 1990s can help interrogate the ways in which aspects of the secular, including law, science, and scholarship, emphasize "neutrality, impartiality, factuality, rationality and reason" while disavowing the "emotional, affective and sensorial" dimensions of these activities. Borrowing somewhat from Charles Hirschkind, if someone claims that "atheism is a world view," what of the spaces in which atheism is taken for granted—spaces such as operating theaters and factory assembly lines? Does their godless materiality implicate or constitute a body, and if they do, what kind of embodied viewing or seeing do such settings enable?

Finally, "atheism," "religion," "belief system," and "world view" all presuppose a subject—that is, a self that believes (or that doesn't believe), that sees (or views), and that acts. This subject or self is the foundation of most theories of religion and atheism. But what if it is nothing more than a host, a container to which can be added various beliefs that in turn make it speak and move? Alternatively, what if it is a puppet on a string, its words and actions generated by social forces and cues? Could an account of "atheism" be generated that did not presuppose the subject, and if so, what would atheism-without-a-subject look like? Such an account might begin not with subjects that believe or that entertain world views but with events through which subjects come to articulate themselves as such.

About the author

Paul-François Tremlett is a senior lecturer in religious studies at the Open University. He is interested in classical and contemporary theory and has conducted ethnographic research in the Philippines, Hong Kong, Taiwan, and the United Kingdom. His research attends to religion and processes of rapid social change.

Suggestions for further reading

In this book
See also chapters 2 (difference between the terms), 6 (measuring), and 12 (atheistic religions).

Elsewhere

Hirschkind, Charles. "Is There a Secular Body?" *Cultural Anthropology* 26(4) (2011): 633–647.

Lee, Lois. "Observing the Atheist at Worship: Ways of Seeing the Secular Body." In *Secular Bodies, Affects and Emotions: European Configurations*, edited by Monique Scheer, Nadia Fadil, and Birgitte Schepelern Johansen, 43–59. London: Bloomsbury, 2020.

Luhrmann, Tanya. *Persuasions of the Witch's Craft: Ritual Magic in Contemporary England*. Cambridge, MA: Harvard University Press, 1989.

Munro, Rolland. "Agency and 'Worlds' of Accounts: Erasing the Trace or Rephrasing the Action?" In *Agency without Actors? New Approaches to Collective Action*, edited by Jan-Hendrik Passoth, Birgit Peuker, and Michael Schillmeier, 67–86. London: Routledge, 2014.

Scheer, Monique, Nadia Fadil, and Birgitte Schepelern Johansen, eds. *Secular Bodies, Affects and Emotions: European Configurations*. London: Bloomsbury, 2020.

Society, politics, and media

22

What are the most atheistic societies?

Isabella Kasselstrand

Many picture Northern and Western European countries at the top of the list of "godless" societies—an idea that is largely accurate. However, measuring and comparing levels and trends of atheism across countries is notoriously difficult, as we are confronted with cultural, linguistic, political, methodological, and theoretical obstacles. Sociologist Phil Zuckerman highlights these dilemmas before settling on an estimate of 500 to 750 million atheists, agnostics, and nonbelievers in God globally, which corresponds to about 7.5 percent of the world's population. This figure compares to the 450 to 500 million, or 7 percent, noted by Ariela Keysar and Juhem Navarro-Rivera. Simply put, there is a sizeable nonreligious population in the world, but it is nonetheless distributed highly unevenly across regions and countries.

According to Zuckerman's study, Sweden tops the list of countries with the highest share of atheists, agnostics, and nonbelievers in a personal god. This is followed by Vietnam, Denmark, Norway, Japan, the Czech Republic, Finland, France, South Korea, and Estonia. Using different data, Keysar and Navarro-Rivera show that in terms of nonbelief or uncertainty in the existence of a god, the top ten countries are the Czech Republic, France, Sweden, Germany, the Netherlands, Belgium, Denmark, Norway, the United Kingdom, and South Korea, with 55 percent in the Czech Republic and 28 percent in South Korea. Furthermore, the International Social Survey Programme's 2018 data on twenty-seven countries identify ten countries where more than half of the respondents are nonbelievers in God: Sweden, the Czech Republic, Norway, Denmark, Japan, South Korea, France, Finland, Great Britain, and Germany, with 69 percent in Sweden and 51 percent in Germany. In other words, Europe does indeed dominate these rankings, with only a handful of non-European countries (South Korea, Japan, and Vietnam) stated here.

Yet when we consider the challenges of measuring global atheism, the picture of atheistic societies is complicated further. One issue to contemplate is what we count as atheism. Are we looking at individuals who call *themselves* atheists? Or are we measuring nonbelievers in God, who in theory are atheists and whom *we* may call atheists, regardless of how they label themselves? In fact, when looking at the number of atheists in a particular society, it is important to keep in mind that not believing in God and defining oneself as atheist are often not the same thing. Take the data from the World Values Survey and the European Values Study from 2008 to 2020, for example. On the question of whether the respondent believes in God, the top ten countries that rank the highest for their share of nonbelievers are China, Thailand, the Czech Republic, South Korea, Sweden, the Netherlands, Vietnam, Estonia, South Korea, France, and Norway—ranging from 81 percent in China to 45 percent in Norway. Yet if we look at the question of whether the respondent is a religious person, a nonreligious person, or an atheist, we find that the countries with the highest percentage of atheists are China, South Korea, Japan, Taiwan, Australia, Sweden, France, the Czech Republic, Andorra, and Slovenia—with 34 percent in China and 14 percent in Slovenia. Here, the top five countries in terms of self-labeled atheists are actually in Asia and Oceania, not in Europe.

So why is there only a partial overlap in the two lists of countries with the most atheists and the most nonbelievers, especially when both questions were asked in the same survey? In addition, why do the percentages differ so substantially? In fact, the most nonreligious societies, with the fewest people believing in God and where religion does not have much influence, may actually have more people being indifferent about religion and therefore rejecting the atheist label. A Scottish nonbeliever expressed to me that atheism is an active form of disbelief and is "about stating your case." In this way, a society may paradoxically be the most nonreligious when religion is so weak that no one even thinks about their religiosity—or lack thereof.

There are also challenges in comparing measures across countries and cultures. For example, are we looking at societies where governments are enforcing atheism—or a particular religion, for that matter? If doing so, how can we make meaningful comparisons to democratic societies with a high degree of religious freedom? When looking at China, Zuckerman cautions that the estimate for this country may have low validity but that the percentage of atheists, agnostics, and nonbelievers in a personal god is around 8 to 14 percent. At the same time, data from the World Values Survey suggest that 34 percent are self-defined atheists in this country. History, politics, and social expectations are all factors that play a role in how individuals report their (non)beliefs. When making cross-cultural comparisons, we also need to consider language differences, question wording, issues of translation, and the connotation of the word "atheist," especially in societies that are not historically Judeo-Christian or monotheistic.

If we expand our analysis beyond the countries and regions in the "top ten" lists explored above, we also see low or falling levels of belief in God in other regions, such as in North and South America. Despite any challenges in comparing religious decline globally, and despite distinct characteristics and processes, most highly developed or developing countries around the world are currently seeing declining levels of belief in God. Nevertheless, countries in Northern and Western Europe and in East Asia do seem to be the furthest down such a path.

About the author

Isabella Kasselstrand is a lecturer in sociology at the University of Aberdeen. Using quantitative and mixed methods, her research examines secularization and nonreligion in northern Europe and the United States.

Suggestions for further reading

In this book
See also chapters 18 (Muslim countries), 23 (why are societies atheistic), and 64 (future).

Elsewhere
Bullivant, Stephen. "Not So Indifferent After All? Self-Conscious Atheism and the Secularization Thesis." *Approaching Religion* 2(1) (2012): 100–106.

Davie, Grace. *Europe: The Exceptional Case—Parameters of Faith in the Modern World*. London: Darton, Longman and Todd, 2002.

Kasselstrand, Isabella. "Secularity and Irreligion in Cross-National Context: A Nonlinear Approach." *Journal for the Scientific Study of Religion* 58(3) (2019): 626–642.

Keysar, Ariela, and Juhem Navarro-Rivera. "A World of Atheism: Global Demographics." In *The Oxford Handbook of Atheism*, edited by Stephen Bullivant and Michael Ruse, 553–586. Oxford: Oxford University Press, 2013.

Zuckerman, Phil. "Atheism: Contemporary Numbers and Patterns." In *The Cambridge Companion to Atheism*, edited by Michael Martin, 47–65. Cambridge: Cambridge University Press, 2007.

23

Why are some societies more atheistic than others?

Teemu Taira

It is simple to say that the societies in which atheist expressions are allowed have more atheists than societies where they are prohibited. Imagine a theocracy in which everyone is expected to adhere to the religious rule of the state. There may well be people who do not believe in God and even people who regard themselves as atheists, but because such expressions are not allowed, we would not know exactly how atheistic the population in such a society might be. In any case, such a state could not be understood as a very atheistic society. Now imagine an atheistic state, such as the former Soviet Union. People might have religious beliefs, and some might regard themselves as religious, but it would be difficult to know how many because such expressions are restricted and many practices and gatherings deemed religious are prohibited. Such a state is an example of an atheistic society in the sense that religiosity is strongly privatized or restricted.

Things get more complicated in societies in which neither religious nor atheist expressions are strictly prohibited. One of the boldest theories offering an account of atheism and secularity that applies to such societies in particular is offered by Pippa Norris and Ronald Inglehart, who suggest that the rise in the level of existential security decreases religious commitment, meaning that the more existentially secure the society, the less religious it is. If a society is existentially insecure, the level of religiosity should be higher. This argument is based on survey findings that indicate that more affluent societies are less religious than poor ones. However, high income in itself does not explain this sufficiently because some wealthy countries are relatively religious, like the United States. These anomalies need an additional component; namely, wealth should be combined with a relatively high level of social welfare or strong supportive networks to provide existential security.

In addition, in recent years, scholars have emphasized that fertility rates are relatively good indicators of the level of religiosity in particular societies. Typical examples of what we have come to call religions have encouraged high fertility norms. However, when the fertility rates have declined in Europe and North America and also in several South American and Asian countries, the popularity of religion has declined. This is not a causal relation, but it suggests that fertility rates—nowadays typically low and even less than the replacement rate in existentially secure societies where children also have a better chance of surviving than in other societies—can be a useful lens for theorizing people's religious commitments on a global scale.

One of the issues that remain unanswered here is why some people identify as atheists. The theory concerning existential security simply posits a positive correlation between a low level of religiosity and a high level of existential security, but people in most secularized societies may not have much interest in atheist identification. It should also be noted that the theory does not apply to individuals as such; it focuses on societies and does not claim that every individual whose situation becomes existentially insecure is going to become more religious.

If Norris and Inglehart provide an example of a general universal pattern, other competing or complementary explanations have highlighted historical reasons to answer why some societies are more religious than others. Generally, these theories assume some kind of standpoint regarding modernity, suggesting either that modernizing societies tend to become more atheistic (or at least less religious) or that there are more particular national and regional reasons for the situation.

Sociologist of religion Steve Bruce has been one of the strongest supporters of the idea that modernity and secularization go hand in hand. He has qualified his views by arguing that he offers a historical explanation rather than a universal pattern of modernity. He maintains that modernity tends to have a secularizing effect and that this is still the strongest likelihood for the path that modernizing countries will follow, but he admits that there is also a potential element of surprise: when people have seen what happens in already modernized societies in relation to religion, they may actively work against it and change the course that modernization might otherwise take.

While Bruce does not address the issue of identification, he maintains that a high level of atheism does not have to be the end point of modernizing societies. Rather, people become indifferent toward religious beliefs and maintain interest in them only if there are some other functions that religious institutions uphold.

A slightly different view has been presented by Berger, Davie, and Fokas, who have argued that modernity does not explain how atheistic societies are. They argue rather that modernization may take more or less religious paths, thus supporting the idea of multiple modernities. In other words, modernity is not a singular path that each society follows in a similar manner; instead, societies can become modern in various ways. Their comparison of a "secular Europe" and a "religious America" leads them to suggest that Europe is not secular because it is modern. Europe is secular because of specific historical changes, due to which the idea of Christendom has dried up and Christian monopolies have lost their ground. This does not mean that the rest of the modernizing world necessarily follows Europe.

All these theories offer useful general frameworks for answering why some societies are less religious. They do not, however, answer directly why people find atheism a relevant form of identification in some countries and irrelevant in others. Therefore, recognizing and theorizing the importance of historical filters that direct secularizing tendencies represent one possible way forward. In other words, there are also historical reasons why certain nations and regions are more atheistic than others. What those reasons are is an empirical question that requires detailed historical examination. It does not mean that such an examination would not allow us to formulate theoretical patterns that may be tested in other societies. One such proposed pattern is that a high level of atheist identification may be found in countries whose majority church has not been integrated with the national identity. This could explain why atheism is popular in Estonia and the Czech Republic, for example. The sense of what it means to be Estonian or Czech has not been attached to belonging to a particular church, whereas in societies where the sense of national identity has been historically tied to the dominant church (e.g., Finland), the level of atheist identification tends to be less pronounced.

Which of these frameworks answers the question best is still an open issue, and more work should be done to figure out how they may be complementary or connected. We do not know whether one of these views will clearly become the dominant one in the end, but in the debate between them, we will learn more about the complexity of the historical and social variables related to atheism.

About the author

Teemu Taira is a senior lecturer in the study of religion at the University of Helsinki.

Suggestions for further reading

In this book
See also chapters 22 (most atheistic societies) and 64 (future).

Elsewhere
Berger, Peter, Grace Davie, and Effie Fokas. *Religion America, Secular Europe? A Theme and Variations*. Farnham: Ashgate, 2008.

Bruce, Steve. *Secularization: In Defence of an Unfashionable Theory*. Oxford: Oxford University Press, 2011.

Jenkins, Philip. *Fertility and Faith: The Demographic Revolution and the Transformation of World Religions*. Waco: Baylor University Press, 2020.

Keysar, Ariela, and Juhem Navarro-Rivera. "A World of Atheism: Global Demographics." In *The Oxford Handbook of Atheism*, edited by Stephen Bullivant and Michael Ruse, 553–586. Oxford: Oxford University Press, 2013.

Norris, Pippa, and Ronald Inglehart. *Sacred and Secular: Religion and Politics Worldwide*. Cambridge: Cambridge University Press, 2004.

Zuckerman, Phil. "Atheism: Contemporary Numbers and Patterns." In *The Cambridge Companion to Atheism*, edited by Michael Martin, 47–65. Cambridge: Cambridge University Press, 2007.

24

Has the internet made atheism more popular?

Teemu Taira

It is very difficult, if not impossible, to demonstrate beyond a reasonable doubt that the ever more ubiquitous internet positively affects the popularity of atheism. The internet has become such an integrated part of our everyday lives in many parts of the world that separating it as a causal factor is not easy. However, this does not prevent scholars from constructing plausible and useful frameworks for theorizing the possible role the internet may have in fostering atheism.

So far, scholars have paid more attention to the internet and religion than the internet and atheism. Existing studies suggest that religious institutions have lost some of their authority, but they also argue that the internet provides new opportunities for renewing religious expression and authority structures beyond traditional religious institutions. This is why scholars are somewhat divided in their assessments of whether the internet enhances secularization or opens up new areas for religions to flourish. I would suggest that the internet itself might be seen as a medium that advances secularization, at least to a moderate degree, because of the way in which it is structured and the way it is used. The easy availability of information and entertainment, mental stimulation, searching, looking and clicking, time wasting, and constant networking and communication may undermine religion's ability to hold one's interest. While it could be argued that the same dimension of distraction may also apply to difficulties in forming and maintaining atheist identities and communities, leaving people without stable identities, the general answer according to the existing scholarship is that the internet offers possibilities for the empowerment of atheistic identities, as well as plausibility structures for them, through communication and interaction in virtual communities.

According to an old stereotype, in a religious village, there was always one grumpy atheist who was disliked by everyone else who lived there.

The stereotype demonstrates the idea that atheists are alone, surrounded by people who have different ideas yet isolated from the rest of the community. The internet, however, allows people to connect with like-minded folks. This means that the internet and social media networks provide structures that facilitate the expression and maintenance of atheism and offer continuous peer support even when face-to-face contact is rare.

Partly because atheists have been able to find one another online, the internet has been dubbed the "atheist agora." One of the most popular atheist bloggers, Hemant Mehta, has stated that the worst enemy of religion is the internet. He has called the internet a "religion destroyer" because of its ability to both offer information that is detrimental to religion and reorganize atheism into a social and political force. At least among blogging atheists, there is a strong belief that their work and chosen medium matter. Most studies demonstrate that social media sites strengthen atheists' sense of belonging, largely through finding a community of like-minded people or a forum where lively debate can be cultivated.

The internet—or particular sites and platforms, to be more precise— forms a kind of atheistic counterpublic, at least an imagined one, to mainstream discussion, and it transcends traditional boundaries between private and public. In such a space, people are able to find other doubters and atheists who help them understand that they are not alone in their thoughts and that there is nothing wrong with them. The internet works effectively as an echo chamber for those looking for confirmation for their doubts, although in most cases, people need some kind of offline stimulus to begin seeking interaction with atheists.

There are also forms of social media that combine virtual interaction and face-to-face encounters. An online dating site tailored specifically for atheists, Atheist Passions, has remained a minor curiosity, and some atheists have criticized the service or made fun of it in online discussions. Many atheist groups have been formed at Meetup, which enables and encourages people to arrange offline meetings. For some atheists, however, the relevance of the internet lies in its ability to offer space for imagining the atheist community in a way that still allows anonymity and participatory flexibility. Online involvement empowers atheists in their everyday life and helps in maintaining atheist identification. Furthermore, if there is such a thing as atheist mobilization, it happens primarily on the internet and social media platforms rather than through friends and neighbors in a local community.

The empowering dimension of the internet for atheists is something that practically everyone agrees on. The disagreements arise when questions are asked about the viability and sustainability of atheist identifications and their wider societal influence. Web-based atheism can be more of an example of a temporary discourse than a movement, community, or institution, as it survives through the attention it gets. When the attention decreases or is not continually renewed, the community practically ceases to exist. In addition, there is a constant danger of the growing fragmentation of atheist online communities. There are examples of cases in which people have put an end to their atheist activism after growing weary of the argumentative and provocative nature of atheist online communities or founded new platforms that better suit their purpose. While the proliferation of new niche communities may offer the right stimulus for some individuals to "come out," the general image of belligerent atheists does not make people more interested in getting involved in the atheist cause.

Most of what has been said about the relevance of the internet for atheists and atheism potentially applies to religious communities too. This is why it is too early to definitively say what the long-term offline impact of the internet on atheism will be. The ephemeral nature of many atheist online communities should be further examined, as it may add a significant qualification to the role of the internet in fostering atheism, but the overall trend seems to be that atheists have found the internet to be very beneficial to them. This is even more the case in countries where atheism and its public expressions are forbidden or repressed; in such contexts, available testimonies of people who have become atheists mention the internet frequently. It should be emphasized, however, that the internet is rarely the only reason that people become atheists. Therefore, the internet does not make people atheists, but in combination with other factors, it can easily offer support for and even enhancement of the doubts individuals may already have.

About the author

Teemu Taira is a senior lecturer in the study of religion at the University of Helsinki.

Suggestions for further reading

In this book
See also chapters 44 (media), 46 (popular culture), and 49 (becoming an atheist).

Elsewhere
Cimino, Richard, and Christopher Smith. *Atheist Awakening: Secular Activism and Community in America*. Oxford: Oxford University Press, 2014.

Laughlin, Jack C. "Varieties of an Atheist Public in a Digital Age: The Politics of Recognition and the Recognition of Politics." *Journal of Religion, Media and Digital Culture* 5(2) (2016): 315–338.

Lundmark, Evelina. *"This Is the Face of an Atheist": Performing Private Truths in Precarious Publics*. Uppsala: Uppsala University, 2019.

Taira, Teemu. "The Internet and the Social Media Revolution." In *The Cambridge History of Atheism*, edited by Stephen Bullivant and Michael Ruse, 1024–1039. Cambridge: Cambridge University Press, 2021.

Taira, Teemu. "Media and Communication Approaches to Leaving Religion." In *Handbook of Leaving Religion*, edited by Daniel Enstedt, Göran Larsson, and Teemu Mantsinen, 335–348. Leiden: Brill, 2019.

25

What makes atheists different from the rest of the population, if anything?

Teemu Taira

It is a truism to say that atheists are more critical of religion than theists and religious people. Similarly, atheists tend to hold in favor whatever is seen (rightly or wrongly) as other than religion, such as science. It is less clear what else makes atheists different from the rest, and it is even more complicated to explain why differences exist, but some patterns emerge when sociodemographic characteristics and attitudes are examined. Some differences are local, related to a particular nation or region, and some are more common across societies. However, what makes cross-national comparisons difficult is that studies have used different conceptualizations of atheists, such as those who do not believe, those who self-identify as atheists, or those who are religiously unaffiliated. In addition, sometimes the classification differs from one study to another: some compare two categories—atheists and theists—and some use three (e.g., religious, nonreligious, atheists) or four (e.g., atheists, agnostics, culturally religious, and nonaffiliated believers as secular types). These matters make the comparison of different studies, even within one nation, quite laborious. However, despite these conceptual and methodological differences, several studies provide relatively similar results, making scholars more confident in stating something quite general about the characteristics of atheists.

The most consistent distinctive markers of atheists are related to age and gender. Atheists are likely to be young men. This is mostly a generational issue; several studies from Europe and North America have shown how younger generations are less religious than older ones.

Women are more religious than men, almost everywhere and by most measures. Similarly, men are overrepresented among atheists in most countries. In Finland, Spain, Uruguay, and the United States, for instance, about 60–70 percent of atheists are men. Globally speaking, the gender difference in the 2016 Pew Research Center survey "The Gender Gap in Religion around the World" was 59 and 41 in favor of men, and in some highly secular countries, the gender difference has practically vanished. In the same Pew Research Center survey, only 49 percent of French atheists were men.

If nonreligion is a leftover category, appearing as an answer option to the question "What is your religion, if any?" then at least in the United Kingdom, the gender difference almost disappears among young people. This is rarely the case among those who identify as atheists, however. Even when surveys surprise us and show that men younger than thirty are more religious than young women, like in contemporary Finland, young men are far more likely to identify as atheists. In this case, there was an increased popularity in nonreligious identification among young women but no similarly significant increase in atheist identification.

Atheists are also less likely to be married. This is because a large proportion of atheists are young, but even within that segment, marriage seems to be slightly less tempting for atheists. Likewise, atheists tend to have fewer descendants than theists or religious people. Atheists are also likely to live in urban areas; people living in rural areas are markedly more religious.

Other factors are more contestable, and they can differ significantly from one country and region to another. A considerable proportion of what is known about atheists is still based on the United States, so it remains a critical question to what extent such knowledge applies to the rest of the world. Several US studies have noted that atheists are slightly better educated (leading to higher income and class status) than those who are actively religious, but the results are not clear in all countries. In the United Kingdom, we find a U-pattern between religiosity and education, meaning that people who are certain about their atheist or religious identity are the most educated; in Finland, atheists are overrepresented among the very educated and very uneducated ones. These differences do not take away the fact that worldwide, atheists tend to be more educated than religious people, but the differences are moderate within nations, and they suggest the need to be cautious in our attempts to generalize globally.

In Western countries, atheists tend to be white, although the proportion of atheists among Asians can exceed that demographic (especially among second-generation Asians). In the United States and in Canada, atheists are also less likely to be foreign born. In countries with a large proportion of white people, Asians, or Latinos, Blacks are typically among the least atheistic ethnicities.

In addition to the social characteristics of atheists, some patterns emerge when the attitudes of atheists are analyzed. Political preferences differ from one country to another, but in general, atheists are more likely to be liberal (particularly regarding issues of family and sexuality), support gender equality, and be left leaning than the average person in a particular country. In the United States, atheists are more likely to vote for Democrats or register as independent than vote for Republicans; in the United Kingdom, atheists are more likely to vote for Labourites than Conservatives; in Finland, there is an overrepresentation of atheists among the Greens and the Left Alliance. More recently, there have been indications that atheists are less inclined to value national identity and maintain national pride than the rest.

U-patterns have been found when life satisfaction and happiness are examined, meaning that very pronounced views—be they atheist or theist views—tend to correlate with better life satisfaction and happiness. However, the differences are usually small when sociodemographic characteristics are controlled. While caution should be exercised in attempts to generalize, at least such results suggest that atheists do not find everything in life to be meaningless or empty. Thus, they are not different from others in that regard.

Why do these differences matter? One answer is in our interest in knowing whether atheism is a significant variable in the population. The answer is affirmative regarding some issues and attitudes but not others. What is more, knowing these things about atheists is useful in theorizing about the stereotypes that people have about atheists. Given that atheists in reality are relatively far from the negative perceptions of common stereotypes about them, such knowledge offers a possibility to challenge the basis of the stigma and discrimination that atheists encounter in various societies from not just individual citizens but governments and other societal institutions.

It is expected that if atheism gets normalized—becoming more common in society and losing the stigma it has in many countries—atheists will be relatively indistinct from the rest of the population. There are some signs pointing to such development in the most secular societies, but for the majority of the nations in the world, atheists are regarded as different from the rest. Still, it is expected that negative views concerning religions (and especially the public presence of religious institutions) will remain a visible marker of atheist identification.

About the author

Teemu Taira is a senior lecturer in the study of religion at the University of Helsinki.

Suggestions for further reading

In this book
See also chapters 26 (young people), 27 (gender), 28 (Black), and 34 (political leaning).

Elsewhere

Baker, Joseph O., and Buster G. Smith. *American Secularism: Cultural Contours of Nonreligious Belief Systems*. New York: New York University Press, 2015.

Beit-Hallahmi, Benjamin. "Atheists: A Psychological Profile." In *The Cambridge Companion to Atheism*, edited by Michael Martin, 300–317. Cambridge: Cambridge University Press, 2007.

Cragun, Ryan T., Joseph H. Hammer, and Jesse M. Smith. "North America." In *The Oxford Handbook of Atheism*, edited by Stephen Bullivant and Michael Ruse, 601–621. Oxford: Oxford University Press, 2013.

Taira, Teemu. "More Visible but Limited in Its Popularity: Atheism (and Atheists) in Finland." *Approaching Religion* 2(1) (2012): 21–35.

Woodhead, Linda. "The Rise of 'No Religion' in Britain: The Emergence of a New Cultural Majority." *Journal of the British Academy* 4 (2016): 245–261.

Zuckerman, Phil. "Atheism, Secularity, and Well-Being: How the Findings of Social Science Counter Negative Stereotypes and Assumptions." *Sociology Compass* 3(6) (2009): 949–971.

26
Are atheists typically young people?

Sarah Wilkins-Laflamme and Joel Thiessen

The short answer is, on average, yes. Let's dig into it a bit. In the majority of countries worldwide, a larger proportion of young people do not believe in God or a higher power, compared with older generations. For example, in the United States, an estimated 14 percent of young adults ages eighteen to thirty-four say they do not believe in God or a higher power in the 2018 General Social Survey (GSS), compared with only 10 percent among thirty-five- to sixty-four-year-olds and 7 percent among respondents sixty-five years or older. Not all atheists are currently young people, but a higher proportion is. Figure 26.1 contains more data from the 2018

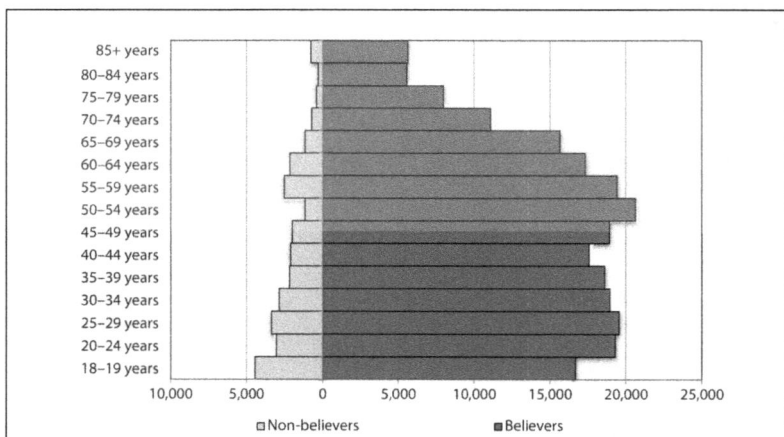

Figure 26.1. Population estimates (in thousands) by age group, US General Social Survey and Census Bureau Data, 2018

GSS, with age pyramids for those who do believe in God or a higher power and those who do not. These age pyramids are top and middle heavy for believers (more believers among older adult groups) and bottom heavy for nonbelievers (more nonbelievers among younger adult groups).

Table 26.1 in turn contains the average age of believers and nonbelievers in forty-five nations included in the 2008 and 2018 International Social Survey Programme (ISSP). In almost all forty-five countries, nonbelievers are younger on average than believers, with the exceptions (in *italic*) of those in Bulgaria, the Dominican Republic, East Germany, Israel, Slovenia, Thailand, Turkey, Ukraine, and Venezuela.

Table 26.1. International Social Survey Programme data

Country	ISSP survey wave	Average age of respondents who *do not* believe in God or a higher power	Average age of respondents who *do* believe in God or a higher power
Australia	2008	49.5	51.6
Austria	2018	47.0	52.6
Belgium	2008	44.7	50.3
Bulgaria	*2018*	*57.8*	*57.4*
Chile	2018	34.7	49.0
Croatia	2018	42.3	45.1
Cyprus	2008	37.4	41.7
Czech Republic	2018	50.9	55.9
Denmark	2018	42.2	48.1
Dominican Republic	*2008*	*38.2*	*37.9*
Finland	2018	39.9	47.2
France	2018	53.1	57.0
Germany—East	*2018*	*54.0*	*53.3*
Germany—West	2018	46.6	51.2
Great Britain	2018	49.2	55.4
Hungary	2018	44.9	50.3
Iceland	2018	41.3	51.1
Israel	*2008*	*52.5*	*49.1*

(continued)

Table 26.1. International Social Survey Programme data
(*continued*)

Country	ISSP survey wave	Average age of respondents who *do not* believe in God or a higher power	Average age of respondents who *do* believe in God or a higher power
Italy	2008	46.0	53.6
Japan	2018	51.2	54.4
Latvia	2008	38.9	45.6
Mexico	2008	33.2	39.1
Netherlands	2008	48.3	52.2
New Zealand	2018	47.8	49.3
Northern Ireland	2008	46.1	49.3
Norway	2018	45.9	51.5
Philippines	2018	41.1	43.4
Poland	2008	37.8	46.2
Portugal	2008	37.0	49.9
Republic of Ireland	2008	40.5	45.3
Russia	2018	43.2	46.7
Slovakia	2018	36.6	49.0
Slovenia	*2018*	*52.6*	*51.8*
South Africa	2008	36.7	40.6
South Korea	2018	50.9	51.1
Spain	2018	43.2	51.1
Sweden	2018	51.7	54.6
Switzerland	2018	44.5	49.5
Taiwan	2018	46.8	48.5
Thailand	*2018*	*48.6*	*45.7*
Turkey	*2008*	*40.4*	*39.6*
Ukraine	*2008*	*52.6*	*48.1*
United States	2018	40.4	49.4
Uruguay	2008	41.2	47.4
Venezuela	*2008*	*43.1*	*38.7*

When researchers have investigated further, many have found that, among those who switch from believing to nonbelieving, this transition tends to happen during their late teen and young adult years: often (not always) when parents give more choice over involvement in certain religious practices (e.g., attending religious services), when individuals develop their own circle of friends, when they move out of their parents' home, and when they attend college or university. In these settings, they begin to question the religious beliefs that they were raised with, a process sometimes aided by their peers, social media interactions, and higher education. Regardless of whether individuals are raised without belief in God in the first place or transition to it as teens or adults, in most cases, this nonbelieving then tends to last a lifetime. It is not just something specific to young adult years; it also sticks around later in life as well for most individuals.

So why are atheists younger on average then? For many decades now, each successive birth cohort (generation) in Western as well as in some non-Western nations has been less believing on average than their parents and grandparents. The secular transition framework in the field of sociology of religion highlights this *generational effect*. Although the timing may vary between regions and countries due to their distinct sociohistorical contexts, once underway, a process begins where each successive birth cohort is less religious than the preceding one. This phenomenon is aided by a range of complex and interrelated social realities, including social and religious pluralism; the diminished role of religion in key social institutions, such as education, politics, law, or health care; advances in science and technology; strengthened economic standing; and a growing value for individualism and choice in society. This secularization process achieves fruition when parents, with weakened religiosity from their now more secular social environment, have children of their own and raise their children without explicit religious socialization in markedly more secular surroundings. According to the secular transition framework, this generational decline affects all elements of religion and spirituality. Most religious beliefs, including the belief in God or a higher power, are also on the decline across birth cohorts, along with religious identity and behavior. This does not mean that religion is going to completely disappear from our societies anytime soon, but it does mean that coexistence between believers and nonbelievers is the new name of the game moving forward.

About the authors

Sarah Wilkins-Laflamme is an associate professor in the Department of Sociology and Legal Studies at the University of Waterloo (Canada). She completed her DPhil (PhD equivalent) in sociology at the University of Oxford in 2015. Her research interests include quantitative methods, sociology of religion, immigration and ethnicity, and political sociology. She has authored or coauthored two books, including *Religion, Spirituality and Secularity among Millennials: The Generation Shaping American and Canadian Trends* (Routledge, 2022) and *None of the Above: Nonreligious Identity in the US and Canada* (New York University Press, 2020).

Joel Thiessen is a professor of sociology at Ambrose University (Canada). He has authored or coauthored several books, including *None of the Above: Nonreligious Identity in the US and Canada* (New York University Press, 2020), *The Millennial Mosaic: How Pluralism and Choice Are Shaping Canadian Youth and the Future of Canada* (Dundurn Press, 2019), and *The Meaning of Sunday: The Practice of Belief in a Secular Age* (McGill-Queen's University Press, 2015).

Suggestions for further reading

In this book
See also chapters 25 (what makes atheists different), 48 (upbringing), and 64 (future).

Elsewhere
Manning, Christel. *Losing Our Religion: How Unaffiliated Parents Are Raising Their Children*. New York: New York University Press, 2015.

Taylor, Charles. *A Secular Age*. Cambridge, MA: Belknap Press of Harvard University Press, 2007.

Thiessen, Joel, and Sarah Wilkins-Laflamme. *None of the Above: Nonreligious Identity in the US and Canada*. New York: New York University Press, 2020.

Voas, David, and Mark Chaves. "Is the United States a Counterexample to the Secularization Thesis?" *American Journal of Sociology* 121(5) (2016): 1517–1556.

27

Why are men more likely to be atheists than women?

Tiina Mahlamäki

While women tend to be more religious than men, men are more commonly atheists than women. They leave their church, do not practice religion, and do not believe in any deity as often as women. Those who reject God and identify as atheists tend to be male, white, highly educated, urban, and politically liberal. But the situation is changing.

Several social, biological, and evolutionary models have been advanced to explain the gender difference. The studies have usually wondered why women tend to be more religious, as if it were somehow exceptional. Studies have not typically asked, however, what it is in atheism that appeals to men or displeases women. But while none of the existing explanatory models are unanimously accepted, they can, taken together, at least offer some points of consideration.

Some models that have sought to explain the gender gap in religious orientation—such as structural location theories (different social roles and positions lead to differences in religiosity), the compensator model (both costs and rewards of religiosity are gendered), and psychological theories on personality differences between men and women—have not received sufficient empirical support. What has been demonstrated through demographic analysis is that nonreligious and atheist people tend to enjoy a privileged standing in society: they are often male, white, educated, and of higher socioeconomic status. They do not suffer oppression, nor do they need the social or soteriological support that religious beliefs, organizations, or communities might offer.

One explanatory factor closely connected with both privileged status and gender is *education*. Historically, women have received less education than men, and more educated women tend to be less religious than their less-educated sisters. Education could be seen to shield individuals from adopting supernatural beliefs, thus associating a lack of education with vulnerability and ignorance. *Socialization* is another explanatory factor. In the same way that women are taught to be more submissive, passive, and obedient than men, they are taught to be more religious. The stronger religiosity of women is often connected to women's traditional roles as caretakers. The fact that women are more involved in the upbringing of children, maintaining the chain of memory and traditions, and caring for sick and dying persons puts them into a more immediate relationship with the ultimate questions of life and death—and God.

Sociological models consider if different modes of socialization or different kinds of social obligations projected for women and men might explain the difference. Some explanatory models ask, Do women and men simply differ from each other in some basic and fundamental way, be it biological or social? Some of these approaches have been overly simplifying, dividing humans into just men and women. Other recent studies indicate that gender differences in religiousness, while caused by biological and psychological factors, might be explained within each sex. These models do not divide humans into men and women but discuss mere roles and attitudes as well as attributes connected with masculinity and femininity and see gender division as socially constructed and maintained.

Several studies show a significant relationship between *gender orientation* and being religious; masculinity and femininity are identified as important determinants of both women's and men's religiosity. Social constructions of masculinity or "maleness" emphasize aggressiveness, logic, rationality, goal orientation, and competitiveness, while femininity or "femaleness" is associated with nurturing, gentleness, submissiveness, and community building. According to several studies, these attributes drive masculine people to align with secular beliefs and feminine people with religious ones.

The standards of masculinity within Western culture encourage men to seek adventure, brave dangers, and take risks. In some studies, the gender difference in religiousness is explained by *risk preferences*: men or masculine people are more likely to commit crimes, behave violently, drive at high speeds, hunt large and dangerous animals, and so on. According to these studies, nonreligiosity and rejecting God are part of typically masculine risk-taking behavior. These results can be interpreted in many ways. They might lead us to assume that atheists tend to be masculine risk-takers. But there are gaps in this explanation. This theory assumes that all individuals are calculating costs and rewards when choosing whether to turn toward religion or away from it. Empirical examinations have demonstrated that both men and women take risks, but the risks are of a different kind. Analyses of the datasets of the General Social Survey and World

Values Survey regarding the impact of gender and belief in an afterlife on religiousness have revealed results that contradict the risk-preference theory. They found that risk preferences were related to religiousness, but they did not find indications that the relationship between risk-taking and religiousness was linked to gender.

Penny Edgell, Jacqui Frost, and Evan Stewart, who have developed the risk-preference approach, emphasize that it is *social risk* and not existential risk that explains why nonreligion, and especially atheism, is more socially risky for women and other marginalized groups. They see religiosity, nonreligiosity, and gender as contextually embedded practices and argue that women more often than men face greater risks for similarly socially stigmatized choices. That means that women are more likely than men to experience social costs for embracing nonreligious beliefs, identities, and practices.

The nonreligion as a social-risk model applies best in the United States, where religiosity, national identity, and civic virtue are closely connected. At the same time, atheists are discriminated against, disliked, and distrusted. Rejecting religion in the United States is socially risky, and it is often women who bear the social costs of stigmatized nonreligious choices. This is because atheism is seen as violating gendered expectations of women being moral, nurturing, and religious, while men do not risk appearing less masculine when rejecting religion. Men who choose atheism are also more likely to be in privileged positions (educated, for instance), so they are more able to avoid stigma.

Marta Trzebiatowska and Steve Bruce have pointed out that secularization processes have affected men before women, and when secularization processes impact women as well, the number of nonreligious women will grow. Thus, they suggest that there is a time differential in the gender gap. This has, to some extent, proved to be the case because the number of nonreligious and atheist women is growing. And while higher levels of atheism are clearly linked to the promotion of egalitarianism, gender equality, and women's empowerment across nations, this direction is plausible.

About the author

Tiina Mahlamäki earned her doctorate in the study of religion, specializing in civil religion and gender. She is a senior lecturer on the study of religion at the University of Turku, Finland. Her research and publications focus on contemporary religion, atheism, Western esotericism, and creative writing.

Suggestions for further reading

In this book
See also chapters 25 (what makes atheists different), 42 (activism), and 43 (feminism).

Elsewhere

Brewster, Melanie Elyse. "Atheism, Gender, and Sexuality." In *The Oxford Handbook of Atheism*, edited by Stephen Bullivant and Michael Ruse, 511–524. Oxford: Oxford University Press, 2013.

Edgell, Penny, Jacqui Frost, and Evan Stewart. "From Existential to Social Understanding of Risk: Examining Gender Differences in Nonreligion." *Social Compass* 4(6) (2017): 556–574.

Trzebiatowska, Marta, and Steve Bruce. *Why Are Women More Religious Than Men?* Oxford: Oxford University Press, 2012.

28
Why are there so few Black atheists?

Daniel Swann

Across many societies that use "Black" as a racial category, there appears to be a trend of Black people in these societies identifying as atheists at lower rates than their fellow residents. Take the United States, for example. There are several reasons why there are fewer Black atheists in America than atheists of other races and ethnicities. Culture and cultural history, the stigmatization of atheist identities by Americans at large and African Americans specifically, demographics, and social factors can all help explain the question "Why are there so few Black atheists?"

Although most of the work done about Black atheists has been culturally situated in the United States, it is likely that other societies with similar histories and similar racial constructs of the category "Black" have some level of applicability with these findings. An example of such a society that shows similar patterns to the United States in terms of the racial disparities in identifying as atheist is the United Kingdom.

Religion, particularly Christianity, has been central to African American culture and its development. Early Negro spirituals drew upon biblical traditions, churches and religious spaces were among the freest spaces for Black Americans, and early Black literature often appealed to biblical notions of bondage, deliverance, and freedom. Given this set of circumstances, one could see why the Black church developed into such a central institution for Black Americans. Additionally, this important religious and cultural institution has in many ways doubled as an activist base for positive social change in African American life, further engraining it as centrally situated in the majority of Black communities.

Parts of the abolitionist movement as well as the civil rights movement, often in the form of respectability politics, used Christianity as a way to humanize Black Americans in the eyes of White Americans. These portrayals of Black Christianity in successful and generally fondly remembered movements influenced—and continue to influence—the way in which blackness is seen in contemporary America.

In fact, the acceptance of the centrality of religion, particularly Christianity, as an important element of Black culture is so widely accepted that the racial category "Black" actually transmits religiosity in the United States; that is, when people are informed someone is Black, they are more likely to attach a presumptive religious belief to that person. A helpful analogy is that the category "NBA player" transmits the idea of tallness in a way "MLS player" does not. So in addition to having to overcome the cultural and stigmatizing consequences of being atheist, Black atheists also violate a major assumption of Americans at large. This also holds true for the perception of Black Americans by other Black Americans.

"Atheist" is one of the most highly stigmatized identities in the United States, and this is consistent across most demographics. Thus, Black atheists often knowingly take on a double stigma: two highly stigmatized identities of Black and atheist. This has profound effects on Black atheist identity development, expression, and presentation. However, Black Americans stigmatize atheists even more and distrust atheists even more than do their fellow residents. Not only are atheists hyperstigmatized in Black communities broadly, but there appears to be a particular kind of racialized stigma that many Black atheists face from other Black Americans.

Among their fellow Black Americans, Black atheists often experience challenges to their authenticity for identifying as atheist. The ideas that atheism is a "white thing" and that "Black folks don't do atheism" are fairly widely distributed, can also be found in some Black cultural productions, and serve to reinforce the idea that religiosity is an essential component of blackness in the United States. The idea that one cannot be authentically Black was one that many Black atheists report encountering, both directly and indirectly. Some of them report hearing the idea that Christianity is "a part of us" and a "part of who we are." To a group that has a highly salient racial identity, this challenge to authenticity is no doubt a consideration that might lower the rates of individuals who identify as atheist.

Many Black atheists also link the stigma to potential consequences in interpersonal relationships with parents and grandparents, other family members, and potential romantic partners. There is research that suggests many Black atheists feel that at least one interpersonal relationship has been negatively affected by their identity, including the dissolution of relationships.

Additionally, Black Americans and Blacks in many other countries are stigmatized within their respective society. Adopting another highly

stigmatized identity is a decision that is probably made with more trep-
idation than making such a decision without having to consider other
stigmatized identities or visible markers of stigma.

Social factors that correlate with atheism, such as higher incomes,
higher levels of education, white-collar work, and regionality (Blacks
disproportionately live in the more religious Southern states), are not
associated with African Americans. That is, the social factors that correlate with being religious and with higher levels of religiosity also correlate
with the average social outcomes of African Americans. Most of the
disparities that we see in racial outcomes can be traced back to historical
race relations, discrimination, and structural racism. But the fact that
Blacks are among the lowest incomes of any racial group, have lower
levels of wealth, are less likely to hold college degrees, and are less likely
to hold white-collar jobs almost certainly relates to their lower rates of
identifying as atheist.

Blacks are more likely to be raised religious and form a religious
identity and are less likely to see atheism presented in a positive or even
neutral way. Given these circumstances alone, we would expect to see
fewer Black atheists than atheists of other races. However, to understand
why these circumstances exist in the first place, one needs to examine
the interplay among history, stigma, culture, race relations, and contemporary understandings of race—namely, the way in which Blacks were
marginalized and the spaces of freedom that they were given produced
a culture in which spirituality, particularly Christianity and particularly
Black mainline Protestantism, was and remains central.

The lived experiences of Black Americans regarding atheist identities are qualitatively different from the lived experiences of many other
demographics. They have a unique set of circumstances, a unique set
of considerations, and potentially a unique set of consequences that all
contribute to why there tend to be so few Black atheists.

About the author

Daniel Swann is a sociologist from Goucher College who completed his
graduate studies about Black atheists at the University of Maryland. He
researches and writes about religion, atheism, race, politics, and rhetoric.

Suggestions for further reading

In this book
See also chapters 31 (racism), 38 (discrimination), and 63 (health).

Elsewhere

Cragun, Ryan T. "Who Are the 'New Atheists'?" In *Atheist Identities: Spaces and Social Contexts*, edited by Lori G. Beaman and Steven Tomlins, 195–211. Cham: Springer, 2014.

Hutchinson, Sikivu. *Moral Combat: Black Atheists, Gender Politics, and the Values Wars*. Los Angeles: Infidel Books, 2011.

Pinn, Anthony. *The End of God-Talk: An African American Humanist Theology*. New York: Oxford University Press, 2012.

Pinn, Anthony. *What Is African-American Religion?* Minneapolis: Fortress, 2011.

Swann, Daniel. *A Qualitative Study of Black Atheists: "Don't Tell Me You're One of Those."* Lanham, MD: Rowman & Littlefield, 2020.

29
Does migration make people less religious?

Tuomas Martikainen

International migration is one of the key reasons why we speak of religion these days. Immigrant Islam has become a salient political topic in many countries around the world. But are there grounds besides popular debates for associating international migrants with high levels of conservative, or even radical, religion and religiosity? What about secular and atheist migrants? Do they exist in any other role than that of an apostate or a vocal critic of her migrant fellows' religious behavior? Does migration make people less or more religious/secular, or does it make any difference at all? In order to answer the above questions, let us consider three main areas: migrants' country of origin, the migration and settlement process, and migrants' country of destination.

The world's countries have very distinct religious and secular profiles. Therefore, it is crucial to understand what the starting point for a migrant is, as it is a sociological truism that the society and family in which one has grown up and lived the early parts of one's life leave permanent marks on one's behavior and world view. However, no country in the world is singular for its citizens' way of life. All societies have internal differences that are too many to address here but are nevertheless significant for an individual's disposition and opportunities. All countries have secularists and atheists, no matter how religious the countries' populations on average are.

Thus, knowing the migrant's country of origin is only a starting point. This is accentuated by the fact that migration is a selective process. The usual international migrant is a young adult in her twenties or thirties. The main reasons for migration are related to work, family, and educational opportunities, which all indicate life stages that may relate to the migrant's world view. For example, married migrants may soon establish a family and have children, where issues of the child's educational world view soon become relevant. Conversely, work migrants may mostly focus on gaining as much money as possible and leave other considerations in the background.

The selectivity of emigration even relates to religious and political issues, as groups having another ideological disposition than that in power in the country of origin may lead to higher-than-average emigration in these groups. History is full of examples of both religious and secular people who have been forced to leave their motherland for ideological reasons. Still today, atheism is not tolerated in many countries. Besides individual exiles, even large groups have been the targets of hostility for political and religious reasons. Refugees constitute approximately 10 percent of the world's international migrants.

Knowing a migrant's origin provides us with some clues, but migration itself is a transforming process. One leaves behind the certainties of everyday life and is confronted with a stressful period of learning to live in a new place and society. For many, this coincides with young adulthood, which is also a critical period in personality development. Some scholars suggest that religion becomes more important due to immigration, but more recent studies have challenged this. Still, migration's potential to create personal change is obvious.

As much as the country of origin, so does the country of destination and settlement affect migrants. Its role increases over time, even though transnational connections can stay lively for a prolonged time through media, travels, and local migrant communities. However, here again we need to remind ourselves that all societies are pluralistic regarding the ways of life present in them. In Western societies, in particular, people have considerable freedom in organizing their lives according to their wishes, including the selection of with whom they socialize. Nevertheless, Western societies are also relatively open and do have extensive publicly funded interventions that, from primary to higher education through to social and other policies, include many measures aspiring to influence the population. Recent research provides strong support that the context in which one lives influences one strongly. This also applies to religious and secular issues.

Whereas migration itself can be a disruptive process on an individual level and can lead to a more or less religious or secular life, it seems that the main direction of change is to become increasingly similar to the majority population. While not yet confirmed in all types of societies, it is plausible that these changes take place most smoothly in open societies that include considerable interaction with the majority population. In the case of repressed groups, we may expect a stronger opposition to change, whereby one's preexisting world view remains stronger in order to protect the groups' integrity. However, even such exclusive world views are not immune to change, as studies of the substantive changes in migrants' children's world views tell us. European studies show that migrants' children are less religious than their parents though still more religious than the average native born. The least religious of all are the children of mixed marriages.

Finally, after we have considered these various societal- and migrant-specific issues, we also need to ask whether some religions are more prone to change, including changes leading to secularization. No definite answer to this question exists yet. On the one hand, some religions support remaining apart from the surrounding society and thereby from its secularizing forces. Such views are common among many religious sects that aim to preserve distance from outsiders. On the other hand, no religion has been immune to change, whereby we have many examples of at first highly exclusive groups that later have become more open.

To answer the main question—Does migration make people less religious?—the answer is that migration opens a window of opportunity for change in many directions, but at least it makes evident for the migrant that her own world view is not the only one that matters. It makes one's beliefs, whatever they are, vulnerable. For those who worry about a "religionizing" trend in Western societies, as people from more religious parts of the world arrive, my message is simple: If you value secularity and atheism, make the society such that it allows people of other convictions to remain without fear of attacks on their beliefs. At the same time, show these newcomers that a secular and atheist way of life is worth pursuing and interact with them at all levels of social life, including being willing to marry them. Exclusion is the best recipe for perpetuating devout beliefs, whatever they are; being inclusive does just the opposite.

About the author

Tuomas Martikainen is a senior researcher at the University of Eastern Finland. He has done research on migrant integration and religions.

Suggestions for further reading

In this book
See also chapters 22 (most atheistic societies), 49 (becoming an atheist), and 64 (future).

Elsewhere

Connor, Phillip. *Immigrant Faith: Patterns of Immigrant Religion in the United States, Canada and Western Europe.* New York: New York University Press, 2014.

Kasselstrand, Isabella, and Setareh Mahmoudi. "Secularization among Immigrants in Scandinavia: Religiosity across Generations and Duration of Residence." *Social Compass* 67(4) (2020): 617–636.

Pew Research Center. *Faith on the Move: The Religious Affiliation of International Migrants.* Washington, DC: Pew Research Center, 2012.

30
How has atheism related to politics?

Steven Kettell

At first glance, atheism might not appear to be especially political. Compared to ideologies like liberalism or socialism, it is hard to see how a mere belief in the nonexistence of god(s) can provide the basis for a political cause. Yet atheism is political in a number of ways. Atheism has been seen historically as a threat to the social order, has inspired a range of political campaigns to challenge religious power and privilege, has been linked (often wrongly) to repressive political forces, and in recent years, has been turned into a social movement with its own sense of identity and internal power dynamics.

Atheism is usually said to have emerged in Greece sometime during the fifth and sixth centuries BCE. Initially limited to a small number of thinkers, atheism was nevertheless considered to pose a challenge to the existing power structures of the ancient world. Social order at this time was grounded in religious rites and rituals designed to ensure the security of the Greek (and later the Roman) state, and atheists were criminalized for having heretical beliefs.

Atheist ideas continued to be suppressed throughout the medieval era. With European society now dominated by the Roman Catholic Church, the predominant view among political and theological elites was that enforcing the moral teachings of Christianity was essential to maintain social stability. Being an atheist during this time was extremely dangerous, with harsh punishments (including death) being meted out for blasphemy.

Atheist ideas began to grow in popularity from the sixteenth century following a weakening in the power of the church. By the eighteenth century, atheists were directly challenging religious power and privilege. Viewing religion as a barrier to social and political progress, many atheists were publishing works criticizing religious beliefs and aligning themselves to political campaigns for progressive social causes, such as women's emancipation, voting reform, equal rights for nonbelievers, and secularist ideas for the formal separation of church and state. Organized groups aiming to promote explicitly nonreligious ideas also began to develop.

Twentieth-century atheism is connected to politics in different ways. A key assertion made by critics of atheism is that it helped drive the totalitarian political ideologies of fascism and communism. Here, the loss of a religious moral code is seen as a direct contributor to an outbreak of global repression and conflict. The reality, however, was rather different. Totalitarian regimes can be seen not as manifestations of atheism but as political religions, drawing on core aspects of religious systems (such as mass rites, mythologies, and sacred texts and symbols) to invoke the worship of the state. And while communist regimes certainly promoted atheism as part of their official doctrines, their despotic nature cannot be explained by an absence of religious belief. Indeed, claims of a link between atheism, immorality, and violence are refuted by the postwar growth in the popularity of atheist ideas. The decline of religious beliefs and practices in Western Europe, for example, coincided with the expansion of democratic politics, individual freedom, and human rights.

Atheism remains a political force in places where religion holds political power. At the present time, over seventy countries have blasphemy laws directly repressing atheist ideas. Against this backdrop, atheists are closely linked to a variety of political causes. These include campaigns to promote free speech and expression (such as the abolition of blasphemy laws), to establish legal and civil rights for nonbelievers, to promote individual freedom and equality on issues such as sexual orientation and reproductive rights (e.g., promoting the legalization of same-sex marriage and access to abortion, both of which remain stridently opposed by most religions groups), and to promote and uphold the values of secularism, including campaigns to disestablish state religions and abolish faith schools.

Atheists seek to achieve these objectives in various ways. Promotional activities include the publication of books, articles, and magazines about atheism; the production of media programs such as atheist podcasts and content on platforms such as YouTube; and awareness-raising campaigns such as International Darwin Day and the use of atheist advertisements on billboards and public transport, the most famous of which was an "atheist bus" campaign launched in London in 2009 with the slogan "There's Probably No God. Now Stop Worrying and Enjoy Your Life." Atheists also lobby governments and seek to change public opinion through a range of nonreligious campaign organizations.

In recent years, atheists (particularly in the United States) have sought to transform atheism into a politically active social movement. In doing this, atheists have made direct comparisons to previous social struggles for equality (such as the civil rights movement), arguing that nonbelievers need to become empowered by developing their own sense of community and identity. This process has involved the creation of nonreligious social action groups (such as Non-believers Giving Aid), the promotion of community gatherings (such as the Atheist Film Festival), and the use of irreligious symbols and imagery (such as the satirical Flying Spaghetti Monster) to create a sense of group belonging.

This attempt to construct a social movement based on atheism has also led to a number of internal tensions and schisms around its goals, strategies, and direction. One key issue has centered on the topic of branding and the nature of atheist identity itself. This has involved a debate on whether atheists should continue to call themselves "atheists" or adopt a different label, such as "Brights." Another critical debate has centered on the kinds of political strategies that atheists should use. A critical distinction here has been between people who favor the use of a confrontational approach toward challenging religion and promoting atheist ideas and those who prefer to adopt more moderate and conciliatory strategies, including alliances with progressive religious groups on issues of shared concern, such as climate change.

Social-movement atheism also faces tensions around issues of diversity. One of the main problems here is that atheism remains excessively white, elitist, and male, with a notable lack of representation from ethnic minority groups and women. Critics claim that this lack of diversity threatens to inhibit the long-term growth of atheism and undermines its ability to achieve its political aims. A pressing issue for the atheist movement at the present time is to find ways of bringing in underrepresented groups and broaden its appeal.

About the author

Steven Kettell is a reader in politics and international studies in the Department of Politics and International Studies, University of Warwick. His primary research interests are focused on the politics of secularism, nonreligion, and the role of religion in the public sphere. He is a coauthor of *The Politics of New Atheism* (with Stuart McAnulla and Marcus Schulzke; Routledge, 2018).

Suggestions for further reading

In this book
See also chapters 32 (peace), 33 (communism), 34 (political leaning), 35 (president), and 42 (activism).

Elsewhere

Buckley, Michael J. *At the Origins of Modern Atheism*. New Haven, CT: Yale University Press, 2009.

Hyman, Gavin. *A Short History of Atheism*. London: I. B. Tauris, 2010.

McAnulla, Stuart, Steven Kettell, and Marcus Schulzke. *The Politics of New Atheism*. London: Routledge, 2018.

Thrower, James. *Western Atheism: A Short History*. New York: Prometheus, 2000.

31

What is the historical relationship between atheism and racism?

Nathan G. Alexander

Racism has not always been with us. Many historians have now suggested that it was not until the modern period (roughly after 1500) that ideas arose that some races were superior or inferior to one another. Earlier people noticed others who had different skin colors or hair forms, for example, but they did not attribute the same kind of value to these differences as modern people did.

But this begins to change after 1500, when the ideas of race and racism emerged in the West. The question then becomes, Why did racism arise, and did secularization have anything to do with it? Some historians have seen Christianity itself as central in the creation of racism; others have held the decline of Christianity responsible for the rise of racism. But the situation is more complicated than either of these simple stories.

There is no question that as the dominant cultural force in Western societies, Christianity shaped the way race was understood. Anti-Semitism, the hatred of Jews, slowly shifted from a religious prejudice in the medieval period into a biological or racial one in modern times. In other words, the hatred toward the Jews morphed from being about their religion to being about their imagined race.

The development of the Atlantic slave trade, in which millions of African slaves were shipped to the Americas, further cemented ideas about race. Slavery predated the development of racist ideology, but Christianity acted as an early justification on the grounds that Africans were heathens and could therefore rightly be enslaved. Passages from the Old and New Testaments further provided legitimacy to slavery. The need to spread the Gospel to so-called heathens likewise justified imperialism and territorial conquest around the globe.

Thus far, it seems as though Christianity played an important role in the development of racism, but secular thought too had a role to play.

Beginning particularly in the eighteenth-century Enlightenment, there was an urge among scientists to classify everything in the natural world. This can perhaps best be seen in the species classification system of the Swedish botanist Carl Linnaeus in the first half of the eighteenth century. He popularized and standardized the system of combining genus and species names (e.g., *Homo sapiens*) that we still use today. Scientists who considered humans part of the natural world, not special creations of God, wished to extend their classification schemes to the different varieties of humanity. Various divisions of humanity into distinct races—sometimes three main races, sometimes four, sometimes five, sometimes over sixty!—proliferated over the 1700s and 1800s. These schemes often saw—erroneously—different racial groups as permanently distinct in terms of their physical and mental features.

Paradoxically, however, in the eighteenth-century Enlightenment, secular ideas about the equality of humanity were also born. One thinks, for example, of the American Declaration of Independence of 1776 ("all men are created equal") or the French Declaration of the Rights of Man and of the Citizen. At the same time, as thinkers divided up humanity into racial groups, other thinkers (and sometimes the very same ones) were proclaiming on secular grounds that all humans were equal.

The racial divisions of humanity also had a theological element—namely, in the debate over monogenesis and polygenesis. Monogenesis said that all humans came from a single origin, Adam and Eve, as the Bible said. Polygenesis meanwhile said that each human race had its own separate origin, meaning that all the races were originally and permanently distinct. As a general rule, monogenesis seemed to act against racism, since it said all people, no matter their race, were ultimately related, whereas polygenesis maintained fundamental distinctions between races. Again, as a general rule, it was more often Christians who supported monogenesis, while atheists and other secular people supported polygenesis.

The division between monogenesis and polygenesis became less important following the publication of Charles Darwin's theory of evolution in 1859. In his scheme, humans were not specially created by God but had evolved from an ape ancestor. In this way, he was a monogenist, but not a Christian one. Darwin himself hated slavery and the cruelties of imperialism, which he saw as justified in part by the theories of polygenesis. This hatred of polygenesis provided an impetus for his own theories about the unity of humanity.

But different thinkers drew both antiracist and racist lessons from Darwinism about race. For some, differences between races were superficial and unimportant, developed too recently in humanity's past to matter much. For others, some races were at a higher stage of biological or cultural evolution than others, and their moral worth was therefore based on their imagined level of evolution.

A related issue is eugenics, founded in the late nineteenth century by Darwin's cousin, Francis Galton. Eugenics said that certain traits were heritable, and therefore, one could weed out undesirable traits and boost desirable ones. Eugenics programs ranged from encouraging supposedly "fitter" people to have more children, to encouraging the availability of birth control, to forced sterilization, and even to genocide as in Nazi Germany. It was true that Galton and some of his early followers were secular, but it is also true that eugenics found support across the religious spectrum.

How did secular activists relate to questions of racism? Take, for example, the nineteenth-century American freethinker Robert Ingersoll, dubbed the Great Agnostic. Ingersoll was probably the most famous freethinker of his era, and he used his platform to protest against racism. In the late nineteenth century, in the wake of the end of slavery, Ingersoll protested as newly won rights for African Americans were rolled back. Ingersoll deplored racial segregation and condemned the practice of lynching—the murder of supposed Black criminals by a mob. What was more, Ingersoll spoke for the value of intercultural exchange and against the movement to prohibit Chinese immigration.

One can cite examples of atheists who supported racist policies and ideas, but especially as we approach the present, these people became increasingly fringe figures to the main currents of atheist thought.

It is clear that if one tries hard enough, one can find arguments for or against racism in Christianity or in secular thought. It would be too simplistic to suggest that either is *inherently* racist or antiracist. But atheists' widely shared rationality, humanistic values, and skepticism could lead them in antiracist directions.

About the author

Nathan G. Alexander is a writer and historian from Canada. He is the author of *Race in a Godless World: Atheism, Race, and Civilization, 1850–1914* (New York University Press / Manchester University Press, 2019).

Suggestions for further reading

In this book
See also chapters 9 (Darwin), 28 (Black), and 38 (discrimination).

Elsewhere

Alexander, Nathan G. *Race in a Godless World: Atheism, Race, and Civilization, 1850–1914*. New York: New York University Press, 2019.

Bethencourt, Francisco. *Racisms: From the Crusades to the Twentieth Century*. Princeton, NJ: Princeton University Press, 2013.

Fredrickson, George M. *Racism: A Short History*. Princeton, NJ: Princeton University Press, 2002.

Kidd, Colin. *The Forging of Races: Race and Scripture in the Protestant Atlantic World, 1600–2000*. Cambridge: Cambridge University Press, 2006.

32
Does atheism promote peace?

Stacey Gutkowski

Since 9/11, academics have extensively researched whether religions promote violence. They have found a mixed picture: sometimes yes but most often no. For comparison, they have examined "atheist" regimes, like the USSR. Whether a state promotes peace or violence has little to do with how religious a population or politicians are. Beyond the government, whether a nonstate group or individual promotes peace or violence also has very little to do with the group's creed or the individual's beliefs.

Before considering whether atheism promotes peace, we must start with another question: "Does religion promote violence or peace?" This leads us to further questions: What do we actually mean by "religion"? (This is a very complicated question, as others in the book have described.) Are we talking about religious texts? Does it matter when and by whom those texts were written and what authority they carry among followers? If a text says something open to interpretation, then what interpretation is most authoritative? Who gets to decide? Are we talking about how religious leaders use religious texts or symbols to promote a political message? Are we talking about how political leaders use religious symbols to back whatever point they want to make to rally their followers?

Scholars agree that the relationship between religion and political violence is deeply complex. They agree that across the globe since the 1980s, there has been an uptick in those actors, states, nonstate groups, and individuals who use religious idioms and symbols to justify violence. They agree that these symbols are rarely used in isolation but are part of a matrix of other factors—the striving for national sovereignty, economic grievances, racist sentiments—that are used to justify violent action. They agree that disputes that become "religionized"—where potentially incommensurable values, laws, ontological beliefs, or sacred spaces are in play—are the hardest to resolve through negotiations rather than battlefield victory. They agree that very few disputes actually become religionized. Wars are still, as they always were, about guns, land, and money.

The question "Does atheism promote peace (or violence or something in between)?" raises a similar set of questions. However, the difference is that very few political actors, including states, have set out a political program to actively promote atheism among the population. On this front, we can identify state-sponsored atheism in the USSR and its ideological satellites in Eastern Europe and Central and East Asia. However, it would be a mistake to say that such state-sponsored atheism played any causal role in state repression of political opposition movements. Rather, the best way to understand these things is to ask, Who holds power in any given political context, who wants power, and what do they think is the best way to rally people to their cause? That is a different question from asking, What does any actor believe about the ultimate state of the universe and the purpose of human life?

Authoritarian regimes, regardless of creed, use violence as a brutal suppression tactic against any credible opposition to their rule. That was the case in the USSR and has been the case under other communist regimes. In another example, Marxist-influenced fighters seeking to overthrow the old political order in the Catholic, Spanish-speaking world in the twentieth century violently attacked priests. But they did so because clerics were allies of the regime, not because the fighters were atheistic or antireligious. In the Middle East from the 1920s to the 1970s, regimes aiming to modernize newly formed states suppressed clerical opposition while at the same time claiming Islamic legitimacy for themselves. All these regimes aimed to promote stability and maintain their own power, including through the use of force by the police and intelligence services. This is not the same as promoting peace, what Norwegian sociologist Johan Galtung calls negative peace (absence of violence) or positive peace (structural equality).

To summarize, we cannot come to any sound conclusions about a causal relationship between atheism and peace. But we can begin to ask other interesting questions about the relationship between peace, violence, and atheism.

For example, in my own research, I have been intrigued by the question, How does violence (including political violence) feel to those who describe their beliefs as atheist? Beyond atheists, I have also been interested in agnostics or humanists or people who, in their own words, are "not very religious" or "rational" or "skeptical." Does violence feel different if you do not believe a higher power can reliably be called upon to save you or care? So far, I have no definitive conclusions. But it seems that violence feels the same regardless of your philosophical beliefs because we all bruise and bleed in roughly the same way. What differs is how we describe violence and what it means to us. Here, many factors are in play: personal belief framework as well as other factors like political leanings, gender, geography, and so on.

The popular adage "There are no atheists in foxholes" coined by Ernie Pyle, Pulitzer Prize–winning American war correspondent during World War II, is pithy. However, there is actually very little academic research on how living through war affects philosophical and ethical beliefs or vice versa. The consensus of that research is that whatever you were going into the "foxhole"—an ardent believer (in God or not), indifferent, confused—is what you will end up when you come out. As far as what happens in the "foxhole," anything goes. Some people see God. Others see only human brutality and evidence for Nietzsche's conclusion that God is dead. What is also interesting is what people do. Research from cases around the world shows that soldiers will carry spiritual talismans for good luck into battle regardless of what, if, or how they believe. The same is true for civilians hoping just to survive.

About the author

Stacey Gutkowski is a reader in peace and conflict studies and deputy director of the Centre for the Study of Divided Societies, King's College London. She is the author of two books, *Religion, War and Israel's Secular Millennials: Being Reasonable?* (Manchester University Press, 2020) and *Secular War: Myths of Religion, Politics and Violence* (I. B. Tauris, 2013), as well as articles and book chapters on the relationships among politics, security, religion, and secularism in Jordan, Israel/Palestine, Lebanon, Iraq, Egypt, Afghanistan, the United States, and the United Kingdom. She is coeditor of the book series Religion and Its Others: Studies in Religion, Nonreligion and Secularity (DeGruyter) and was codirector of the Nonreligion and Secularity Research Network (2008–2020).

Suggestions for further reading

In this book
See also chapters 20 (dialogue), 30 (politics), and 33 (communism).

Elsewhere
Gutkowski, Stacey. "Jewish Atheists in Foxholes? Existential Beliefs and How War Feels." *Secular Studies* 1(1) (2019): 34–73.

Gutkowski, Stacey. *Religion, War and Israel's Secular Millennials: Being Reasonable?* Manchester: Manchester University Press, 2020.

Gutkowski, Stacey. "Secularism, Security and War." In *Beyond Religion*, edited by Phil Zuckerman, 203–221. New York: Macmillan, 2016.

Skabelund, Aaron, and Akito Ishikawa. "Japan." In *Religion in the Military Worldwide*, edited by Ron E. Hassner, 23–44. Cambridge: Cambridge University Press, 2014.

33
How has atheism related to communism?

Atko Remmel

Communism refers to an ideology that seeks to establish a communist society, which is characterized by common ownership of production and a lack of social classes, money, and other features that characterize capitalist societies. In its stance toward religion, communism comes in various formations, varying from complete entwinement (Christian communism) to negative attitude (Marxist communism). Even within Marxist thinking, notable differences can be found, as in the case of the "God-builders" at the beginning of the twentieth century, who advocated for the creation of a new religion grounded in science. Yet most of the communist movements of the twentieth century, especially those based on Marxism, have included some form of atheism in their agenda.

Marxism is based on the theories of German philosopher Karl Marx (1818–1883), who saw the development of societies as based on class struggle. Tensions arose between the ruling classes that owned the means of production and the working classes who sold their labor in return for wages. Religion, according to Marx, creates false consciousness by teaching that human misery is God's will, whereas in reality, it is a result of the exploitation by the ruling classes. Thus, religion makes suffering a virtue, and by teaching that it will be rewarded in life after death, religion functions as a means of protecting the stability of the system. It prevents the development of class consciousness—that is, an understanding of one's position in the chain of power and the first step toward the revolution that would replace capitalism with communism. Therefore, Marx, in his *Critique of Hegel's Philosophy of Right* (1843), compared religion to opium:

> Religion is the sigh of the oppressed creature, the heart of a heartless world, and the soul of soulless conditions. It is the opium of the people. The abolition of religion as the illusory happiness of the people is

the demand for their real happiness. To call on them to give up their illusions about their condition is to call on them to give up a condition that requires illusions. The criticism of religion is, therefore, in embryo, the criticism of that vale of tears of which religion is the halo.

It has been argued that by using this metaphor, Marx pointed out that opium was not only a painkiller; it was a source of profit and utopian visions. As opium does not cure anything, in order to improve the situation, one should not fight religion per se but instead try to change the social conditions that call for the existence of religion. In turn, religion dissolves itself, as there is no need for it anymore.

Practice—the criterion of truth according to Marxist understanding—however, turned out to be much more complicated than the theory anticipated, as religion proved to be persistent even after, in Lenin's words, "cutting off its social roots." The followers of Marx had to deal with the problem, but depending on the time and place, they chose different strategies. Extreme cases, such as the cultural revolutions of Stalin, Mao, and Pol Pot, sought to eradicate religion completely, although these attempts were short-lived. In most cases, both sides, religion and state-sponsored atheism, were accommodated and developed, learning—or trying to learn—from each other in everyday life and also during the Marxist-Christian dialogues in the 1960s and 1970s. Therefore, despite the common root, there are very different constellations of atheism and communism not only in different countries but even within one communist project.

Let us turn to look at the example of the Soviet Union, one of the best-known communist experiments. The Bolsheviks saw religion as an obstacle to their monopoly on political, ideological, and spiritual authority. Even though a commitment to atheism remained a constant in Soviet religious policy, its implementation and interpretation depended primarily on the political needs of the day, which differed from one period to another. This also influenced the methods for dealing with religion, which ranged from direct repression, to control exerted through legal and administrative means, to wide-scale propaganda and replacement of church traditions with new Soviet customs. Mostly, religion was dealt with in the form of campaigns that were bloody and directed toward demolishing the church organization before the Second World War, whereas the campaigns from the late 1950s onward focused more on atheist propaganda and ideological content. Thus, in the words of Victoria Smolkin, the party had neither a systematic approach to managing religion nor a clear sense of the role that atheism would play in the Soviet project. This produced very different "atheisms":

1. For the Communist Party officials, "atheism" meant a militant attitude toward religion. In everyday usage of the party officials, "atheism" was used to denote the propaganda of atheism through lectures, media, and education. Even the process of educating and training people to become distributors of atheist propaganda and conducting secular rituals that were to substitute religious ceremonies fell into the category of "atheism."

2. In order to demonstrate freedom of belief to the world as a part of foreign policy, the state tried to present itself as neutral toward religion and declared religion a private matter. However, since the executive power was in the hands of the Communist Party, and as the Leninist approach was that "religion is not a private matter in relation to the workers' party," the principle of neutrality became democratic-sounding nonsense, as the party ideology and state policy were hopelessly mixed. Therefore, the state policy was actually "atheistic"—that is, it focused on eradicating religion. Meanwhile, from the perspective of the various churches, almost every activity originating from the state counted as "atheism."

3. The ideological goal of getting rid of religion produced "scientific atheism," a semiacademic discipline for studying religion (and atheism) from psychological, historical, and sociological perspectives in order to assist in the process of making religion disappear from society. "Scientific atheism" also referred to an ideal set by the party, a systematic and conscious antireligious world view based on science and materialistic philosophy. Yet despite the efforts invested in the atheist upbringing of the populace, the reality was quite far from the ideal. Therefore, scientific atheists distinguished themselves from the lower-level "spontaneous atheism" that emerged as a result of life experience.

These different "atheisms" point out the twofold nature of the atheism in the Soviet system: a destructive part focused on getting rid of religion and a constructive part that dealt with providing a new world view. In retrospect, the Soviet atheism did much better on the destructive part, quite effectively subordinating the churches, cutting off religious socialization, and relocating religion deep into the private sphere. For the constructive part, the Soviet atheist project could be considered a fiasco, as it failed to provide a meaningful world view and justify the position of atheism in this system, which did not proceed beyond the level of a slogan.

In conclusion, when talking about atheism and communism, one should distinguish between atheist convictions (i.e., about the existence of God), antireligiosity, and anticlericalism, both on a personal and state-sponsored level. These three are often delivered in one package, but not necessarily. Therefore, there is no uniform relationship between communism and atheism, as proven by the histories of communist regimes, which have adopted a wide range of stances in their attitude toward religion.

About the author

Atko Remmel is an associate professor at the University of Tartu and a senior research fellow at the University of Tallinn, Estonia. He has published on antireligious policy and atheist propaganda in the Soviet Union, (non)religion and nationalism, secularization and religious change, and contemporary forms of (non)religion and spirituality. He has carried out fieldwork among nonreligious populations in Estonia and on people's relationship with nature.

Suggestions for further reading

In this book
See also chapters 30 (politics), 32 (peace), and 34 (political leaning).

Elsewhere
Boer, Roland. *Red Theology: On the Christian Communist Tradition.* Leiden: Brill, 2019.

McKinnon, Andrew M. "Reading 'Opium of the People': Expression, Protest and the Dialectics of Religion." *Critical Sociology* 31(1–2) (2005): 15–38.

Ngo, Tam T. T., and Justine B. Quijada. "Introduction: Atheist Secularism and Its Discontents." In *Atheist Secularism and Its Discontents: A Comparative Study of Religion and Communism in Eurasia*, edited by Tam T. T. Ngo and Justine B. Quijada, 1–26. Cham: Palgrave Macmillan, 2015.

Remmel, Atko. "Ambiguous Atheism: The Impact of Political Changes on the Meaning and Reception of Atheism in Estonia." In *Annual Review of the Sociology of Religion*, edited by Roberto Cipriani and Franco Garelli, 233–250. Leiden: Brill, 2016.

Smolkin, Victoria. *A Sacred Space Is Never Empty: A History of Soviet Atheism.* Princeton, NJ: Princeton University Press, 2018.

34

Is contemporary atheism leaning politically to the right or the left?

Stuart McAnulla

Being an atheist does not commit you to hold any kind of political perspective. Indeed, atheism is often defined as an *absence* of belief, specifically an absence of belief in the existence of any gods. A lack of belief in God does not in itself mean that atheists will have any particular views on politics—for example, whether tax rates should be lower or whether governments should do more to tackle climate change. Similarly, being an atheist does not determine whether you think religious groups should be listened to when governments make public policy. Atheists, much like everybody else, have political attitudes that are shaped by a wider range of factors, including, educational background, economic circumstances, geographical location, and cultural influences. Some atheists may develop views that can be considered "right wing" (e.g., belief in strong immigration controls), while others may form "left-wing" attitudes (e.g., being in favor of reducing economic inequalities). These political beliefs will be shaped by their background and life experiences rather than being determined by nonbelief in God.

However, historically speaking, the emergence of atheist ideas has often been perceived as a threat to political and religious systems. For instance, in many predominantly Christian and Islamic societies, belief in a God has been so widespread and fundamental to the prevailing moral codes that atheists have been considered a dangerous threat to social order. Indeed, in some countries, being an atheist is still considered to be a crime punishable by death. Even in contemporary democratic nations such as the United States, atheists are considered by many to be an untrustworthy minority. Within these countries, they can find themselves subject to prejudice or discrimination within strongly religious communities. It is therefore unsurprising that many contemporary atheists are critical of institutions and social attitudes that they believe favor religion or those who have a belief in God. Broadly speaking, "left-wing" views are often understood to be attitudes that argue for social and political change to achieve a more equal and inclusive society. For this reason, there is often an association made between advocating atheism and political views that lean more to the political left. However, it is certainly possible for atheists to have political views that tend to have a more "right-wing" inclination to want to preserve the status quo in most respects.

Many modern-day atheists hold "secularist" political attitudes. Secularists argue that the government and state should be totally separate from religious institutions. The hope is that if politics and religion are kept distinct from each other, then the likelihood of discrimination against atheists and other minority groups will be reduced. Secularism is often viewed as a "left-wing" or liberal tendency, as it seeks to reduce or limit the power of traditional religious institutions. Certainly, some types of political conservatism are hostile to secularism, which they fear acts to undermine traditional forms of morality and values. Through asserting the social and political rights of nonbelievers, secularism is often linked with broader liberal-left movements for the extension of rights and protections for those with minority identities. This said, not all secularists hold left-wing views. For example, in the United Kingdom, the prominent historian David Starkey has staunchly argued for the disestablishment of the Anglican Church but more generally holds conservative views that defend traditional institutions such as the monarchy of the United Kingdom.

Over the last fifteen years or so, a more far-reaching kind of atheist viewpoint has been widely publicized in the form of "New Atheism." Rather than be content with arguing for the secularist separation of church and state, New Atheists such as Richard Dawkins and Sam Harris have argued for the public denunciation and mockery of both the belief in God and monotheistic religion. Following the impact of forms of Islamic and Christian fundamentalism on global politics during the twenty-first century, New Atheists have argued that religion and the belief in God must be overtly challenged and, if possible, largely eliminated through persuasion. Certainly not all atheists share these hard-line views concerning religion, but in places like the United States, a large majority of atheists do appear to believe that religion does more harm than good. New Atheism does not promote any political party or generally define itself in terms of a left-right political scale—indeed, such atheists tend to be more concerned with promoting science as providing grounds for alternative world views to that offered by religions.

However, some commentators have interpreted New Atheism as having links to types of right-wing politics. For example, Ayaan Hirsi Ali is a strong critic of Islam and is associated with the neoconservative political movement that has advocated military intervention by the United States to overthrow authoritarian Islamic regimes in the Middle East. She and several other prominent New Atheists have been accused of holding views that not only criticize Islam as a set of ideas but may slide into opinions that could encourage negative attitudes toward those who practice the religion. In turn, this is considered to reinforce the dangerous idea of Western elites assuming that they are more enlightened than populations in other parts of the world.

Nonetheless, there is considerable political diversity within groups and individuals who publicly advocate atheism and challenge religion. For example, feminists such as Jey McCreight have argued for the promotion of atheism to be tied to the wider political campaigns for equality regarding race, gender, and sexuality. Their view is that progressive, left-leaning politics needs to be ready to rigorously criticize religious beliefs and practices where these may perpetuate inequalities.

Evidence suggests that in general, atheists tend to be more left-liberal in their political views than those who are affiliated with a religion. For example, according to a Pew Research Center report in 2020, atheists, agnostics, and those unaffiliated with a religion are more likely to identify with the political left, especially in the United States, Canada, and Spain. In the United States, a large majority of atheists support the Democratic Party, hold socially liberal attitudes, and advocate for more government spending on public services. To conclude, atheists may indeed be thought to lean more to the left politically, but the nonbelief in God is also compatible with many types of right-wing political perspectives.

About the author

Stuart McAnulla is an associate professor in politics at the University of Leeds. He has research interests in the politics of contemporary atheism, ideological change in British politics, and social/political science metatheory. His books include *The Politics of New Atheism* (coauthored with Steven Kettell and Marcus Schulzke; Routledge, 2018) and *British Politics: A Critical Introduction* (Continuum, 2006).

Suggestions for further reading

In this book
See also chapters 11 (New Atheism), 30 (politics), and 35 (president).

Elsewhere

McAnulla, Stuart. "Radical Atheism and Religious Power: New Atheist Politics." *Approaching Religion* 2(1) (2012): 87–99.

McAnulla, Stuart, Steven Kettell, and Marcus Schulzke. *The Politics of New Atheism*. London: Routledge, 2018.

McGrath, Alister. *The Twilight of Atheism: The Rise and Fall of Disbelief in the Modern World*. London: Rider, 2004.

Zuckerman, Phil, ed. *Atheism and Secularity*. Volume 1, *Issues, Concepts, and Definitions*. Santa Barbara: Praeger, 2009.

35

Is it possible for an atheist to become a president or a prime minister?

Stuart McAnulla

Becoming a president or a prime minister is an accomplishment that few politicians ever achieve, despite the ambition that many possess to win these positions. Obtaining the executive leadership of a nation-state tends to require skills of communication and organization and a distinctive style. Even when a politician has great ability or widespread support, they may still require a considerable fortune to rise to the very top. At times, though, the path to becoming president or prime minister can become blocked, even for a talented leader, if they have characteristics or personal attitudes that too many voters find unacceptable in a candidate for a high office. The religious context within which they run for election can be significant for leaders, playing a role in how they are judged by electors. Unsurprisingly, then, politicians will often reflect carefully on how they may reference God and religion in their campaigning to appeal to diverse groups in society. This can present leaders who are atheists with challenges—in most cases, they will be in an apparent minority in their nonbelief, and so they must hope this factor is not held against them by large numbers of people.

Broadly speaking, in twenty-first-century modern democracies, leaders who are atheists now have improved chances of winning elections compared to the previous two centuries. This is due to the impact of secularizing trends, which means religious practices often play a less central role in the lives of families and individuals than previously. However, there is a great variation between the religious contexts faced by aspiring national leaders. For example, in the United States, it is expected—indeed, assumed—that presidential candidates will reference God and religion in their speeches. However, in the United Kingdom, this is less common. Indeed, an adviser to former prime minister Tony Blair (1997–2007) once famously declared, "We don't do God," despite Blair's own deep Christian faith. The differences arise in part from the relative numbers in each country who openly identify with and practice religion. The United Kingdom is now a much more secular country than in earlier centuries, with historically low numbers of people now attending church or identifying as religious. A growing number of Britons have no religious faith or are atheists, even though a majority still retain a Christian identity of some kind. Successive recent UK prime ministers have been Christian—for example, Gordon Brown, David Cameron, and Theresa May—but they have generally been cautious in speaking at length on religious matters, as the British public tends to expect leaders to generally steer clear of these. However, recently, several political party leaders have been atheists, including former Labour leader Ed Miliband and Liberal Democrat leader Nick Clegg. Neither became prime minister, but their failure to do so had little to do with their attitudes to God. It therefore appears perfectly possible that the United Kingdom could elect a declared atheist leader to the role of prime minister, especially if they remain respectful of religion in a society that now has multiple practicing faiths. In fact, there have been a few previous prime ministers who may have been privately atheists. For example, although Clement Attlee (prime minister from 1945 to 1951) advocated for Christian values, he dismissed wider Anglican beliefs as "mumbo jumbo."

Within Europe, there have now been a few instances of atheists becoming national leaders. French president François Hollande (2012–2017) was openly atheist, as was Greek prime minister Alexis Tsipras (2015–2019). In Australia, atheist Julia Gillard served as prime minister (2010–2013) following the precedents set by a number of previous atheist or agnostic leaders. In much of the democratic world, we see that being an atheist is now not a "deal breaker" for aspiring leaders, even if they may occasionally have a disadvantage when competing against religious rivals who may be able to win support more easily from certain faith-based groups. It should also be highlighted that it is possible for a leader to have a firm religious identity but still not have a personal belief in God, as appears to have been the case with the Jewish former Israeli prime minister Golda Meir.

A question remains, though, regarding whether we are likely to ever see an atheist elected to be president of the United States. As a relatively religious modern democratic society, there is a long history of atheists being portrayed as morally deficient in America. The argument is made that if atheists have no belief in God, then they have no solid foundations or compelling reasons to behave in a moral way. Former president George Bush (1988–1992) even suggested that atheists should not be considered patriots, since the United States is "one nation under God." This kind of antiatheist prejudice was reinforced during the Cold War, as liberal capitalist America competed against the "Godless Communism" of the Soviet Union. In 2019, a Gallup poll found that only 60 percent of Americans would vote for an atheist to be president, compared to 80 percent who would vote for an Evangelical Christian and 76 percent who would vote for a lesbian/gay candidate. This is a context that could make it very difficult for an openly atheist politician to win a mainstream party nomination for president.

However, there are certain developments that could give American atheists a glimmer of hope. Bernie Sanders competed strongly in the Democratic primaries in 2016, despite being a relatively secular candidate. A Pew Research Center survey in 2020 found that a majority of Americans didn't consider incumbent president Donald Trump to be very religious, yet he won over seventy-four million votes in the presidential election that year, the highest ever popular vote for a losing candidate. While the prospects of an overt atheist winning the US presidency anytime soon appear remote, it might be that a candidate who held some private atheist leanings could win a presidential nomination if they successfully courted support from a coalition of religious and other groups.

About the author

Stuart McAnulla is an associate professor in politics at the University of Leeds. He has research interests in the politics of contemporary atheism, ideological change in British politics, and social/political science metatheory. His books include *The Politics of New Atheism* (coauthored with Steven Kettell and Marcus Schulzke; Routledge, 2018) and *British Politics: A Critical Introduction* (Continuum, 2006).

Suggestions for further reading

In this book
See also chapters 30 (politics), 34 (political leaning), and 38 (discrimination).

Elsewhere
Crines, Andrew S., and Kevin Theakston. "'Doing God' in Number 10: British Prime Ministers, Religion and Political Rhetoric." *Politics and Religion* 8(1) (2015): 155–177.

Schmidt, Leigh Eric. *Village Atheists: How America's Unbelievers Made Their Way in a Godly Nation.* Princeton, NJ: Princeton University Press, 2016.

36

Do laws about religion take atheism into account?

Lori G. Beaman

There is no simple answer to this question. First, we need to ask what we mean by "laws about religion." These may be human rights guarantees of things like freedom of religion or conscience or nondiscrimination based on a number of grounds, including religion. These guarantees exist at the international level and at the state level. At the international level, the UN special rapporteur on freedom of religion or belief, Ahmed Shaheed, has been very clear that he understands the mandate of his office and the Universal Declaration of Human Rights protection of freedom of religion or belief to include nonbelief. At the state level, there may be benefits and privileges extended to religion, like tax breaks. Or there may be exceptions to laws of general application, like clergy exemption from performing same-sex marriage. Some countries have formal recognition systems for religions wherein religions must apply for recognition and the benefits that attach to those. In some countries, it is mandatory to include one's religious affiliation on state identity cards. In many of those countries, being an atheist has negative consequences. Further, some countries have state religions, like England or Norway. The simple fact of the existence of a state religion does not mean that atheism is not legally protected. The inclusion of atheism in legal protections varies from context to context, so there is no one response that captures the approach from country to country.

One of the factors that is important to consider in thinking about atheism and the law is that the number of people who identify as nonreligious (this is a broader category than atheist and includes humanists, agnostics, freethinkers, the spiritual but not religious, and the indifferent) has increased rather dramatically during the past few decades. This increase has meant that law is increasingly called upon to consider the interests of nonreligious people as they seek equality of treatment.

This leads to a second consideration in answering this question: What does "taking atheism into account" mean? This might include legal protection for freedom of conscience on par with freedom of religion, although some courts have interpreted atheism as a system of beliefs analogous to religion. This approach warrants the extension of rights and freedoms to atheists on the basis of religious freedom rather than through the conscience route. Taking atheism into account might also mean the inclusion of atheism in educational programs aimed at religious literacy or the possibility of affirming rather than swearing on a "holy" book, such as the Bible, when giving evidence in court. Some core areas of concern include the protection of the nonreligious from hate (including by state actors), the protection of nonreligious children from discrimination by their parents or guardians, the freedom from proselytization, equal access to social services, and the privileging of religion over nonreligion. This last area often takes relatively subtle forms. For example, court-mandated treatment programs for alcohol or drug addiction may only use religiously rooted programs like Alcoholics Anonymous, thus effectively forcing nonreligious people into religious programming in which they are obliged to recognize a "higher power." Another example is the religious exemption for physicians who do not wish to offer information or services around birth control or abortion. The very private nature of these services means that women who do not receive the services they need are very likely to go undetected. While not all of these women are atheists or nonreligious, there is a potential privileging of particular religious views when those physicians exercising an exemption refuse to refer women to alternative medical caregivers who offer the services they need. A similar issue arises in those jurisdictions in which medical assistance in dying is available.

In many countries, social institutions—hospitals, schools, and other social services—have been built by or in collaboration with religious organizations. Even in contexts in which these have been "secularized," this historical foundation leaves a structural religious residue that shapes institutional practices and can effectively exclude atheists. Let's take two related and increasingly common examples in countries that have historically been dominated by Christianity to give this a concrete form: first, the display of religious symbols such as crosses, crucifixes, and religious artifacts such as statues in places like publicly funded hospitals, public schools, and places of government business, such as parliaments, legislatures, and municipal councils; second, the recitation of prayers before state activities, including parliamentary sessions, the swearing in of police officers and military personnel, and perhaps most commonly (and least visible), local town hall meetings. Humanist and atheist organizations have often challenged these practices, noting that despite the claims of some religious people, such symbols and practices are not "universal" and do not represent the nonreligious. The most common defense of these symbols and practices is that they are not really or predominantly religious but are part of that particular region's culture, history, and heritage. This claim to heritage and culture attempts to erect a protective shield around practices and symbols that might otherwise be interpreted as violations of freedom of conscience, religion, or equality provisions on the ground of religion or nonreligion, which can occur when people are disfavored or excluded on the basis of their (non)religious identity. In some cases, courts have upheld prayer and symbols on the grounds that they are part of a nation's history and part of "our culture." Such an approach often erases groups who do not fit into the Christian profile of the imagined "us."

In addition to these more overt entanglements of atheism and law, there is arguably a more subtle way in which law is taking nonbelief or atheism into account. Shifts in laws around medical assistance in dying, for example, seem to appropriate concepts such as the sanctity of life to reconstitute them as nonreligious, stripping them of religiously loaded meaning (including the good of suffering) to argue that making decisions around the time and place of one's death and the preservation of dignity are at the core of the sanctity of life. These shifts are more difficult to track and link to nonbelief, and it is important not to oversimplify. Nonetheless, the growth of nonreligion may be shifting legal analytical frameworks.

About the author

Lori G. Beaman is the Canada Research Chair in Religious Diversity and Social Change at the University of Ottawa. She is the principal investigator of the Nonreligion in a Complex Future project and author of *The Transition of Religion to Culture in Law and Public Discourse* (Routledge, 2020).

Suggestions for further reading

In this book
See also chapters 18 (Muslim countries), 38 (discrimination), and 41 (organization).

Elsewhere
Beaman, Lori G., Cory Steele, and Keelin Pringnitz. "The Inclusion of Nonreligion in Religion and Human Rights." *Social Compass* 65(1) (2018): 43–61.

Lerner, Natan. *Religion, Secular Beliefs and Human Rights* (2nd rev. edition). Leiden: Brill, 2012.

McAdam, Marika. *Freedom from Religion and Human Rights Law: Strengthening the Right to Freedom of Religion and Belief for Non-religious and Atheist Rights-Holders*. London: Routledge, 2018.

37

Why do some atheists want to convert others?

Steven Kettell

Not all atheists actively seek to change people's minds about religion. Contrary to the image that is sometimes presented by both pro- and anti-religious activists, most nonbelievers are content to live their lives and have no interest in converting (or rather, deconverting) others. Those that do want to promote atheist ideas often do so for three main reasons: because they consider religious views to be irrational and wrong, because they see religion as a negative and potentially dangerous force, and because they want to secure equal rights for nonbelievers.

The first reason some unbelievers seek to promote atheist views is that they consider the core claims made by religion to be false. Atheists typically put a high value on the use of reason and rationality and argue that truth claims about the nature of reality should only be accepted when verifiable evidence to support them is provided. From this perspective, because religious beliefs are ultimately based on faith (in other words, a belief in something that cannot be shown to be true) rather than evidence, they are said to be unable to meet these standards and are therefore rejected. While theologians often maintain that religious views are largely inspirational or metaphorical and are not meant to be taken literally, atheists argue that many religions do make truth claims about the nature of reality. These include assertions about the divine creation of the universe, the existence of an afterlife, and the performance of miracles, such as virgin births, res-urrections, the healing of the terminally ill, the fulfillment of prophecies, and so on. According to many atheists, claims such as these are capable of being scientifically tested (at least in principle), and no convincing evi-dence to support them has ever been provided. Additionally, atheists also frequently argue that religion itself can be explained as a human creation. Throughout history, human societies have created a huge variety of diverse religions, making an assortment of different and often mutually exclusive claims. Since all of these beliefs cannot, by definition, be true, atheists contend that there is no convincing reason to believe in any of them.

The second reason atheists seek to (de)convert others is that they see religion as a predominantly negative force. Although it is true that religious beliefs can inspire good deeds and ethical forms of behavior, such as encouraging people to become involved in community projects (e.g., helping the poor or the homeless) or donating to charitable organizations, atheists contend that religious beliefs also often lead to harmful and dangerous consequences, both for the individuals who hold them and for the wider societies in which they live. These negative outcomes include cases of parents denying lifesaving medical treatments for their children on the grounds of their religious beliefs; institutional scandals such as the cover-up of child abuse by the Roman Catholic Church; religious support for restrictions on free speech and expression through the use of blasphemy laws; acts of religiously inspired violence such as terrorist attacks carried out by groups, including al-Qaeda or Boko Haram; disorder between religious communities in places such as Northern Ireland and India; and instances of discrimination against people on the basis of their gender and/or sexual orientation. Key examples here include support for restrictive policies on reproductive rights (e.g., opposing the use of contraception and the liberalization of abortion laws), a refusal to allow women to hold senior roles in religious organizations, and the promotion of negative attitudes toward homosexuals (e.g., opposing the right of same-sex couples to adopt children or get married). In addition to this, many atheists also highlight religious opposition to scientific and medical advances with the potential for reducing human suffering, such as the development of treatments for incurable and debilitating diseases based on research using embryonic stem cells or the liberalization of laws on assisted dying.

These issues are especially problematic in places where religion wields significant political or social power. This can be clearly seen in countries where religion has a direct and central role in the system of government, such as Saudi Arabia or Iran, but also includes countries (such as Argentina, Poland, and Russia) where the size of the religiously active population or the close connection between political and religious institutions allows religion to shape political decision-making, leading to repressive laws around issues such as sexual orientation and gender equality.

None of this is to say that religion is the only belief system capable of producing harmful behavior. Political ideologies such as fascism or nationalism can have similarly negative effects, and misogynistic and racist attitudes can be found in every society. Nevertheless, many atheists claim that religion provides a uniquely dangerous combination, giving negative attitudes a sense of cosmic importance by connecting them to ideas of the afterlife and eternal salvation. This allows religions to promote an extraordinarily strong sense of group belonging, making it easier to demonize and dehumanize anyone deemed to be an "outsider." For these reasons, many atheists claim that turning people away from religion and reducing the influence of religious beliefs and organizations would lead to a more tolerant, peaceful, and rational world.

The third reason nonbelievers seek to promote atheist ideas is that they want to normalize nonbelief and secure equal legal and civil rights for atheists. These motivations are particularly strong in countries where religion holds political influence and where atheists face ongoing issues of prejudice and discrimination. At the present time, atheism remains illegal in many parts of the world (being punishable in some cases by death), and even in some advanced liberal democracies, atheism remains a marginalized view. Studies in the United States, for example, have found that atheists are frequently considered to have a low social status and are often regarded as "un-American." Until very recently, polls consistently showed that a majority of Americans would refuse to vote for an atheist president, highlighting the low regard in which atheism is often held. Many atheists claim that attitudes such as these will not change until nonbelief itself becomes a powerful social force.

About the author

Steven Kettell is a reader in politics and international studies in the Department of Politics and International Studies, University of Warwick. His primary research interests are focused on the politics of secularism, nonreligion, and the role of religion in the public sphere. He is a coauthor of *The Politics of New Atheism* (with Stuart McAnulla and Marcus Schulzke; Routledge, 2018).

Suggestions for further reading

In this book
See also chapters 11 (New Atheism), 20 (dialogue), 30 (politics), 39 (religious people), and 49 (becoming an atheist).

Elsewhere
Hitchens, Christopher. *God Is Not Great: How Religion Poisons Everything.* London: Atlantic, 2007.

Klug, Petra. "Varieties of Nonreligion: Why Some People Criticize Religion, While Others Just Don't Care." In *Religious Indifference: New Perspectives from Studies on Secularization and Nonreligion*, edited by Johannes Quack and Cora Schuh, 219–237. Cham: Springer, 2017.

McAnulla, Stuart, Steven Kettell, and Marcus Schulzke. *The Politics of New Atheism*. London: Routledge, 2018.

Silverman, David. *Fighting God: An Atheist Manifesto for a Religious World*. New York: St. Martin's, 2015.

Stenger, Victor J. *God, the Failed Hypothesis: How Science Shows That God Does Not Exist*. New York: Prometheus, 2008.

38

Is there discrimination against atheists?

Ryan T. Cragun

The answer to this question requires the defining of some terms. "Discrimination" is treating a certain group or category of people differently—typically in a negative fashion—based only on the fact that they belong to that group or category. Discrimination is rooted in prejudice, which is when people hold specific attitudes or views toward a group or category of people and those views are not based on compelling evidence. Greater interest is usually given to negative prejudices rather than positive prejudices. In short, prejudice refers to attitudes; discrimination refers to behavior.

Scholars have documented widespread prejudice against atheists in many parts of the world using a number of different methodologies. For instance, in the United States, scholars have asked people if they think atheists (along with lots of other religious, sexual, and racial/ethnic categories) agree with their vision of American society. Over 40 percent of Americans say that atheists do not share their vision of American society, compared to 7 percent who say Jews do not share their vision of American society. Using a different approach, scholars asked people in thirteen countries around the world if a serial murderer was more likely to be an atheist than a religious believer. In twelve of those thirteen countries, people said that the serial murderer was more likely to be an atheist than a religious believer. Studies like these demonstrate that there is widespread prejudice against atheists.

Does widespread prejudice translate into discrimination? Yes, it does. However, demonstrating discrimination is more challenging than demonstrating prejudice. To measure prejudice, you can ask people directly or indirectly what they think about atheists and measure their attitudes. But people are much less likely to admit to treating others poorly and may not even recognize that their mistreatment of others is unethical or discrimination. As a result, discrimination is usually captured by asking the targets of prejudicial attitudes whether or not they have experienced discrimination.

Scholars have documented discrimination against atheists. One study showed that roughly 40 percent of atheists in the United States reported experiencing discrimination in at least one of six contexts—family, workplace, school/college, military, social setting, volunteer organization—in the prior five years. Other studies have illustrated that this discrimination takes a variety of forms. Milder forms of documented discrimination include observing people on TV misrepresent the views or behaviors of atheists or suggesting that nonbelievers are the cause of modern social problems. Another form of discrimination reported by atheists is when religious family members visit the homes of atheists and insist on praying over meals. Not only does this show disrespect for the views of the nonbelieving family member, but it also illustrates the presumption and privilege of religious individuals who often assume that everyone should be subjected to their beliefs, values, and behaviors. Such prayers commonly include language that sanctimoniously condemns the nonbelieving family member for their nonbelief as well, adding insult to injury.

More serious forms of discrimination have also been documented. Atheists have lost custody of their children in divorce proceedings because their former partner is religious and a believer and they are nonreligious and an atheist. People have lost their jobs because their religious bosses found out that they were an atheist. Some countries maintain that only those who belong to a specific religion or believe in a deity can be elected to public office. Even when that is not the case, when individuals choose not to vote for atheist candidates for political office, they are discriminating against atheists.

The most serious forms of documented discrimination against atheists include physical harm. Atheists have been the victims of crimes, and upon reporting the crime to the authorities, police officers have refused to investigate or sided with the religious believer upon finding out that the victim is an atheist. As of 2020, fourteen countries outlaw atheism, making nonbelief a crime that can result in the nonbeliever being imprisoned or killed. Atheists have been physically attacked because of their nonbelief, and threats have been made against the lives of many atheists. At times, those threats are acted upon, and numerous individuals around the world—in India, Pakistan, Indonesia, Egypt, and many other countries—have been killed because of their atheism. There is widespread discrimination against atheists.

An important question to ask about discrimination against atheists is, Is discrimination against atheists universal? While prejudice against atheists is widespread, there are some countries where people do not perceive atheists as being less moral than are religious believers, like Finland. That there is variation in views toward atheists illustrates that prejudice toward atheists is not innate; it is learned. This is particularly fascinating given that children are born without a belief in a god or higher power, meaning children are naturally atheists. Parents and religions that teach children to believe in a god, gods, or higher powers often also teach their children—intentionally or not—that atheists are inferior to religious believers, should not be trusted because they do not believe a deity is always watching their behavior, and warrant discrimination.

Finally, given the relatively benign nature of atheism—a simple lack of belief in a deity—it is also worth considering why religious believers hold such negative attitudes toward atheists. The most plausible answer is that many religious believers are afraid. They are not afraid of atheists; most atheists are not scary individuals. They are rarely willing to blow themselves up or kill for a cause, as they believe death is the end. No, religious believers are afraid that atheism and atheists are correct—that there are no gods and no afterlife. They are afraid that they are wrong and that all the time they have spent in devotion to their god or religion has been for naught. Atheism is terrifying to religious believers because it gives the lie to their entire world view.

About the author

Ryan T. Cragun is a professor of sociology at the University of Tampa. His research focuses on Mormonism and the nonreligious and has been published in various scholarly journals. He is also the author of several books.

Suggestions for further reading

In this book
See also chapters 18 (Muslim countries), 28 (Black), 36 (law), and 39 (religious people).

Elsewhere
Cragun, Ryan T., Barry A. Kosmin, Ariela Keysar, Joseph H. Hammer, and Michael E. Nielsen. "On the Receiving End: Discrimination toward the Non-religious." *Journal of Contemporary Religion* 27(1) (2012): 105–127.

Downey, Margaret. "Discrimination against Atheists: The Facts." *Free Inquiry* 24(4) (2004): 41–43.

Hammer, Joseph H., Ryan T. Cragun, Karen Hwang, and Jesse Smith. "Forms, Frequency, and Correlates of Perceived Anti-atheist Discrimination." *Secularism and Nonreligion* 1 (2012): 43–67.

Humanists International. *The Freedom of Thought Report 2019: A Global Report on the Rights, Legal Status and Discrimination against Humanists, Atheists and the Non-religious.* https://fot.humanists.international/download-the-report/.

39
What do religious people think of atheists?

Petra Klug

Not all religious people think about atheists in the same way. But although they are usually a small minority, many believers see atheists as a huge threat. This antiatheism, which will be my main focus here, also includes that the accusation of atheism or secularism is used as a way to mute religious or political dissenters. Atheists have been persecuted throughout history and still face discrimination and violence in many parts of the world. Today, there are huge differences between regions and religions. In some mainly Muslim-majority countries, atheists are threatened with the death penalty. In the United States, they are used as scapegoats for tragedy, school shootings, the coronavirus pandemic, and even religious terror attacks by those who see such events as God's punishment. Antiatheist views vary greatly between different religious affiliations and age groups, but for a long time, atheists were the most despised group in terms of religion—viewed more negatively than Muslims, who have been under constant attack because of Islamic terrorists. However, in the younger generations, atheists moved up on the sympathy thermometer and are viewed now more positively than Mormons by adults below the age of fifty. Atheists are rated most warmly by the group of the unaffiliated and by Jews and most negatively by Evangelical Christians, according to a 2017 Pew Research Center survey.

Historically, atheists have been portrayed as agents of Satan and as archenemies of the believers. However, today, antiatheism usually comes in more subtle forms. While some believers still condemn atheists outright, others are more restrained in their judgment, and yet others do not want to be judgmental but imply negative assessments of atheists nevertheless. Even if many believers imagine themselves as inclusive, religion creates a division between righteous believers and everybody else. In orthodox or conservative faiths, the out-group entails everyone who differs from one's own religion. But even more liberal interpretations of religion, like ecumenism or the interfaith movement, typically exclude those who do not hold any supernatural beliefs. That makes the atheist the ultimate outsider.

Ascriptions of atheists vary tremendously—to the extent that they directly contradict one another. Historically, atheists have been associated with divergent political views, including fascism, communism, anarchism, capitalism, and liberalism. A rather typical ascription toward atheists is that they are too intellectual. At the same time, people also hold prejudices against atheists as less or even anti-intellectual and as boisterous. They sometimes merely call them ignorant, dumb, or foolish. Atheists are seen sometimes as lazy but more often as ambitious, greedy, and success oriented.

Atheists are often described as untrustworthy or selfish and are associated with betrayal and criminal behavior, including rape and murder. This goes back to the thought that people cannot be moral if they don't fear the principle of reward and punishment that many religions entail. To many believers, atheists seem to lack empathy, love, compassion, conscience, and moral guidelines. Sometimes, respondents see atheists as ungrateful, unable to forgive, and revengeful.

However, the prejudices that believers have about atheists go beyond the lack of trustworthiness. In the imagination of many, atheists go out a lot, party, flirt, and have fun. They are very often connected to immoral sexual behavior, drug use, and alcoholism and are associated with superficiality, consumerism, fashion, and pop culture. A frequent accusation is that atheists either worship other things, like money or success, or make gods out of themselves. They are often seen as immature, pitiable, or in need of help. They are described as sad and fearful cowards who have no direction in life.

At the same time, atheists are depicted as aggressive, rebellious, destructive, and degenerate. They are seen as hateful, angry attackers of the religious, who hurt their religious feelings and take away their rights. They are imagined as lacking respect and being offensive and are associated with deviance, trouble, and chaos. As such, they are seen not as victims of the modern and secular society but as the reason for the societal change behind it. They are portrayed as politically dominant, as a major influence upon society as well as a threat to religious and personal freedoms.

If we inquire into the reasons for those negative ascriptions, it is apparent that some might be rooted in the actual behavior of atheists: when belief in God is the societal norm, not believing is indeed an expression of deviance. However, some believers also think that atheists are more likely to be criminals than believers, have a lot of power, and want to control the government. Hence what believers ascribe to atheists actually may tell us more about the believers themselves than about the atheists. Ascriptions and prejudice often reflect the believers' own repressed desires. Wishes that the believers cannot act on because that would be—for better or worse—against the norms of their faith are projected into the atheists, who then are condemned for that. This includes in particular sexual associations like homosexuality, promiscuity, and sexual abuse but also many topoi that are linked to individuality and a free lifestyle.

Many of these stereotypes and behaviors have a model in religious scriptures. But antiatheism is so powerful because it is the result of the human psychological makeup, as it develops out of the patriarchal family structure. Religion can be seen as a means to cope with the insecurity of the world by imagining one's surroundings as dependent upon a good, reasonable, and approachable authority like God. If monotheist religions emphasize the dependence upon God, this resembles the situation in early childhood when a child fears their parents, particularly their father, but also depends on their protection. The idea of a good and protective father-god gives believers the hope and security that everything will turn out good in the end—whether this end is understood as being on earth or in the alleged hereafter. Questioning this authority—as atheists do—for believers, then, is more than a difference in opinion: it threatens their hope and security. Therefore, in order to keep their faith unquestioned, some believers simply deny that atheists even exist. To avoid having to confront their arguments intellectually, such believers accuse atheists of lying about their atheism and call them mentally disturbed or just angry at God.

All this leads to the exclusion and derogation of atheists but also to more subtle expressions of superiority—namely, the talk of love and compassion. In particular, the latter allows the believers to elevate themselves to a higher position from which they can belittle atheists and try to convert them to their faith, no matter if the atheists are interested or not.

About the author

Petra Klug obtained a master's degree in sociology and cultural studies, a master's degree in the study of religion from the University of Leipzig, and a PhD from the University of Bremen. In 2019, she was a guest professor for critical theory at Justus-Liebig University Gießen, and currently she is an assistant professor at the University of Bremen and is working on her project on religion and patriarchal violence.

Suggestions for further reading

In this book
See also chapters 20 (dialogue), 37 (converting), 38 (discrimination), and 40 (members).

Elsewhere
Edgell, Penny, Joseph Gerteis, and Douglas Hartmann. "Atheists as 'Other': Moral Boundaries and Cultural Membership in American Society." *American Sociological Review* 71(2) (2006): 211–234.

Gervais, Will M., Azim F. Shariff, and Ara Norenzayan. "Do You Believe in Atheists? Distrust Is Central to Anti-atheist Prejudice." *Journal of Personality and Social Psychology* 101(6) (2011): 1189–1206.

Klug, Petra. *Anti-atheism in the United States*. Bremen: Staats- und Universitätsbibliothek Bremen, 2018.

Norenzayan, Ara. *Big Gods: How Religion Transformed Cooperation and Conflict*. Princeton, NJ: Princeton University Press, 2013.

Pew Research Center. "Americans Express Increasingly Warm Feelings toward Religious Groups." 2017. https://www.pewresearch.org/religion/wp-content/uploads/sites/7/2017/02/Feeling-thermometer-report-FOR-WEB.pdf.

40

Why do some atheists remain members of religious groups?

Isabella Kasselstrand

Atheists are often seen as a group of individuals who think negatively about religion and who reject any ties to religious organizations. After all, if they do not believe in a god, why would they preserve a connection to the organized and institutional aspects of religion? This question may be particularly pertinent as churches and other places of worship, especially in the West, are currently facing considerable difficulties in retaining followers. Yet in reality, a significant share of individuals who do not believe in God do identify with organized religion—which in some cases includes membership and financial commitments—even in countries where religious belonging and participation are presently in decline.

In fact, the 2018 data on religion that the International Social Survey Programme collected in twenty-seven countries suggest that around a third (32.3 percent) of the nonbelievers in God at the same time identify with a religious group. This phenomenon is particularly common in Scandinavia (55.3 percent in Denmark; 34.5 percent in Norway; and 47.5 percent in Sweden), where many retain a connection to the national churches; in Israel (87.9 percent), where most nonbelievers identify with the ethnocultural aspects of Judaism; and in locations such as Thailand (99.7 percent), where a Buddhist identity does not necessarily assume a belief in a deity. Nevertheless, "belonging without believing" is prevalent in most other countries in the survey, beyond the contexts mentioned here—and beyond undemocratic societies where religious identity is a matter of coercion. So why do some atheists choose to belong to a religious group if they don't believe in its theological content?

The term "cultural religion" describes individuals who do not necessarily believe in God but who adhere to a religion as a matter of cultural heritage and tradition. This idea was put forth by N. J. Demerath III, who describes this phenomenon in three different nations: Sweden, Northern

Ireland, and Poland. Despite differing levels of religious beliefs and partic-ipation, religious attachment can, in these societies, often be described as nostalgia surrounding a historical legacy. This is akin to Phil Zuckerman's comparison of Scandinavian culture to Jewish culture in Israel and in the United States, witnessing a lack of supernatural beliefs but nevertheless a deep commitment to religious traditions and rituals. This sentiment was expressed in my own conversation with a Swedish atheist and church member who herself noted that she had a "very romanticized image of the church" and its heritage, speaking warmly of her father's desire to arrive at midnight mass by a horse-drawn antique sled through the snow-covered forest.

Another reason why atheists might want to stay in a religious group can be explained by "cultural defense." In situations where there is tension between religious or ethnic groups or where a group feels threatened, it can reinforce the sense of connection to that particular identity, regardless of held religious beliefs. Sociologist Steve Bruce uses the relationship between Catholics and Protestants in Northern Ireland and Scotland as an example of cultural defense. In my own conversation with a Scottish-Irish woman about this matter, she noted that the Irish Catholic community in Glasgow has a strong sense of identity because they have historically had to fight for their social rights but that "many of them don't actually believe."

The third reason for atheists to be members of organized religion is rooted in family, social life, and community. The recent religious decline is often described as a generational shift whereby the younger generations are less religious than their parents. In these cases, many nonreligious children remain members to respect or not disappoint family members who view this institution as a focal point in their lives. In short, a place of worship brings people together, and some atheists value the social aspects of religion, in particular when it is important to loved ones. There can also be practical benefits to belonging to a religious group. As an example of this, a Scottish woman expressed that the church in her village offered great services, like the "mother and baby group" that she attended when she had a newborn. The practical aspects are also demonstrated by the fact that religious institutions provide resources for immigrants and vulnerable members of the community who are looking for help, guidance, and social connections.

Finally, atheists who do not themselves need the services that are offered may still feel compelled to support a religious organization due to its charitable work and the sociopolitical values that it embodies. For example, I spoke to atheists in Sweden who felt a collective solidarity with others who may need the church. They also explained that they chose to continue to pay for their membership to show their support for an organization that represents love, humanity, and inclusion, especially in a social climate that is increasingly individualistic and competitive.

It is a persistent misconception that all or most atheists dislike organized religion. Of course, some atheists do, but what we are finding is that atheists around the world have their own unique and important reasons for staying connected to a religious institution. It is this group that typically remains overlooked in popular media and in current research. So despite all that we know about why nonbelievers stay in the church, a bigger question now is whether these dynamics will eventually lead to further religious decline. When younger, more secular generations raise their own children, the expectation to maintain a connection to a religion for family reasons will diminish, and when the public importance of religion declines and the historical state churches are abandoned, the identification with a church for cultural reasons will likely also wane. Yet regardless of future trends, it is clear that religious beliefs, belonging, and membership are characterized by distinct trends and changes that do not always go hand in hand. Therefore, when we hear of someone being an atheist, the reality of what that means may be more complex and nuanced than what it initially appears.

About the author

Isabella Kasselstrand is a lecturer in sociology at the University of Aberdeen. Using quantitative and mixed methods, her research examines secularization and nonreligion in northern Europe and the United States.

Suggestions for further reading

In this book
See also chapters 39 (religious people), 61 (attitudes toward religions), and 62 (value in religion).

Elsewhere
Bruce, Steve. "Secularization and Its Consequences." In *The Oxford Handbook of Secularism*, edited by Phil Zuckerman and John R. Shook, 55–70. Oxford: Oxford University Press, 2017.

Day, Abby. *Believing in Belonging: Belief and Social Identity in the Modern World*. Oxford: Oxford University Press, 2011.

Demerath, N. J., III. "The Rise of 'Cultural Religion' in European Christianity: Learning from Poland, Northern Ireland, and Sweden." *Social Compass* 47(1) (2000): 127–139.

Kasselstrand, Isabella. "Lived Secularity: Atheism, Indifference, and the Social Significance of Religion." In *Beyond Religion*, edited by Phil Zuckerman, 37–52. New York: Macmillan, 2016.

Kasselstrand, Isabella. "Nonbelievers in the Church: A Study of Cultural Religion in Sweden." *Sociology of Religion* 76(3) (2015): 275–294.

Zuckerman, Phil. *Society without God* (2nd edition). New York: New York University Press, 2020.

41
How are atheists organized?

Richard Cimino and Christopher Smith

It has been said, often by atheists themselves, that "trying to organize atheists is like herding cats." Atheists are considered too individualistic and independent to form a well-structured small group, let alone a cohesive movement. But as atheists and other secularists have established a stronger identity in recent years due to resistance to the influence of the religious right and their adoption of minority-identity politics, they have developed greater acumen in starting organizations that cater to a wide range of needs and interests. It is also the case that secularists—whether they were called freethinkers, rationalists, or humanists—have had a history of creating groups and organizations for support and activism, particularly in Great Britain and the United States. Organized "free thought" and atheism emerged in the eighteenth century, as seen in antireligious tracts, such as Thomas Paine's *The Age of Reason*, and antireligious groups, such as the Infidel Society. Meanwhile, another strain sought closer connections to traditional forms of religion. These denominations and quasi denominations organized secularists into congregation-like subgroups. The Unitarian Universalists (UUs) were considered theistic liberals and humanists, but one segment of Unitarianism has been more hospitable to nontheists (now known as the UU Humanists). Nontheists and agnostics of Jewish background started the Society for Ethical Culture in the late nineteenth century. In England and in much of northern Europe, there were similar "secular churches," such as the National Secular Society (founded in 1866) and the Norwegian Humanist Association, one of the largest secular humanist organizations in the world.

Those nontheists known as "religious humanists," which means that they cultivated rituals and secular beliefs and world views, started the American Humanist Association (AHA) in 1941. A group of more strict secularists broke off from the AHA in 1978 to form the Council for Secular Humanism. The American Atheists organization, started by Madalyn Murray O'Hair in 1963, also tends to disdain any taint of religion and even shies away from promoting "humanism" in the way of promoting democracy and human rights and focuses on debunking the belief in God and supporting atheists. These organizations are membership-based groups and tend to run local chapters in different parts of the United States and Canada. There are also more activist- and advocacy-oriented groups, such as the Freedom from Religion Foundation, founded in 1978. It should be noted that while there remain significant differences between these groups, it is not uncommon to find participants attending each other's events and even holding membership in more than one organization.

Up until recently, secularist leaders often complained that atheists and fellow travelers lacked the organizational vitality and unity of their religious antagonists. This changed with the advent of New Atheism in the early 2000s. Although it was a noninstitutional phenomenon, New Atheist authors and spokesmen, such as Richard Dawkins and Sam Harris, injected a good deal of self-confidence into the wider atheist movement at a time when secularists felt besieged by the rising influence of the religious right. The galvanizing role of the New Atheists in the United States could be seen in the Godless March in Washington event in 2002, which brought together different groups of secular humanists and atheists to press for their rights and the strict separation of church and state. Secularists also increasingly organized online through a host of websites, blogs, and forums that created new forms of community that in some cases extended offline. Such virtual forms of community have been particularly important for atheists in more rural areas. Another atheist rally in Washington in 2012 drew a much larger crowd of about fifteen thousand participants and demonstrated the stronger organizational ties that had developed in the previous decade. The American Atheists, the Ethical Culture Society, the AHA, and the Council for Secular Humanism, which is now part of the umbrella group Center for Inquiry (CFI), cooperated to make the event one of the largest public gatherings in atheist history. Other organizations came into being in the early 2000s, such as the Secular Coalition for America, which advocates for atheist rights in Washington, and the Secular Student Alliance, which organizes atheist activity and education in universities. There has even been the formation of secular humanist charities and the first atheist political party in the United States, known as the Secular Party. Atheists living in non-Western countries that may be highly religious and restrictive organize and meet in the virtual space of social media, especially Facebook. There are now Facebook groups of atheists in such countries as Afghanistan, Algeria, Egypt, Indonesia, Iran, Iraq, Libya, Pakistan, Tunisia, and Turkey. There are also online ex-Muslim groups that have large numbers of atheists and agnostics.

Some observers say that the internal differences among secularists will challenge their ability to press their political claims. But others challenge the portrayal of organized secularism as a competitive and conflict-ridden world where cooperation between the different groups has been difficult. Instead, they argue that in recent years, a new generation of secularist leaders have learned to cooperate and that the diversity in the movement shows its vitality rather than its disorganization and schismatic nature.

About the authors

Richard Cimino is a visiting professor in sociology at the State University of New York at Old Westbury. He is also the editor of *Religion Watch*, a monthly publication reporting on new research and trends in contemporary religion. He is a coauthor of *Atheist Awakening: Secular Activism and Community in America* (Oxford University Press, 2014).

Christopher Smith is an independent scholar, a coauthor of *Atheist Awakening: Secular Activism and Community in America* (Oxford University Press, 2014), and the author of other articles on atheism.

Suggestions for further reading

In this book
See also chapters 30 (politics), 36 (law), and 42 (activism).

Elsewhere
Cimino, Richard, and Christopher Smith. *Atheist Awakening: Secular Activism and Community in America.* New York: Oxford University Press, 2014.

Cragun, Ryan, Christel Manning, and Lori Fazzino, eds. *Organized Secularism in the United States.* Berlin: De Gruyter, 2017.

Zuckerman, Phil, ed. *Atheism and Secularity.* Volume 2, *Global Expressions.* Westport, CT: Praeger, 2010.

Zuckerman, Phil, Luke W. Galen, and Frank L. Pasquale. *The Nonreligious: Understanding Secular People and Societies.* New York: Oxford University Press, 2016.

42

Are atheist activists mostly men?

Richard Cimino and Christopher Smith

Yes and no. Statistically speaking, more men than women self-identify as atheists, and therefore, atheist activists are more likely to be men. In terms of religiosity, men have consistently rated lower than women, at least in the West. This faith gap has been explained in various ways—from genetics to differences in socialization—but the role of men and women in atheism has been shaped by the history of this diffuse movement.

Historically, women have more often played the role of caregiver, which often included maintaining ties with the extended family and broader community, where Christian churches functioned as an integral social institution in many regions of the world. This is one reason why we may see more men champion the cause of nonbelief historically. The social phenomenon of the "New Atheists," represented by scientists and polemicists such as Richard Dawkins and Sam Harris, inadvertently presented a skewed, heavy-bravado, male-gendered view of a much broader, multifaceted movement. Moreover, we believe when you take the emphasis off atheist activism and look at social activists who are also atheists, then the gap between males and females likely decreases, especially among millennials, with research showing more engagement among females than males. Yet even within the movement, there are women of prominence.

Historically, there is Madalyn Murray O'Hair, founder of American Atheists and activist for getting compulsory prayer stricken from public schools in the 1960s. More recently, women atheists have gained prominence in atheist institutions and activism, including Greta Christina; Robyn Blumer, director of the Center for Inquiry, the largest secular humanist organization; Lyz Liddell, director of campus organizing for the Secular Student Alliance; Debbie Goddard, director of African Americans for Humanism; Kathleen Johnson, founder of the Military Association of Atheists and Freethinkers; and Annie Laurie Gaylor, cofounder and current copresident of the Freedom from Religion Foundation, an organization devoted to upholding the strict separation of church and state.

Additionally, there is a growing cadre of female entertainers that could rival the "New Atheist" authors in terms of irreverence and putting forward a vitriolic antireligious discourse.

The growth of atheist activism among women has been met with some controversy in recent years. In the early 2000s, at various atheist gatherings and conferences as well as in online venues, atheist women charged that they encountered sexual harassment and a general attitude of sexism from the predominantly male leadership and participants. The incidents became notorious enough to find their way into the media and cause a great amount of debate and attention in secularist groups. This also led to a new wave of organizing among women to create their own space and set an agenda distinct from "establishment" atheism. The Center for Inquiry has sponsored Women in Secularism conferences in Washington, DC, since 2012. Past conferences have stressed social activism. This call for greater social involvement in atheism dovetails with what New Atheist polemicist P. Z. Myers calls a "third wave" of atheism (which would follow New Atheism). Myers's joining of social justice concerns with atheism is part of a larger debate in secularist circles about the role of feminism and progressive politics within the movement. This is clearly on display in issues of *Free Inquiry*; the magazine has published special issues devoted to women and atheism, and its articles on feminism that we studied tended to focus on fighting sexism and pressing for greater inclusion and leadership within secularist organizations. The reform movement Atheism+ also includes "social justice" in its platform, with a strong feminist thrust.

To conclude, although it is the case that the majority of individuals who self-identify as atheists are men and therefore most atheist activists are men, in the last analysis, there is not only a legacy of women atheist activists we can point to, but there is reason to believe that as more women enter the secularist fold, they will contribute in equal measure to men in terms of activist engagement in atheist causes.

About the authors

Richard Cimino is a visiting professor in sociology at the State University of New York at Old Westbury. He is also the editor of *Religion Watch*, a monthly publication reporting on new research and trends in contemporary religion. He is a coauthor of *Atheist Awakening: Secular Activism and Community in America* (Oxford University Press, 2014).

Christopher Smith is an independent scholar, a coauthor of *Atheist Awakening: Secular Activism and Community in America* (Oxford University Press, 2014), and the author of other articles on atheism.

Suggestions for further reading

In this book
See also chapters 25 (what makes atheists different), 27 (gender), 41 (organization), and 43 (feminism).

Elsewhere
Christina, Greta. *Why Are You Atheists So Angry?* Durham, NC: Pitchstone, 2012.

Cimino, Richard, and Christopher Smith. *Atheist Awakening: Secular Activism and Community in America.* New York: Oxford University Press, 2014.

Garst, Karen, L. *Women beyond Belief.* Durham, NC: Pitchstone, 2016.

Hensley, Melody, ed. "Women in Secularism." Special issues, *Free Inquiry* 33(1) (2013) and 34(1) (2014).

43

Do atheists and feminists support each other?

Tiina Mahlamäki

Feminism is usually categorized in terms of three waves. The first wave, which took place during the early twentieth century, promoted women's political rights and particularly the right of women to vote. For many of the first-wave feminists, religious faith was a natural part of their world view. The second wave of feminism, during the latter part of the twentieth century, included both activism—especially women's rights concerning their own bodies (e.g., abortion)—and academic research, notably women's studies. Many of the second-wave feminists distanced themselves from religion and took a secular stance. The now ongoing third wave consists of multiple feminisms, such as standpoint feminism and intersectional feminism. It concerns the rights of all oppressed and marginalized groups, such as people of color and LGBTQ+ communities. Academic research has expanded into gender studies.

At the heart of feminism is the question of emancipation—that is, revealing and criticizing political, social, cultural, and religious structures of dominance. The main values behind the concept of emancipation, at least in the Western context, can be listed as equality, self-determination, liberation, and individual responsibility. Very often, these also mean freedom from religion and its power structures, misogyny, and patriarchalism. These values are appreciated on a larger scale in atheist milieus as well, which in general support gender equality and women's rights. Feminism is one of several social issues important to many atheists.

In particular, it is the second-wave feminists who in many ways agree with atheists when it comes to religion. They both perceive practices associated with religious traditions as harmful for women, especially norms that restrict women's lives, agency, and sexuality: restrictions in birth control and prohibitions around abortion, same-sex marriage, and divorce. Women with feminist orientations are often alienated from religious traditions.

Of today's younger feminist generations, many have grown up in secular families, from which it follows that they do not reject religion but also do not consider it an important part of their lives. The majority of Western feminists declare that they are atheists, agnostics, or nones. However, feminism and nonbelief do not always coincide, and various versions of spiritual and religious adherence have also been identified in feminist circles.

The fact that religious traditions usually tend to oppress women in multiple ways may lead feminist women to turn their backs on religious traditions. Some have suggested that all feminists should be atheists, as feminism is incompatible with Christianity, which in most instances treats women as inferior. On the other hand, the values of feminism are identical to those of atheists: rationality, reason, justice, and equality.

Thus, feminists can be atheists but are not necessarily so. As a matter of fact, many feminists who identify themselves as atheists have experienced the discussion culture within atheist circles to be quite masculine and misogynistic; they perceive atheism as a project belonging to white Western men. If the values of feminism and atheism are fully compatible, why do many female atheists feel uncomfortable in atheist circles, both on the internet and in real-life situations? The atheist movement has been plagued with accusations of misogyny, sexual harassment, and general hostility toward women; atheists can be just as patriarchal as their religious peers. Accordingly, there may be a disconnect between atheist men's verbal support of gender equality and their actual behavior.

The main voices within the contemporary atheist milieu—such as Richard Dawkins, Sam Harris, and Ayaan Hirsi Ali—support equal human rights and promote women's rights. However, they usually promote women's rights primarily in order to highlight the lack of rights within conservative Christianity and Islam. The sexism of the atheists' online community is especially well known, one example being Carl Benjamin's YouTube channel Sargon of Akkad.

Misogynistic attitudes within atheist circles are not a new phenomenon. Already in the meetings of freethinkers during the nineteenth century, female participants had to struggle hard to gain attention and acceptance. They were regarded as a threat to the (natural) gender order, and they were thought to be immoral and unfeminine. The same kinds of accusations can also be found in twenty-first-century organized secularism and atheism in the forms of sexual harassment and general hostility toward women.

The world of atheists is internally contradictory with regard to gender: there are large numbers of atheists who support gender equality and women's rights, but atheist men can be as patriarchal as religious men. Neither atheistic nor religious communities exist outside of, or apart from, social and cultural phenomena but reflect them, which gives one explanation for androcentrism and misogyny in both the religious traditions and the atheist milieus.

One of the most well-known and debated incidents is from 2011, when Rebecca Watson told about being approached by a male atheist. Her vlog caused a sort of "internet war" in the atheist community. Some thought the incident was not remarkable, while others thought it was a reflection of the sexist culture in the atheist community, mostly consisting of white, male heterosexuals. The relationship between atheism and feminism is still controversial. In addition to misogynistic attitudes within atheist milieus, there also exist cissexist views. For instance, Dawkins has questioned whether transgender women were "really women" based on their chromosomes. Atheist milieus may not always offer either cis- or transgender women a safe space.

Leaving a religion may no longer be a huge social risk for women, at least in the Western world. Being nonreligious or an atheist causes little to no loss of status or social exclusion. But still, even in the Western world, it is not always easy or self-evident for women to identify themselves as both feminists and atheists. The terms are controversial and contested, although they are becoming more and more acceptable. Atheism and feminism are both devalued identities in society when embraced by women. This leads atheist women to adjust their utterances and actions in a way that minimizes the social risks involved. They want to keep themselves safe from the possible reactions coming from society at large or, in particular, the atheist community.

The fact that some atheists do support feminism but some do not leads some atheist feminists to silence their voices.

About the author

Tiina Mahlamäki earned her doctorate in the study of religion, specializing in civil religion and gender. She is a senior lecturer on the study of religion at the University of Turku, Finland. Her research and publications focus on contemporary religion, atheism, Western esotericism, and creative writing.

Suggestions for further reading

In this book
See also chapters 25 (what makes atheists different), 27 (gender), 30 (politics), and 42 (activism).

Elsewhere
Brandt, Nella van den. "Secularity, Gender and Emancipation: Thinking through Feminist Activism and Feminist Approaches to the Secular." *Religion* 49(4) (2019): 691–716.

Stinson, Rebecca D., Kathleen M. Goodman, Charles Bermingham, and Saba R. Ali. "Do Atheism and Feminism Go Hand-in-Hand? A Qualitative Investigation of Atheist Men's Perspectives about Gender Equality." *Secularism and Nonreligion* 2 (2013): 39–60.

Trzebiatowska, Marta. "'Atheism Is Not the Problem. The Problem Is Being a Woman.' Atheist Women and Reasonable Feminism." *Journal of Gender Studies* 28(4) (2018): 475–487.

Trzebiatowska, Marta, and Steve Bruce. *Why Are Women More Religious Than Men?* Oxford: Oxford University Press, 2012.

44

How are atheists represented in the media?

Teemu Taira

It is a widely spread assumption, at least in Europe and North America, that the mainstream media is somewhat antireligious. Even scholars have wondered whether atheists are overrepresented among the educated elite, including media professionals.

It can be generalized that media professionals are slightly less religious than the general population. This may lead us to think that they are atheists and wish to promote their views in their profession. However, in the United States, for instance, those "focused producers" among media professionals who frequently deal with religion in their work tend to be highly religious and markedly more religious than their peers. Many consider religion to be extremely important, and most of them affiliate with a religious tradition. The pattern is not that clear in Europe, and there is also a lack of comparative and comprehensive studies, but it appears similar that antireligious atheists do not usually end up being focused producers of religion-related media material. It is true that religion and atheism are increasingly being covered by media professionals whose main expert area is something else (e.g., politics, culture, local issues), but so far, there is no convincing evidence that media professionals are biased toward favoring atheism and atheists. This applies especially to societies in which the values of dominant religious institutions are widely shared in society, but it also applies to many of the most secular societies.

However, one cannot infer the nature of media representations on the basis of the religiosity or irreligiosity of journalists because there are other factors contributing to how atheism and atheists are represented. Despite the ideal of objective journalism, ownership structure, the political profile of the media, advertisers, and (expectations concerning) readership are all key issues when seeking to determine the general approach of the media. Just like the rest of us, media professionals have internalized some attitudes and conceptualizations from the surrounding society and the institution that pays their salary, and they are conscious of only some of them. Even work factors, such as lack of time, can be crucial because media professionals, like others, tend to use already familiar templates in framing their stories, especially if their schedule does not allow for reflecting on and questioning the traditional approach. Therefore, a closer look at the media content is needed. There are not many major studies focusing on representations of atheists in the media, but most of the existing research offers relatively similar conclusions: mainstream media representations are not particularly favorable toward atheists.

A study of British media found that, in particular, the most popular tabloids have been very critical of atheists and have portrayed them as aggressive, noisy, and even insane left-wingers who are ruining the Christian country. Among this segment, it is hard to find any positive or even nuanced stories about atheism. The representations were more moderate in terms of media outlets with more liberal, left-of-center positions. In such media, atheists were offered more space to articulate their views. These outlets even had columnists who every now and then wrote in favor of secularism, though the editors made clear that they opposed what they called aggressive secularism. While being an atheist was clearly seen as an accepted position, highlighting the freedom of conscience and freedom of (and from) religion, and being understood as a normal part of the British religious landscape, atheist activism that heavily criticized religiosity or aimed for social change was more likely to be ridiculed and approached with caution. This was particularly the case during the papal visit to Britain in 2010, when one of the most famous atheists and generally appreciated defenders of the natural sciences, Richard Dawkins, received an unusual amount of negative media coverage because of his harsh criticism of the pope and the Catholic Church.

Probably the best opportunity for an international comparison of media representations of atheism in the twenty-first century is the atheist bus campaign that originated in Britain in 2008 and 2009. The slogan "There's Probably No God. Now Stop Worrying and Enjoy Your Life" was used on buses. The campaign was later adopted—or there was an attempt to adopt it—by local atheist organizations in more than a dozen other countries, with varying degrees of success. The media was keen to cover the case and monitor the debate around it, but there is very little evidence of mainstream media outlets providing support for the campaign and its message.

As hinted at by these examples, the presence of atheism among the media is primarily made up of organized atheists and a few celebrities and public intellectuals who tend to be more critical of religion than typical atheist individuals. Most atheists are not organized and do not have an active role in the media as such. Therefore, it should be noted that only some types of voices represent atheism to the larger public, and one topic for further reflection is what social consequences such representations may have.

In the light of existing studies, it is clear that despite the fact that media professionals in general are less religious than the rest of the population, the mainstream media, while offering space for debate on religion and atheism, is usually not on the side of outspoken atheists. Rather, the media tends to support liberal Christianity, especially if it is in the dominant position in society and if media professionals share most of its values. The negativity of representations tends to increase when the atheists portrayed are very assertive in their cause. They are seen as provocative, aggressive, or intolerant, and their reasons are belittled. This more commonly happens in conservative and right-wing media. However, the most vocal and articulate atheists can get their message out, especially in more liberal media, so they are not silenced in or ostracized from the media sphere in general. They are even able to raise issues for discussion, but it is rare to see mainstream media providing full support for atheist activities.

The situation is very different in countries where atheist expressions are not allowed in the public sphere. Especially in some Muslim-majority countries, mainstream media representations of atheism are very limited and predominantly very negative. More nuanced representations are limited even on social media and the internet, but they provide a means for those who wish to gain information to do so. Social media and the internet are also important in regions where atheist expressions are allowed because they offer space for atheist self-representations and discussion and sometimes even a channel to feed new and more heterogeneous representations to the mainstream media.

About the author

Teemu Taira is a senior lecturer in the study of religion at the University of Helsinki.

Suggestions for further reading

In this book
See also chapters 24 (internet), 45 (literature and arts), and 46 (popular culture).

Elsewhere

Cimino, Richard, and Christopher Smith. "How the Media Got Secularism—with a Little Help from the New Atheists." *Oxford Handbooks Online*. https://doi.org/10.1093/oxfordhb/9780199935420.013.15.

Knott, Kim, Elizabeth Poole, and Teemu Taira. *Media Portrayals of Religion and the Secular Sacred: Representation and Change*. Farnham: Ashgate, 2013.

Laughlin, Jack C. "Varieties of an Atheist Public in a Digital Age: The Politics of Recognition and the Recognition of Politics." *Journal of Religion, Media and Digital Culture* 5(2) (2016): 315–338.

Taira, Teemu. "Media and the Nonreligious." In *Religion, Media, and Social Change*, edited by Kennet Granholm, Marcus Moberg, and Sofia Sjö, 110–125. London: Routledge, 2015.

Tomlins, Steven, and Spencer Culham Bullivant, eds. *The Atheist Bus Campaign: Global Manifestations and Responses*. Leiden: Brill, 2017.

van der Veen, A. Maurits, and Erik Bleich. "Atheism in US and UK Newspapers: Negativity about Non-belief and Non-believers." *Religions* 12 (2021): 291.

45

What is the historical role of atheism in literature and the arts?

James Bryant Reeves

Humans are narrative beings. We understand ourselves and our world not simply by examining empirical data or constructing philosophical arguments but by telling stories about our lives, our communities, and our values. Attitudes toward atheism are therefore largely dependent upon the stories we tell about unbelief, the ways we *imagine* godlessness. In Western Europe, stories about atheism became more and more common during the early modern period, which lasted from approximately 1500 or so until the end of the eighteenth century. To understand the historical role atheism has played in literature and the arts, we can start by investigating how authors and artists from this period portrayed unbelief.

When poets, playwrights, and novelists wrote about atheism in the seventeenth and eighteenth centuries, they imagined godless characters and worlds that many of their contemporaries considered impossibilities. Until very recently, atheism was not a widely held world view, and many thinkers from the 1600s and 1700s doubted the possibility of a true, honest unbeliever. Belief in God was considered natural, commonsense, and necessary for preserving social order. As a result, laws often prohibited public declarations of unbelief and promoted particular state religions (the Church of England, for instance). So it makes sense that unbelievers were hesitant to out themselves and that authors therefore had to be inventive when creating characters who doubted God's existence.

Given the lack of public atheists in these centuries, visual depictions of atheism are rather sparse, though there are notable exceptions like James Gillray's political cartoons of the 1790s. In caricatures like "Smelling Out a Rat; or The Atheistical Revolutionist Disturbed in His Midnight 'Calculations'" (1790) and the "Presentation of the Mahometan Credentials, or, The Final Resource of French Atheists" (1793), Gillray (1756–1815) depicts atheism as unruly, absurd, and seditious. Like many conservative Britons at the time, he associated unbelief with the French Revolution and the social unrest that accompanied it. Yet while atheism was largely absent in visual arts before the nineteenth century, it was surprisingly prominent in imaginative literature. Plays like Cyril Tourneur's *The Atheist's Tragedy* (1611) and Thomas Otway's *The Atheist* (1684); poems like Alexander Pope's *The Dunciad* (1743), Edward Young's *Night Thoughts* (1742–1745), and Phillis Wheatley's unpublished "An Address to the Atheist" (1767); and novels like Sarah Fielding's *The Adventures of David Simple* (1744) and Phebe Gibbes's *Lady Louisa Stroud* (1764) portray numerous fictional atheists who openly express their unbelief. In many of these works, and in others like them, atheists are semicomic figures who are simultaneously dangerous and ridiculous. These fictional atheists are quick to betray others, pursue their own wants and desires no matter how negatively this pursuit affects others, and, in the end, give up their unbelief and acknowledge God's existence when faced with the slightest danger or crisis. (For instance, Otway's atheist quickly renounces his unbelief after being scratched by a penknife, a wound that he ludicrously assumes is fatal.) In sum, fictional atheists from the seventeenth and eighteenth centuries are frequently laughable, their atheism feeble and irrational but nonetheless capable of causing harm.

In fact, despite atheism's public absence, and despite the confident dismissals of atheism in literature written between 1600 and 1800, authors were seriously concerned about atheism's emergence. For one, atheistic ideas *did* spread secretly in manuscript tracts and poems intended for circulation only in small, select groups, like those written by the religious skeptic John Wilmot, Second Earl of Rochester (1647–1680), whose poetry frequently questions established social conventions and the reasonableness of organized religion. (Interestingly, Rochester's biographer, Gilbert Burnet [1643–1715], controversially claimed that Rochester experienced a death-bed conversion, just like many of the fictional atheists mentioned above.) In addition, *On the Nature of Things*, a long atheistic poem by the ancient Roman author Lucretius, was first translated into European vernacular languages in these centuries, when licensing laws and rules regulating religious worship became less restrictive, both of which allowed atheistic ideas to spread more easily. On top of all this, many eighteenth-century thinkers advocated various forms of deism, the belief that a supreme being exists but is impersonal and therefore quite different from the Christian God. While atheism itself was still prohibited, then, religious authors worried that such developments would eventually lead to all-out unbelief and widespread rejection of God. With this in mind, it is clear that fictional representations of atheism from this time are not merely two-dimensional putdowns of nonexistent unbelievers (though they certainly are that), but they are also intriguing attempts to imagine what the world would look like without God or, at least, without people who believe in him.

While these fictions often cast atheists as unsympathetic, hateful, and unlovable, suggesting that at least some sort of belief in God is necessary to sustain moral behavior and social cohesion, a few nineteenth-century authors insisted that atheism leads to self-improvement and social well-being. The most outspoken atheist, perhaps, was the Romantic poet Percy Shelley (1792–1822), who was famously expelled from Oxford for refusing to admit to authoring a pamphlet entitled *The Necessity of Atheism* (1811). Unlike many authors before him, Shelley presented atheism as pure common sense, while religion was, for him, both destructive and repressive (as his verse drama about a corrupt Italian family and the Catholic Church's sordid collusion with their misdeeds, *The Cenci* [1819], clearly suggests). In lengthy poetic works like *Queen Mab* (1813) and *Prometheus Unbound* (1820), Shelley likewise celebrates atheism as unselfish, rational, and ecologically beneficial, insisting that religion is the exact opposite in every way. Shelley was an enormously influential author whose portrayal of atheism affected not only his contemporaries (most of whom despised his unbelief) but also later thinkers like Karl Marx and Mahatma Gandhi. And in turn, Marx's religious and economic ideas were highly influential in Soviet Russia, which produced a wealth of atheistic literature, visual art, and propaganda throughout the twentieth century.

Since the nineteenth century, countless authors have also offered nuanced, less one-sided takes on the debate between religion and irreligion. For instance, in the nineteenth century, the poet, essayist, and cultural critic Matthew Arnold (1822–1888) acknowledged his own lack of personal faith while also lamenting that lack (see especially his famous poem "Dover Beach" [1867]). Despite his personal unbelief, Arnold curiously insisted that religion is necessary to provide most people hope, purpose, and social stability. And throughout the nineteenth and twentieth centuries, philosophically minded novelists like Fyodor Dostoevsky (1821–1881) and Albert Camus (1913–1960) explored the ramifications of godlessness at great imaginative length. While Dostoevsky's *Demons* (1872) and *The Brothers Karamazov* (1880) deftly lament the expansion of materialistic, atheistic world views in nineteenth-century Russia, the Algerian-born Camus's *The Plague* (1947) casts nonbelievers as existential heroes in a godless (and therefore absurd) universe. While the two authors reached different conclusions about God's existence, both avoided the straightforward denunciations and insults that characterized many previous literary explorations of godlessness, and they approached God's potential (non)existence as the thorny, complex issue it most assuredly is.

If contemporary novelists like Marilynne Robinson (b. 1943), the critically acclaimed Christian author of *Gilead* (2004), *Home* (2008), and several other novels and essay collections, and Ian McEwan (b. 1948), a renowned atheist and author of novels such as *Atonement* (2001) and *The Children Act* (2014), are any indication, literature will continue to be a fertile space for thoughtful, creative imaginings of unbelief for years to come.

About the author

James Bryant Reeves is an assistant professor of English at Texas State University, where he teaches classes on eighteenth-century British literature, satire, mythology, and more. He has published several essays and articles on literature and religion, and his first book, *Godless Fictions in the Eighteenth Century: A Literary History of Atheism* (Cambridge University Press, 2020), examines fictional portrayals of atheism during the British Enlightenment.

Suggestions for further reading

In this book
See also chapters 7 (identity), 44 (media), and 46 (popular culture).

Elsewhere
Jacob, Margaret C. *The Radical Enlightenment: Pantheists, Freemasons and Republicans* (2nd rev. edition). London: Cornerstone Books, 2006.

Priestman, Martin. *Romantic Atheism: Poetry and Freethought, 1780–1830*. Cambridge: Cambridge University Press, 2000.

Rivers, Isabel. *Reason, Grace, and Sentiment: A Study of the Language of Religion and Ethics in England, 1660–1780* (2 volumes). Cambridge: Cambridge University Press, 1991–2000.

46

Is atheism visible in popular culture?

Teemu Taira

It is safe to suggest that atheism has not been a particularly visible theme in Western popular culture, no matter whether popular culture is defined as a form of culture that ordinary members of society practice and appreciate or as widely appreciated and mediated cultural forms that include films, television, pop music, and games. Nowadays, popular culture is typically seen as referring to the latter characterization, at least if studies in religion (and atheism) and popular culture are used as an example.

What does the relative absence of atheism in popular culture mean? Does it mean that it is not an interesting issue that would draw people's attention? Does it mean that producers and consumers share it as the implicit view and consider religion as the "other"—namely, deviant or exotic? Rather than answering these questions directly, it is possible to start mapping the topic by considering the means to examine the visibility of atheism in popular culture.

One way to start thinking about the possible presence of atheism in popular culture is to focus on the identities of producers of content. When the few existing overviews of atheism in popular culture are reviewed, particularly in films, it can be said that while there are explicitly atheist directors, their take on religious topics is mostly appreciative. In their work, atheistic directors have not decided to focus on representing atheism and atheists.

Another way to think about the question is to review what types of criticism of religion could be counted as supporting atheistic views. For instance, some popular animated television series, such as *The Simpsons* and *South Park*, contain criticism of religion, especially regarding conservative US Christians, Mormons, and Scientologists. Humor is then a means to raise critical issues and sometimes offend religious people. While such representations can be seen as supporting atheism or at least science over religion, they make fun of atheists too; for example, *South Park* features a two-part story arc that includes Richard Dawkins as a character. The creator of *Family Guy*, Seth MacFarlane, is a self-identified atheist, and sometimes proatheist views are manifested in the series.

Criticism of religion combined with implicit or nonarticulated atheism is also the case with some popular films, such as Monty Python's *Life of Brian* (1979). In fact, it is common that atheism and atheists are not represented directly in films, although the treatment of religion could be supportive of atheism. It is telling that the Reel Rundown website lists "The Top 20 Atheist-Friendly Movies" rather than movies about atheists or atheistic protagonists.

Several films' relation to atheism is indirect and distant, but some have explicitly atheist protagonists. For instance, Cecil B. DeMille's *The Godless Girl* (1928) represents an atheist as an intolerant person who has no means to comfort a dying human being and who turns to God at a difficult moment in her life. The viewer may have a lot of sympathy for the young atheist girl who falls in love with a young Christian man because the real villains in the film are the older people who treat them horribly, but atheism itself is portrayed negatively.

One of the films in which the protagonist's atheist identity is portrayed positively is *The Ledge* (2011), whose director, Matthew Chapman, advertised it as the first US proatheist feature film with an openly atheist hero. Since then, there have been biographical drama films about real atheists. An example is *The Most Hated Woman in America* (2017), based on the life of the founder of American Atheists, Madalyn Murray O'Hair (1919–1995), directed by Tommy O'Haver. Its way of describing one infamous atheist does not necessarily qualify as an "atheist-friendly" movie, however.

It is notable that documentaries, rather than fiction films, have become a vehicle for popular atheistic criticism and identity politics in the first decades of the twenty-first century. They address the question of how humans should live from the atheist point of view. In addition to involving celebrity atheists such as Dawkins, the development of media technologies, particularly in terms of distribution, has further facilitated their reach.

While there are multiple studies about religion in popular music, and many of them note how several music genres are often critical in relation to Christianity, especially its institutional forms, there are no substantial surveys on atheism. It is clear, however, that atheism has a significant place in Western popular music. Many heavy metal bands have been labeled antireligious and atheist. The former is obvious, at least in the sense that they are "anti-Christian," but the latter is more contentious. Even black metal musicians who burned churches and preached about the evils of religion have been supportive of pagan traditions, or their atheism is framed in the language of Satanism. Punk is an obvious case. Sociological studies have demonstrated that punks are predominantly nonreligious, and many punk bands have advanced an atheist view in both their lyrics and their interviews. While some British punk artists and bands have occasionally provoked their fans to turn against religion (e.g., Siouxsie and the Banshees, Crass), some American punk bands, such as the Dead Kennedys or Bad Religion, have been critical of religious beliefs and religious people's political views consistently throughout their careers. Bad Religion's singer, Greg Graffin, has even written a book focusing on his science-driven, naturalistic atheist world view.

If the popularity of video games continues to grow, it is likely that at some point, representations of atheism and atheists will become more common. A number of games contain criticism of religion, thus giving an opportunity to analyze their implicit atheism (e.g., *Dishonored*, 2012). Atheism is generally an ineffective asset in games (e.g., researching atheism is considered to be the least useful technology a player can utilize in *Age of Empires II: The Conquerors*, 2000), and while atheist figures can be found in multiple games, their role is rarely central (e.g., in *The Witcher 3: Wild Hunt*, 2015, one has to negotiate with or fight against an atheist).

As this brief survey shows, atheism and atheists are not fully invisible in popular culture, although they are not the themes around which careers are typically built. Popular culture products addressing atheist identities proudly, rather than stereotypically in a negative manner, have become more common, but it is still easier to find examples of implicit atheistic themes, which primarily means criticism of religion. Given that representing atheism from the atheistic point of view has become more common, it is relevant to study how such representations are constructed. It is likely that the work is done by constructing religion as other, but it is also interesting to see what else is embraced or rejected in representations of atheism and whether it remains a minority interest in our time, which has seen a rise in atheist identity politics in other areas of public life.

About the author

Teemu Taira is a senior lecturer in the study of religion at the University of Helsinki.

Suggestions for further reading

In this book
See also chapters 30 (politics), 38 (discrimination), 44 (media), and 45 (literature and arts).

Elsewhere
Barnett, Christopher R. "Film and Television." In *The Cambridge History of Atheism*, edited by Stephen Bullivant and Michael Ruse, 740–759. Cambridge: Cambridge University Press, 2021.

Bird, S. Elizabeth. "True Believers and Atheists Need Not Apply: Faith and Mainstream Television Drama." In *Small Screen, Big Picture: Television and Lived Religion*, edited by Diane Winston, 17–41. Waco: Baylor University Press, 2009.

Feltmate, David. *Drawn to the Gods: Religion and Humor in* The Simpsons, South Park, *and* Family Guy. New York: New York University Press, 2017.

Rautalahti, Heidi. "Disenchanting Faith: Religion and Authority in the Dishonored Universe." *Religions* 9(5) (2018): 146.

Taira, Teemu. "Atheistic Documentaries and the Critique of Religion in Bill Maher's *Religulous*." In *Representing Religion in Film*, edited by Tenzan Eaghll and Rebekka King, 27–39. London: Bloomsbury, 2022.

Beliefs, values, and practices

47
Are children born atheists?

Andrew Ross Atkinson and Thomas J. Coleman III

On this very question, eighteenth-century Enlightenment philosopher Baron d'Holbach, in his book *Good Sense*, argued against the plausibility that God exists. D'Holbach argued that babies held no idea of God because their brains were a blank slate, awaiting parents and society to etch onto it whatever the local norms and beliefs were—in this case, the belief in God. This blank-slate view of a newborn's mind has all but disappeared among scholars since Immanuel Kant and well on into the twentieth century. It is now thoroughly discredited thanks in part to experiments led by cognitive scientists that show in similar Kantian spirit that the mind is far from being void of a priori concepts and intuitions. Could this mean that d'Holbach was wrong—that instead of being born atheists, we are perhaps born with an innate knowledge of God, as some might argue? Before answering these questions, it is important to consider how we define the term "atheist" and unpack some potential assumptions. Ask yourself, How might different understandings of "atheist" influence our interpretation of the science behind what newborn infants (don't) believe?

How these questions are answered depends on how atheism is defined. For example, if an atheist is defined as being without belief in God (i.e., "negative atheism"), as d'Holbach held, then this would include adolescents and adults who are capable of ratiocination on the (non) existence of God and withholding their belief—but also wantonly vomiting, defecating, and slobbering animals, such as newborn infants and the family dog, who are without belief simply because they are unacquainted with the claim God exists for ipso facto lacking the requisite cognitive sophistication. By contrast, if an atheist is defined more narrowly as being capable of thinking that there are no gods (i.e., "positive atheism"), then it would seem fit that it includes adolescents and adults and excludes nonhuman animals but also creates another question confronted by our interlocutor, d'Holbach: At what point is a child mature enough to ratiocinate their (dis)belief?

One of the unexamined assumptions behind defining the atheist positively or negatively is that each requires a certain level of cognitive maturity having been reached. D'Holbach rejected attempts to discern this, in part because he was responding to a philosophical debate that dichotomized the foundation of human knowledge into two philosophical schools of thought—*both* of which were employed in the debate over the (non)existence of God: on the one hand were the rationalists who held that knowledge was derived from reason alone, and on the other were the empiricists who held that knowledge derived ultimately from experience. Rationalists such as René Descartes—unable to proffer sound logical proof for God's existence—deferred to the idea that man is "stamped" with the idea of God at birth. Empiricists such as John Locke leaned more toward the blank-slate view—the mind as tabula rasa. Strange as it may seem, they were both partially correct about some things concerning religious ideas about God. Contrary to d'Holbach's blank-slate view of the individual, children do exit the womb with something—their functioning brain—ready to experience the world *as if* a blank slate, but with just enough cognitive tools for understanding that there are other people in the world (agents) who think and want things (intentionality) like peace and quiet, food, love, and affection. This is called a "theory of mind," and human beings are invariably pretty good at using it to do a whole range of things, from playing chess to understanding the characters in works of fiction. Like a virus or a key fitting into a lock, so basic ideas about supernatural agency easily parasitize our evolved psychology. There are certain elements about the idea of a God that are intuitively easy to grasp. The counterintuitive elements are another matter and perhaps warrant a wholly different kind of attention. The easy-to-grasp parts about deities are agency and intentionality, and those cultural particulates can ride anyone's capacity for a theory of mind, generally—even that of a child.

Without being subjected to significant guiding influences that might provide the necessary cues to theistic reasoning, there is no reason to suppose that major religious ideas about a God will come to the fore in an infant's mind in the absence of, say, a parental cue. Besides currently lacking evidence to show infants and young children spontaneously coming to believe in God, this argument is further strained because it appears children come to adopt—for a time—whatever the culturally prevalent supernatural beliefs are, from the tooth fairy to the monster under the bed and not just God.

Children do not spontaneously invite supernatural concepts during their development—although they may ask very strange questions such as

"Why are rocks pointy?" that might indicate a way of trying to understand the world *as if* it had purpose and design. In attending to such questions with a mind that evolved largely to deal with intentional agents, it is no great surprise that it readily accepts certain kinds of "whodunit" explanations. The fact that supernatural entities are mentioned throughout history and in all cultures is good evidence that such ideas do enjoy cognitively fertile terrain. It does *not*, however, provide evidence for God's existence, as some would indeed have it. The most reliable finding we have is that children come to believe in the God or gods that populate the culture they were born into, adding further support for the idea that such beliefs are culturally inherited.

Children are not *born* atheists or theists and do not have any gumption for either of the two positions. Is the former even a belief set or just the absence of those beliefs implied by the latter? We hold that children are born with an absence of those theistic beliefs waiting out there in various cultures—and in that sense, they *are* atheists. Whereas some biological viruses can be resident at birth and genes are also inherited, religious cultural information, including ideas about God, cannot—otherwise, we might well be able to breed children with religious pedigrees and perhaps new hybrid religions.

About the authors

Andrew Ross Atkinson did his PhD in the philosophy of science at the University of Bristol. He is a postdoctoral researcher in the Society & Cognition Unit at the University of Bialystok, Poland, and a visiting researcher at the University of Agder, Norway.

Thomas J. Coleman III was a research associate at the University of Bialystok, Poland. He did his PhD in psychology of religion at Coventry University in the United Kingdom.

Suggestions for further reading

In this book
See also chapters 48 (upbringing) and 53 (values).

Elsewhere
Banerjee, Konika, and Paul Bloom. "Would Tarzan Believe in God? Conditions for the Emergence of Religious Belief." *Trends in Cognitive Sciences* 17(1) (2013): 7–8.

Boyer, Pascal. *Religion Explained: The Evolutionary Origins of Religious Thought*. New York: Basic Books, 2001.

Jong, Jonathan, Christopher Kavanagh, and Aku Visala. "Born Idolaters: The Limits of the Philosophical Implications of the Cognitive Science of Religion." *Neue Zeitschrift für Systematische Theologie und Religionsphilosophie* 57(2) (2015): 244–266.

Shook, John R. "Are People Born to Be Believers, or Are Gods Born to Be Believed?" *Method and Theory in the Study of Religion* 29(4–5) (2017): 353–373.

48

Do atheist parents have atheist children?

Christel Manning

The answer depends on what you mean by that question. Let's take the term "atheist" first. Strictly speaking, the term refers to someone who does not believe in God. But this tells us nothing about what atheists do believe. Their disbelief in God may be grounded in science or in humanism or in Marxist philosophy or in Buddhism. They may find meaning in spiritual practice such as meditation and nature walks, in rituals like Passover that honor a cultural tradition, or in community service and activism. There are "hard atheists" who take a strong stand against theism and "soft atheists" who may be agnostic or simply indifferent. Like religious people, atheists are diverse, and the values they transmit to their children will reflect that.

This leads us to the meaning of the word "have." Research suggests atheism, like religion, is learned rather than passed on via genetic transmission. So it may be better to ask if parents raise their children to be atheists. Atheist parents, like religious ones, want to pass on values and traditions to their children. But there is much variation in how they go about doing that. Location matters. Raising children in China, where atheism is the official state ideology, is obviously a different enterprise than in the United States, where conservative Christians are a powerful political force and the word "God" is stamped on the currency. And there are regional differences within societies. In the United States, for example, atheist parents living in the Bible Belt have been found reluctant to identify as such because they fear their children will be stigmatized. Such parents were more likely to affiliate with an organization that supports their world view and to enroll their children in secular educational programming than atheist families living in regions they perceived as more tolerant.

Family structure also matters. There are many stakeholders who may seek to influence how a child is raised, not just the father and mother, but stepparents, grandparents, and others. If only one parent is atheist, the religious parent may want to send a child to Sunday school or take them to church. The secular parent may not wish the children to be indoctrinated and may model a questioning attitude. When children grow up in single-parent or blended families, the custodial parent will obviously have a strong influence on world-view transmission, but the visiting parent may expose the children to different ideas. Research on religious transmission shows the mother to have a strong influence, but one recent study found that fathers had a more important role in atheist socialization. Grand-parents can also play a role, either encouraging or pushing back against secular parenting.

A common value among many atheist parents in Western democra-cies is respect for choice. They are wary of indoctrination and assert that their children should decide for themselves. In the United States, many secular parents wish to expose their children to religion, often because of a family heritage. They may outsource religious education by enrolling a child in a religious education program or by letting the child attend services with someone else. Or if one parent is religious, the family may affiliate with a conventional religious organization and may celebrate some holidays at home. As the child grows older, they discover that their parents have different beliefs and realize they can choose.

Other atheist parents seek out a community that affirms secularism, such as humanist associations, Unitarian Universalist associations (UUAs), or more recently, the Sunday Assembly. These organizations encourage families to build their own rituals from traditions that are meaningful to them (e.g., a secular Hanukah, summer solstice celebrations, or Darwin's birthday). UUA offers formal "world-view education" programs, a kind of secular Sunday school that teaches kids about many different religions as well as humanist and atheist philosophies and encourages the child to choose. Secular organizations may also provide summer camps, after-school care, and weekend social justice work that support humanist ethics, including tolerance and compassion.

Parents who want to raise their child atheist have fewer options for community than religious parents do. Although surveys show growing numbers of individuals to be nonreligious, organized secularism has not kept pace. Depending on where they live, atheist families may not have access to a secular organization nearby, or they may not trust organized isms in the first place. Such parents may attempt to transmit an atheist world view on their own, often with the help of internet blogs. They may read books and watch videos with children, have conversations, and create unique family rituals in the home. But without support from a wider community, these parents often struggle to maintain a commitment to the process, and as their children enter adolescence, they may lose interest in these activities.

Finally, some atheist parents do not wish to transmit any particular world view to their children. They do not enroll them in a secular or religious education program, and their home life does not involve any systematic effort to transmit either atheism or belief in God. They celebrate holidays but without reference to any particular ism. There may be gifts at Christmas or Hanukah, bunnies and eggs at Easter, but children learn nothing about the religious significance of these events, nor do parents substitute secular meaning such as solstices or mark explicitly secular events like Darwin Day. These families do impart moral values, but they are grounded in universal principles like the Golden Rule or personal accountability. Whether children choose religion or atheism is up to them.

When do children make that choice? That depends on what we mean by "children." We do not have numbers on how many atheist parents use which strategy or its long-term effectiveness. What we do know is that since the 1960s, more nonreligious parents are transmitting their nonreligious values to their children. Children raised by nonreligious parents are more likely to be nonreligious themselves (five times more likely if both parents are nonreligious). And yet most atheist adults today were raised by religious parents. As young children, they learned to believe in God. But starting in adolescence and especially if they left home for university, they explored alternative world views. They become atheists because they questioned and ultimately rejected a belief in God or because they discovered that they never really believed in the first place. The opposite is also true: many people raised atheist may find their way to religion. We are always our parents' children, but socialization is not destiny.

About the author

Christel Manning is a professor of religious studies at Sacred Heart University and has spent more than a decade studying people who leave religion. Her book, *Losing Our Religion* (New York University Press, 2015), was rated one of the top ten religion titles of 2015 and received the 2016 Distinguished Book Award from the Society for the Scientific Study of Religion.

Suggestions for further reading

In this book
See also chapters 26 (young people) and 47 (born atheist).

Elsewhere

Baggett, Jerome P. *The Varieties of Nonreligious Experience: Atheism in American Culture*. New York: New York University Press, 2019.

Bengtson, Vern L., R. David Hayward, Phil Zuckerman, and Merrill Silverstein. "Bringing Up Nones: Intergenerational Influences and Cohort Trends." *Journal for the Scientific Study of Religion* 57(2) (2018): 258–275.

LeDrew, Stephen. "Discovering Atheism: Heterogeneity in Trajectories to Atheist Identity and Activism." *Sociology of Religion* 74(4) (2013): 431–453.

Manning, Christel. *Losing Our Religion: How Unaffiliated Parents Are Raising Their Children*. New York: New York University Press, 2015.

49

How does one become an atheist?

Julia Martínez-Ariño

Becoming an atheist does not usually happen overnight. It is more frequently a long process whereby a former believer leaves behind a set of beliefs and practices, an identity, and a sense of belonging to a religious community. Sociologists and psychologists have coined the term "deconversion" to refer to this switch from a theist reference framework to an atheist one. This transformation implies some identity work: the person in question must first divest themselves from a previously held religious identity and then construct or adopt the new atheist identity. In doing so, they establish a distinction between the past and the present, their religious and their atheist self. Moreover, this transformation should be understood as not only a personal process but also one that involves the social and cultural environment in which one is located. Becoming an atheist in a society where belief in God is culturally dominant is different from, and likely more challenging and controversial than, undergoing the same process in a society where such a belief represents a minority.

The question of "How does one become an atheist?" can be answered by focusing on two elements: first, the phases a person may go through to become an atheist and, second, the triggers or motivations that initiate or lead to such a process.

In relation to the phases to become an atheist, academic literature highlights a predominant pathway that could be considered the standard one. This transition is characterized by a rather linear trajectory from the status of believer to one of atheist. However, more recently, studies have shown the multiplicity of trajectories toward atheism. Some people who were not raised religious choose to become religious in their teenage or early adulthood years and then reject religion again. Others who had no particularly strong religious upbringing define themselves later in life explicitly as atheists. While the latter two pathways show the fluidity and nonlinear character of an atheist identity construction, I will focus on the most common track.

The standard trajectory could be divided, despite the specificities of each individual process, into four main phases. The first phase is one in which the person in question realizes that the belief in God is something ascribed or given, something the person did not choose but was raised into. The second phase is when the person starts questioning the idea of God and their beliefs in it. This period of doubt is when, I would argue, the triggers and reasons to become an atheist—which I discuss below—become apparent. While for some this period of doubt can be experienced as one of the opening up of new spaces, for others, it might feel like a period of loss, grief, disappointment, or anger with themselves for having believed certain things that now appear implausible. The third phase is that of rejection. According to some sociologists, becoming an atheist is not just a matter of adopting a new, ready-made identity; rather, it implies rejecting beliefs, a previous theistic identity, and, I would add, certain lifestyles, social relations, and spaces. This phase is one in which the person in question defines themselves as atheist. The fourth phase is when the new identity is made public and receives the validation, recognition, rejection, or indifference of the social environment. Some compare this phase with "coming out" of the closet by queer individuals. The sharing of an atheist identity may be done selectively, only in receptive contexts, given the negative connotations associated with atheism in certain societies. However, atheists are frequently outspoken about their identity as a form of claiming what they consider a liberation and transformation they are proud of. This last phase can significantly impact social interactions, family relations, social behavior, and work opportunities. In some cases, this phase may end up in participation with forms of organized atheism.

The second dimension of the question "How does one become an atheist?" refers to the reasons or motivations to leave religion. Sociological research has identified several reasons to become an atheist that can be classified according to their nature as intellectual, social, political, moral, psychological, or emotional. Frequently, a combination of these is what originates the process of deconversion.

Intellectual reasons refer to the incapacity of individuals to make sense rationally of the theistic beliefs they held previously. Several studies and my own research show that access to university is a key moment for changing those beliefs because people are exposed to different world views, have access to new philosophical and scientific ideas, become familiar with new authors, and so on. Moreover, in this period, new relationships are built that challenge one's own upbringing and sense of identity. Therefore, entering into a new social milieu can be a reason to revise one's theistic beliefs and ultimately leave them behind. Political and moral reasons are also frequently mentioned by atheists as the triggers of their doubting and ultimate deconversion. For some, the immorality of certain religious teachings is what has made them question their religious beliefs. The condemnation of homosexuality by a large part of the religious orthodoxy is an example of the mandates that the new atheists find immoral and untenable. Finally, psychological reasons, such as the incapacity to accept the submission to an invisible being, and emotional motivations, such as bad experiences with religious hierarchies, the grounding of their beliefs on the fear of hell, or tough experiences like the loss of a beloved one, may also generate doubts.

In summary, becoming an atheist is far from simple and immediate. Typically, people who become atheists go through a gradual process of identity transformation that is triggered by a variety of reasons and situations. However, most research focuses primarily on atheists who come from Christian backgrounds. Does the process look similar in other religious traditions where beliefs in God are less central? Or does becoming an atheist require a different process in religions where rituals and practices are the most relevant component of the religious identity?

About the author

Julia Martínez-Ariño is an assistant professor of the sociology of religion at the University of Groningen, the Netherlands. Her current research is on apostasy in Spain and Argentina.

Suggestions for further reading

In this book
See also chapters 24 (internet), 29 (migration), 37 (converting), and 40 (members).

Elsewhere
Cottee, Simon. *The Apostates: When Muslims Leave Islam*. London: Hurst, 2015.

Enstedt, Daniel, Göran Larsson, and Teemu T. Mantsinen, eds. *Handbook of Leaving Religion*. Leiden: Brill, 2019.

LeDrew, Stephen. "Discovering Atheism: Heterogeneity in Trajectories to Atheist Identity and Activism." *Sociology of Religion* 74(4) (2013): 431–453.

Lee, Lois. "Ambivalent Atheist Identities: Power and Non-religious Culture in Contemporary Britain." *Social Analysis* 59(2) (2015): 20–39.

Zuckerman, Phil. *Faith No More: Why People Reject Religion*. Oxford: Oxford University Press, 2012.

50
How do atheists reason that God does not exist?

Aku Visala

Atheism comes in different flavors, and not all atheists have attempted to ground their atheism in reason and argument. Some who advocate the belief that there is no God or gods and that one should not engage in religious activity have done so on moral, emotional, and aesthetic grounds. Often-times, atheists and nonreligious people do not think about the grounds for their atheism. For many, there is no need for rational grounding at all. Empirical studies show that those atheists who seek to ground their nonbelief in reason and explicitly argue for it represent only a small minority among the nonreligious. So it seems that only a minority of atheists see the attempt to argue for the nonexistence of God from general empirical and philosophical premises as a worthwhile pursuit.

Those who have taken up this enterprise have developed various strategies for explicitly arguing for atheism. One strategy is to argue that nonbelief in God or gods is the most rational default assumption. We cannot directly observe supernatural agents, and they seldom make pur-ported appearances in our everyday life. Those purported appearances can be explained by other natural factors, like human psychology. In addition, science proceeds perfectly well without assuming the existence of any kind of supernatural entity or force. Scientific methods do not assume God's existence, and generally accepted scientific theories do not feature supernatural agents or forces as theoretical assumptions. Science is, in a word, naturalistic.

So if everyday experience and science are reliable guides to what in fact exists, we should remain agnostic about the supernatural. If some-one wanted to defend their belief in God, they would have to provide some evidence and argument for that belief. Of course, many historical and contemporary arguments have been presented for the existence of God, including the cosmological argument, the design argument, and the ontological argument. What these atheists aim to do is to demonstrate how these arguments fail to give sufficient reason to believe in God. As a consequence, the default stance of nonbelief prevails.

Science has also been central to defenses of atheism in other ways. Some atheists have argued against religion by invoking the trustworthiness of scientific methodology in acquiring knowledge. Before the advent of modern science, the possibility of divine revelation providing some knowledge about the physical world was a plausible option. Moreover, religious experience and revelation could be seen as plausible sources of knowledge about the nonphysical, transcendental world. However, when modern science emerged from the seventeenth century onward, religious ways of knowing about the physical world as well as the world beyond it became suspect. Given the massive success of the scientific method and the development of technologies made possible by this knowledge, religious ways of knowing, like revelation and mystical experience, seem inadequate at best and irrational at worst.

Many nonbelievers from Friedrich Nietzsche and David Hume onward have invoked naturalistic explanations of religion in support of atheism and agnosticism. The most famous historical theories are those of Karl Marx, Sigmund Freud, and Ludwig Feuerbach. Contemporary theorists often refer to sociological or cognitive explanations. While naturalistic explanations of religion do not prove the nonexistence of God or necessarily provide evidence against the theist, they do increase the plausibility of atheism. If atheism is true, the atheist owes us an explanation for why so many people believe in God or gods if such beings do not exist or we have no knowledge of them. A plausible naturalistic account of religion will offer such an explanation, thus making the atheist position more plausible overall.

Rather than simply rebutting theistic arguments and resorting to the sciences, there is another strategy as well—namely, to develop antitheistic arguments. Atheist arguments come in two different types. According to the first, there are empirical features of our world that are either incompatible with the existence of God or make God's existence improbable. In contemporary analytic philosophy, the argument of the existence of excessive or meaningless evil has become the main point of contention. The argument states that since a perfectly good and omnipotent God would seek to minimize suffering and evil in the world, we should not (if theism were true) find the amount of suffering and evil in the actual world than we in fact find. The strong version of the argument suggests that the existence of evil logically entails the nonexistence of God, whereas the evidential version simply invokes evil as evidence against the existence of God.

Another argument along these lines is the problem of divine hiddenness, or nonresistant nonbelief. The idea here is that if God is perfectly good and omnipotent, God will want people to be in contact with him. So we would expect God to maximize the knowledge of his presence so that all who seek him would come to faith eventually. However, we observe that there are people in the world who are sincere but never come to faith. This seems incompatible with God's intentions. Finally, many other atheist arguments (the argument from religious diversity, for instance) have been extensively discussed in philosophical literature.

Notice that such arguments invoke some empirically observable features of our world. There are atheistic arguments, however, that are purely conceptual. Their aim is to demonstrate that the concept of God is, by itself, incoherent. In other words, they attempt to reveal a hidden contradiction in the concept of God, which would naturally lead to the rejection of the possibility of such a being actually existing. The theistic God is conceived as the most perfect being possible—that is, a being that has the widest array of perfections to the greatest degree. He is omniscient, omnipotent, and perfectly good. Antitheistic arguments seek to demonstrate that either these properties themselves are incoherent or their conjunction leads to logical contradictions.

Consider the paradox of the stone, for instance. It seeks to show that there can be no being that has the power to realize all logically possible states of affairs. The paradox is aimed against the view that an omnipotent being can actualize all possible states of affairs. Either God can create a stone he cannot lift or he cannot create such a stone. If God cannot create such a stone, God lacks omnipotence. If God can create such a stone, he cannot lift it, so God again lacks omnipotence. Omniscience has also been criticized: How could a bodiless and timeless being know first-person relative truths about what it feels like to ride a bike, for instance? Finally, there are arguments that seek to show how God's perfect properties cannot be coherently combined. For instance, some have argued that when perfect goodness is combined with omnipotence, God can longer be free to create whatever he wants. Traditional theists maintain that God had the opportunity not to create, but if God wants to maximize goodness, as perfect goodness seems to entail, God would have no option but to create the universe.

About the author

Aku Visala is a research fellow at the University of Helsinki, Finland. He has held postdoctoral positions at the University of Oxford (United Kingdom), Princeton University (United States), and the University of Notre

Dame (United States). His work is located at the crossroads of analytic philosophy, theology, and the cognitive sciences.

Suggestions for further reading

In this book
See also chapters 10 (scientists), 47 (born atheist), and 51 (evil).

Elsewhere

Bullivant, Stephen, Miguel Farias, Jonathan Lanman, and Lois Lee. *Understanding Unbelief: Atheists and Agnostics around the World*. London: St Mary's University, Twickenham, 2019. https://kar.kent.ac.uk/78815/.

Oppy, Graham. *Arguing about Gods*. Cambridge: Cambridge University Press, 2006.

Pals, Daniel L. *Nine Theories of Religion*. New York: Oxford University Press, 2014.

Rowe, William. *Can God Be Free?* New York: Oxford University Press, 2006.

51
How do atheists deal with the problem of evil?

Sami Pihlström

The problem of evil, discussed since antiquity, is generally considered a major challenge for theism. If there is an omnipotent, omniscient, and absolutely benevolent God, then how is it possible that there is so much apparently unnecessary evil and suffering in the world? Indeed, how is it possible that there is any evil and suffering at all? Wouldn't, and shouldn't, a theistic God remove evil from the world he supposedly created—or wouldn't, and shouldn't, he have created a world without evil in the first place? In particular, isn't there something profoundly problematic in God's creating and maintaining a world in which innocent people suffer horrendously?

This problem has been examined by philosophers, theologians, and religious thinkers at least since the Book of Job. While the author of that ancient book was no atheist, many critics of religion (including, say, David Hume in the eighteenth century and several "New Atheists" today) have over the centuries drawn attention to the problem of evil as one of the strongest reasons for maintaining atheism.

The problem can be very simply phrased as a schematic argument along the following lines:

1. If there is a God, he is omnipotent, omniscient, and absolutely good (definition).
2. An omnipotent, omniscient, and absolutely good being eliminates all unnecessary evil and suffering.
3. There is unnecessary evil and suffering (an empirical premise).
4. Therefore, there is no God (of the kind defined in premise 1).

In its simplest form, this is a modus tollens argument: A → B; not B; therefore, not A. Accordingly, philosophers of religion subscribing to the "argument from evil" conclude the truth of atheism (or at least the falsity of theism) from the facts that (1) it follows from a widely accepted conception of God that God, if he existed, would eliminate all unnecessary evil and suffering and that (2) there *is*, as an empirically undeniable fact of the world we live in, unnecessary evil and suffering.

The argument from evil can take different shapes. An important distinction can be drawn between the *logical* problem of evil and the *evidential* problem of evil. Whereas the former claims that atheism logically follows from the kind of premises outlined above (i.e., that theism is logically contradictory in subscribing to the idea of God characterized in premise 1), the latter only claims, more modestly, that the argument from evil presents an evidential challenge to anyone seeking to defend theism. It is, thus, strong evidence against believing in God.

Typical theistic responses to this argument either revise our conception of the divinity, possibly suggesting that there is a sense in which one or more of the characteristics attributed to God in premise 1 must be given up or revised, or suggest that the evil there undeniably is in the world is not "unnecessary" after all but is in some sense unavoidable. The responses of the latter kind are usually called "theodicies" (from the Greek *theos*, "God," and *dike*, "justice"). For example, "free-will theodicies" argue that the reason why some incidents of evil and suffering are actually necessary is that God created human beings with free will, and the misuse of free will leads to moral evil. Thus, while having free will is a very good thing for us, it necessarily brings with it the possibility of moral evil. "Soul-making theodicies," in turn, suggest that there is some good coming out of evil: experiences of suffering provide us with opportunities to grow as human beings by helping the victims of evil and suffering and by developing a deeper understanding of the value of human life.

The atheist typically deals with the problem of evil by critically engaging with these and other theodicies attempting to respond to the argument from evil on behalf of the theist. For example, the atheist may point out that if we really need to pay the "price" of, say, the Holocaust—or some other case of enormous suffering that simply ought never to have taken place—for the sake of our being able to possess a free will or enabling us to develop a more mature "soul," then so much the worse for the latter. It is simply unacceptable for anyone, let alone an all-powerful God, to bring about such a historical event as the Holocaust, or any innocent suffering at all, no matter how good the "purpose" behind it (e.g., creating human beings capable of freedom) might be.

As theists often propose not necessarily theodicies proper—that is, claims that God's reason for allowing evil *is* some alleged X (e.g., creating free will)—but, more moderately, *defenses* suggesting that, *for all we know*, God *might* have such-and-such a purpose in mind when allowing the world to contain evil and suffering, the atheist should critically engage with such "mere defenses" too. Thus, a "free-will defense" does not claim that God allows evil because of free will but that this *might* be his reason for doing so; the burden of proof is here allegedly shifted to the atheist invited to show that this is implausible. The arguments surrounding the problem of evil in contemporary analytic philosophy of religion, in particular, take a relatively complex structure of defenses and counterdefenses.

However, it also needs to be recognized that there are philosophical approaches to the problem of evil and suffering that seek to avoid the opposition between theism and atheism altogether. That is, atheism is not the only alternative to theists' postulations of theodicies. The very debate between theism and atheism in this area can be regarded as "theodicist" in the sense that both the theist and the atheist normatively presuppose that a successful theistic response to the problem of evil and suffering should deliver a theodicy (or at least a "defense"). The theist believes that theism is indeed successful in this, while the atheist denies this. In contrast, an "antitheodicist" approach rejects the theodicist requirement itself and views the problem of evil and suffering not in terms of arguments for and against the epistemic credentials of theism (given the reality of evil) but in terms of ethical acknowledgment of the suffering human being's perspective, including their own account of the meaninglessness of their experience of suffering.

The distinction between theodicism and antitheodicism thus cuts across the one between theism and atheism. Arguably, atheists need to deal with the problem of evil not only by showing that theistic theodicies are problematic but also by demonstrating that antitheodicism can be developed within a secular world view, just as it may be developed within religious outlooks.

About the author

Sami Pihlström is a professor of philosophy of religion at the University of Helsinki, Finland. He has published widely on pragmatism, realism, ethics, metaphysics, transcendental philosophy, and philosophy of religion. His recent books include *Kantian Antitheodicy* (with Sari Kivistö; Palgrave Macmillan, 2016), *Death and Finitude* (Lexington, 2016), *Pragmatic Realism, Religious Truth, and Antitheodicy* (Helsinki University Press, 2020), and *Why Solipsism Matters* (Bloomsbury, 2020).

Suggestions for further reading

In this book
See also chapters 50 (existence of God), 52 (mortality), and 59 (morality).

Elsewhere
Dahl, Espen. *The Problem of Job and the Problem of Evil.* Cambridge: Cambridge University Press, 2019.

Kivistö, Sari, and Sami Pihlström. *Kantian Antitheodicy: Philosophical and Literary Varieties.* Basingstoke: Palgrave Macmillan, 2016.

Sterba, James, ed. *Ethics and the Problem of Evil.* Bloomington: Indiana University Press, 2017.

Trakakis, N. N., ed. *The Problem of Evil: Eight Views in Dialogue.* Oxford: Oxford University Press, 2018.

52

How do atheists cope with mortality?

Jacob S. Sawyer

Death is a natural end to the life cycle, and humans have a 100 percent mortality rate. While no one can say for sure what happens after you die, atheists are far less likely than other groups to believe in life after death. This results in some wondering how atheists cope with mortality and the awareness of death without the comfort that some gain from their religious belief systems about heaven or reuniting with loved ones again. Research suggests that atheists are just as able to cope with mortality as anyone else, though a number of misconceptions remain.

It is often assumed that atheists will ultimately come to accept a higher power when confronted with their own impending death or reminders of their mortality. This assumption is captured in the well-known phrase that there are "no atheists in foxholes." The message conveyed by this phrase suggests that even the most ardent nonbelievers would change their minds once death appears imminent. Despite this assumption, there is no empirical evidence to suggest that atheist people suddenly become believers once they are confronted with their own mortality. On the contrary, recent research comparing death anxiety in religious and nonreligious samples found no significant differences between these groups. Some research appears to suggest that death anxiety is associated with not as much whether or not one believes in God but how *certain* one feels about the existence or nonexistence of God. In other words, those who are more certain that God does *or* does not exist may be less likely to experience death anxiety compared to those who are uncertain in their belief.

For many, the process of bereavement may begin within a religious context. For example, a funeral may be held in a church and may be presided over by a clergy member. The deceased's obituary might include references to them being in heaven or a "better place." Family, friends, and colleagues may make similar references to life after death. All of this would not be applicable to many atheists, who mostly believe that when you are dead, you are in a state of nonexistence that is the same as before you were born. This could be depressing to some, but existentialists have noted that the human ability to be aware of our own mortality is a key element toward striving for a meaningful life. Several recent studies support the idea that meaning in life is associated with more positive outcomes during bereavement. Specifically, meaning in life appears to be associated with less complicated grief (i.e., intense and long-lasting grief) and psychological distress during bereavement. In another study comparing bereavement outcomes between a sample of atheists and those who believe in God, the results found that atheists experienced lower levels of posttraumatic growth during bereavement compared to believers (i.e., experiencing positive changes as a result of the loss), but they also experienced lower levels of complicated grief and psychological distress.

Another common assumption is that atheists are at a disadvantage when it comes to coping during bereavement compared to their religious and theist counterparts. After all, wouldn't the belief that a loved one will be seen again in heaven or that an afterlife exists be an essential component of coping with grief? By extension, would this mean that all atheists are inherently lacking necessary coping strategies for grief? Research has found that there are indeed helpful aspects of religious belief that correspond to better coping during bereavement. For instance, this appears to be true for those who perceive God to be helpful and a source of strength, are able to make sense of the loss based on their religious beliefs, are comforted in the idea of life after death, and experience social support from other churchgoers. Even though religious belief may offer a number of benefits to the bereaved, researchers have noted that belief can also be a source of stress during bereavement. This appears to be true for those who believe death was a punishment by God, believe God did not hear their prayers, and are angry at God. So while atheists would not benefit from positive aspects of religious coping, they would not experience these negative outcomes during bereavement. Simply put, one would not have these negative reactions toward God if one did not believe in God to begin with.

Recent empirical findings have shed light on the experiences of atheists during end of life. For instance, researchers have found that the primary end-of-life preferences for atheists include a desire to find meaning in their lives, maintain a connection with family and friends, and continue to experience and enjoy the natural world. These findings clearly illustrate that factors such as meaning and connectedness are important for atheists and that these concepts are independent of religious belief or belief in God. Richard Dawkins, a well-known proponent of atheism, has stated that it is likely that atheist beliefs provide people with inspiration, explanation, guidance, and consolation in a manner similar to religious belief systems.

The recent evidence related to how atheists cope with mortality indicates that they do it in the same way that others do, minus the religious frameworks. Atheists make meaning of loss, grieve the absence of the deceased, and have good days and bad days during bereavement. While more research is necessary to examine atheist experiences with death, dying, and bereavement, it should not be assumed that atheists are at a disadvantage because they do not believe in God.

About the author

Jacob S. Sawyer is an assistant professor of psychology at Pennsylvania State University, Mont Alto. His research interests include experiences of nonreligious and atheist individuals; psychological factors related to death, dying, and bereavement; and college student mental health.

Suggestions for further reading

In this book
See also chapters 50 (existence of God), 53 (values), and 63 (health).

Elsewhere
Christina, Greta. *Comforting Thoughts about Death That Have Nothing to Do with God*. Durham, NC: Pitchstone, 2014.

Pargament, Kenneth I., Bruce W. Smith, Harold. G. Koenig, and Lisa Perez. "Patterns of Positive and Negative Religious Coping with Major Life Stressors." *Journal for the Scientific Study of Religion* 37(4) (1998): 710–724.

Sawyer, Jacob S., and Melanie E. Brewster. "Assessing Posttraumatic Growth, Complicated Grief, and Psychological Distress in Bereaved Atheists and Believers." *Death Studies* 43(4) (2019): 224–234.

Smith-Stoner, Marilyn. "End-of-Life Preferences for Atheists." *Journal of Palliative Medicine* 10(4) (2007): 923–928.

53
Where do atheists get their values?

Kyle Thompson

While out on a walk, a person notices a child teetering dangerously on the edge of a well. The ancient Chinese philosopher Mengzi famously posited that this person would experience a sudden flash of "alarm and compassion," the small but powerful spark of morality. He suggested that if humans can fan the flames of that ethical ember—and others—into a holistic way of being and acting, then they are walking the path of morality. Of course, developing into a fully moral person is a complicated and difficult affair—it isn't good enough to merely *feel* compassion at the knowledge that someone is about to suffer, we must also take action. Placed into a scientific context, Mengzi's observation suggests that the origin of our morality is a natural capacity for goodness. Indeed, since Mengzi's time, psychologists have even observed budding moral faculties in infants. This means atheists and theists alike have the raw materials for morality in their evolved DNA.

Still, whether out of suspicion or curiosity, we might wonder where atheists get their developed moral values, which are admittedly more complex than flickers of concern. There are two important claims implicit in this question that go unstated and unexamined. The first is that atheists need to provide an account of morality lest they be unable to behave morally. The second is that theists, unlike atheists, have a clear source of their morality in God or religion.

The question about atheistic morality implies that without a clear articulation of where their morals come from, atheists lack a moral compass. It is easy to see how this is false when we consider that atheists can derive their morality directly from religious traditions even if they don't believe in the divinity that supposedly grounds such morality. For example, some people develop their atheistic world view later in life after being raised within a religious tradition. Despite not believing in God, they can still embrace certain moral concepts and embody certain moral behaviors they were introduced to as part of that religious community. Likewise, if we view morality as something people actually do—rather than merely a list of values—then we know there are people who participate in a religious community without believing in God. But even if there weren't any atheists sitting in the pews alongside believers, this wouldn't change the fact that atheists can resonate with values associated with religion without ever receiving a religious education or spending time in a religious community. For example, the reciprocal morality embedded in the Golden Rule, commonly associated with Jesus, makes sense to atheists as much as it does to theists. Belief in God is not required to appreciate the value of feeding the hungry or helping the sick. Most of us would appreciate being aided if we were in need. Simply put, compassion is a human experience, as Mengzi's thought experiment indicates, not necessarily a religious one.

Similarly, one need not believe in God to follow the prohibition on killing in the Ten Commandments—murder horrifically deprives someone of their life, it harms a community, and it can even be destructive to the murderer given the violent and violating nature of the act. To suggest that belief in the God of Abraham is needed for adopting Christian morals discounts the many world religions that uphold similar values—for example, encouraging benevolence while discouraging destructive tendencies. Buddhists, Hindus, and folks who practice Shinto don't believe in the God of Abraham and yet maintain deeply moral lives. This implies morality is foundationally a human enterprise that religions merely codify, not a divine enterprise that falls from the sky upon a small group of humans in one particular time and place in the world.

Now let's examine the implicit claim that theists have a ready-made explanation for where their values come from. When asked, the Christian might say one of the following: "God," "my faith," or "the Bible." Many philosophers are dissatisfied with these responses because they prompt us to ask what makes these things good sources of morality. If we do ask, we introduce a famous philosophical problem called the Euthyphro dilemma, named after Plato's dialogue *Euthyphro* from which it is derived. Framing the dilemma in contemporary language, we can ask the Christian whether an act like murder is bad because God forbids it or if God forbids an act like murder because it is intrinsically bad. It is doubtful the Christian wants to say God *makes* murder bad because then it would be true that God, being all-powerful, could decide to *make* it good on a mere whim. But if the Christian wants to say God forbids murder because it is intrinsically bad, then God isn't the source of morality. If God exists, at most he is a reliable reporter on what we should and shouldn't do. It seems intuitive that what makes murder bad has something to do with what was mentioned previously—that is, the deprivation and harm it causes to a fellow person who deserves moral consideration—and these are things the atheist can recognize just as well as the theist can.

What the Euthyphro dilemma suggests is that the theist and atheist are drawing from a deeper source when reasoning about and acting on morality. In fact, to say that God is good suggests that humans have a clear and intuitive concept of goodness that they can apply to God himself. It is the concept that says we should work to care for one another, to prevent violence, to aim for peace and compassion over separation and hate. It is the concept that makes us righteously angry when we hear about deep injustices.

So where do atheists get their values? I wish I had a one-word answer, but the truth is more complex. According to a standard naturalistic and scientific account of the world, atheists get their values the same place that theists get them: from human reason and cognition as both constrained and supported by cultural traditions, customs, ideas, and expressions as they have gradually developed in concert with the biological evolution of our species and the profound ways it has shaped our minds, dispositions, imaginations, languages, emotions, and preferences for harmony within a community. In other words, we *all* get our moral values from our unique humanity, which emerges from the interplay between biology and culture.

More specifically, atheists get their values from diverse sources given they themselves are a diverse bunch. They get values from their parents, from life experience, from the political values undergirding their society, from being cared for by others, from role models, from kindergarten requirements to share and be kind, from a sense of personal responsibility, from empathy, from weathering obstacles and suffering, from a concern for preventing suffering in humans and other animals, from diverse relationships with family and friends, from philosophy books, from awe of the natural world and cosmos, from virtues they admire in real-life saints and fictional heroes, from organized sports, from their evolutionary dispositions to commune with others, from cultural traditions, from rationally derived principles that encourage fair and equal treatment of others, and sometimes even from religions themselves. The only place they don't get them is from a sustained belief in God.

The question as to where atheists get their values is not fundamentally different from the question as to where humans get their values. Returning to Mengzi's thought experiment about the child and the well, it is clear that the flash of moral concern flares up in *humans*, not atheists only or theists only.

About the author

Kyle Thompson is a philosopher whose research interests center on the intersection between philosophy and the social sciences. He teaches philosophy, religion, and writing as an adjunct instructor at various institutions, including Harvey Mudd College and MiraCosta College.

Suggestions for further reading

In this book
See also chapters 50 (existence of God), 51 (evil), and 59 (morality).

Elsewhere
Baggett, Jerome P. *The Varieties of Nonreligious Experience: Atheism in American Culture*. New York: New York University Press, 2019.

Bloom, Paul. *Just Babies: The Origins of Good and Evil*. New York: Broadway Books, 2013.

Plato. *Five Dialogues: Euthyphro, Apology, Crito, Meno, Phaedo*. Indianapolis: Hackett, 2002.

Van Norden, Bryan W., trans. *Mengzi: With Selections from Traditional Commentaries*. With introduction and notes by Bryan W. Van Norden. Indianapolis: Hackett, 2008.

Zuckerman, Phil, and Kyle Thompson. "Secular Living as a Context for Moral Development." In *The Oxford Handbook of Moral Development: An Interdisciplinary Perspective*, edited by Lene Arnett Jensen, 613–628. Oxford: Oxford University Press, 2020.

54

Do atheists have beliefs in supernatural phenomena?

Jonathan Lanman

While this seems a straightforward question to answer, we should also consider how some interested parties may frame the answer to suit their own interests.

Atheism, by definition, applies to *theism*, which can be interpreted more narrowly to pertain to the classical theistic God of Western tradition or the common personal God of many Christians, Muslims, and Jews or more broadly to mean any God or gods. To provide a straightforward answer to the broad question, then, we can simply examine the views of those who do not believe in the existence of God or gods (atheists) and see if they hold beliefs in the existence of other supernatural entities or processes.

Such an examination was one component of an international research project Lois Lee, Stephen Bullivant, Miguel Farias, and I completed entitled *Understanding Unbelief.* In this project, we surveyed over six thousand atheists and agnostics across Brazil, China, Denmark, Japan, the United Kingdom, and the United States regarding their views on God, religion, mystical experiences, social and religious identities and practices, moral values, and a number of additional supernatural phenomena. These supernatural phenomena included an afterlife; reincarnation; supernatural beings (e.g., ghosts, nature spirits, angels, etc.); astrology; people or objects with the mystical power to heal, harm, or bring good luck; underlying forces of good and evil; a universal spirit or life force; karma; and significant life events happening for a reason. For each phenomenon, participants rated the extent to which they agreed that it was real or true.

Our results indicate that while atheists have, on average, lower levels of supernatural belief than agnostics and the general population, the levels of supernatural belief among atheists do not approach zero in any country or among any demographic group. The percentages of atheists strongly or somewhat agreeing with the existence of an afterlife, for example, ranged from 10 percent in Japan to around 30 percent in Brazil. For astrology, the range was from around 12 percent in Japan to nearly 35 percent in China. And for supernatural beings such as ghosts, angels, and nature spirits, the range was from 15 percent in Japan to over 30 percent in Brazil.

While there was substantial variation both within and between countries in which supernatural phenomena showed the highest and lowest levels of belief among atheists, a few general trends emerged. First, the idea that there are "underlying forces" of good and evil and that "there exists a universal spirit or life force" garnered the most belief among atheists and agnostics globally. Second, Japanese atheists showed the lowest levels of belief in supernatural phenomena and Brazilian and Chinese atheists the highest.

We also calculated the percentage of atheists who are "naturalists": those who either somewhat or strongly disagree with all of the supernatural phenomena statements. In no country did the percentage of atheists qualifying as naturalists reach 50 percent. The highest rate was in the United States, where 35 percent of atheists qualified as naturalists, and the lowest rate was in China, where only 8 percent of atheists qualified as naturalists.

So do atheists believe in supernatural phenomena? Our data indicate that most show some belief in at least some supernatural phenomena but that, in some countries, very sizeable minorities, equating to millions of people, do not hold beliefs in any of the supernatural phenomena listed.

But while this question seems a straightforward one to answer, we should also ask why some individuals would be so interested. Rather than dispassionate scientific curiosity about the minds of atheists, I would suggest much of the public interest in this question stems from the narratives two groups of people wish to tell about the sources of atheist (non)beliefs. For many antireligious atheists in Western countries who view themselves in a struggle with a backward-looking and damaging religiosity, their views about God, gods, and other supernatural phenomena are the product of rational reflection on available evidence. For many conservative religious believers in those same countries, who often view themselves as defending their tradition against an assault of modernity and sociomoral decay, the beliefs of atheists are the product not of rational reflection but of their sinful moral rebellion against a God they know in their hearts to exist.

These two groups have a clear stake in the answer to the question. Antireligious atheists, who champion rationality and evidence and seek to convince religious believers to do the same, would prefer the data to show that atheists have little to no belief in other supernatural phenomena, as this would support their claim that their lack of belief in the existence of God or gods is caused by rational thought and evidence, which would presumably disqualify ghosts, the afterlife, and astrology as well as God. Conservative religious believers, on the other hand, would prefer the data to show atheists to have high levels of belief in other supernatural phenomena, as this would support the claim that it is not rational thought and evidence that have led atheists to their atheism but rather a selfish rebellion against the one true God.

Looking at the data and the wider scientific study of religion, neither group should be rejoicing. For the antireligious atheists, the low percentage of naturalists among atheists would seem to cause problems for the claim that their lack of belief in God is primarily the result of rational reflection on the available evidence. They could argue that only the naturalists qualify as "real" atheists, but this would be to change the definition of atheism to avoid confronting inconvenient evidence. While there is still a definite possibility that a subset of atheists come to their atheism through rational reflection on available evidence, any general claim about the origins of atheism that would also lead to naturalism is not supported by our data.

And for conservative religious believers, while the low numbers of naturalists would seem to support their claims of atheism as a form of moral rebellion, other data emerging from our project cast doubt on such claims. In particular, as detailed in our report, most atheists and agnostics reject moral relativism at rates similar to general population samples and share largely the same values as the general population (e.g., family, freedom, compassion, and truth). We found little evidence, then, of immoral atheists rebelling against God.

While neither narrative of the origins of atheist (non)beliefs is supported by our data—or indeed the wider scientific study of religion—our data do raise interesting questions about how we all come to our beliefs about such phenomena as God(s), ghosts, magic, and fate. To what extent are such beliefs produced by pan-human cognitive tendencies such as mind-body dualism and an intuition that most things are designed for a purpose? To what extent are they produced by socialization or held as symbols of commitments to social relationships and groups rather than as hypotheses? These are questions that many social and behavioral scientists are actively investigating and will continue to investigate.

About the author

Jonathan Lanman is the assistant director of the Institute of Cognition and Culture and a senior lecturer in anthropology at Queen's University Belfast.

His research aims to utilize the tools of both cognitive and social anthropology to examine religion, atheism, morality, and intergroup relations.

Suggestions for further reading

In this book
See also chapters 47 (born atheist), 55 (experience), and 57 (ritual).

Elsewhere
Bullivant, Stephen, Miguel Farias, Jonathan Lanman, and Lois Lee. *Understanding Unbelief: Atheists and Agnostics around the World.* London: St Mary's University, Twickenham, 2019. https://kar.kent.ac.uk/78815/.

55

Do atheists have religious experiences?

Abby Day

While a question about atheists and religious experience initially appears to juxtapose two opposites—atheists and religion—in a contradictory relationship, it is actually a good example of where an apparent contradiction may exist only in the minds of scholars who are being misled by their own misconceptions. Ask an atheist if they believe in god, and they will likely say no. The term "atheist," while open to definition and contestation, means at its most etymologically simple "without" (*a-*) god (*theos*). And so, an atheist may be "without god," but that does not mean that they are without the sense of being swept away by the beauty of a sunset or without feeling the comforting spirit of their deceased loved ones. While most religious people accept a binary distinction between secular/sacred and this world / otherworld, so may a non–god believer. The first time I heard an atheist discuss such an experience was when a man, who had already, during our interview, emphatically described himself as an atheist, said, "I do not believe that there is any all-powerful force that is organizing human destiny. I think that is utterly ridiculous," and then described feeling the presence of his beloved mother on the day of her funeral, saying he believed in "the human spirit." Why, the student may well ask, was it ever to be assumed that this was not possible, that people who reject god could not embrace ghosts? And if that appears to be a contradiction, perhaps it is necessary to ask whether a perceived contradiction is only a pattern that scholars, unlike laypeople, have not yet discerned. The distinction between emic and etic experience and expression may be most evident in the discussion of "religious experience."

Unfortunately, the term "religious experience" is often used by scholars of religion to scoop up the most extraordinary, otherworldly phenomena, such as feeling a sense of awe related to a higher power, perhaps involving a vision, or a voice, or a feeling of being profoundly connected to an often unseen, benign universe. Most scholars do not unpack or define that term too closely but use it to support their arguments that "religion" is still going strong, assuming that everyone agrees that the essence of religion is godlike, and therefore such an emotional, inspiring experience would necessarily emanate from a god and therefore be "religious." It is a circular argument tied to a notion that a god is sui generis—that is, of itself irreducible and preceding human interpretation. And yet one of the earliest and most influential definitions of religion was E. B. Tylor's nineteenth-century formulation based on what he observed as "ancestor worship," arguing that this demonstrated that the origin of religion was "a belief in spirits." Even leaving aside other definitions of religion that did not presuppose belief in a god, such as Émile Durkheim's, the logical progression of Tylor's definition is generally untouched but of significance here—namely, while all religious people may believe in spirits, not all people who believe in spirits are religious. Further, he thought such beliefs were wrong and that as cultures "evolved," people would lose such, in his Victorian-infused view, childlike, primitive ideas. Nearly two hundred years later, in societies generally described as "modern" and "evolved," a belief in spirits continues, markedly among those who describe themselves as nonreligious. Most social surveys show that while belief in a god and hell may be decreasing, belief in a life after death or in a continuing spiritual existence is strong. Those survey scholars may then conclude, wrongly, that such beliefs fall (or, probably more accurately, are shoved and shoehorned) into the category "religious." Further, although the term "ancestor worship" seems non-Western/European, evoking images of shrines in homes or gardens and practices of leaving foods or other gifts on their altars, what should we call the increasingly popular practice in Euro-American countries of lighting candles on graves in modern cemeteries or feeling the sense of a deceased loved one's presence? The common factor seems to be that, more than heaven, hell, or ghosts, most people believe in the continuity of the human soul and the continuing relational ties that bind.

And that, we may argue, is a deeply human experience, although expressing it in words is difficult because most of the words available are embedded in a "this world / otherworld divide": supernatural, paranormal, for example. "Anomalous" is how some scholars describe such experience, meaning that it does not fit within what may be assumed to be ordinary, predictable daily life. Indeed, it may not fit, and yet these everyday ghosts are real to people and are part of their lived experience in ways that gods are not.

When people describe powerful, what I like to call "spirit-full" experiences, they say that the feeling of their deceased loved one's presence was intensely "natural" and "normal." Those experiences are also usually felt, both physically and emotionally, and defy one-word descriptions. Phrases or even sentences may be required to avoid crass reductionism. Based on the stories people tell, it may be easier to use several words in combination: secular, social, sensuous, ordinary yet extraordinary. When I ask my research participants what words they would use to describe their experiences of being visited by their deceased grandmothers, they tend to say, "Being visited by grandma." It is also notable from research like this that people's stories seem rehearsed, polished through retelling. This reveals perhaps one of the functions of such experiences: in the telling and retelling, the living keep alive the memory and, to some extent, personhood of the deceased. The stories are therefore "performative" in that the acts of telling bring back into being the memory and feeling of the deceased relative. As such, they are acts of care and devotion. And atheists, often unfairly cast as hard, cynical, and überrational, may well experience the binding, devotional power of their beliefs in the continuing presence of the people they love, untouched by gods or other divine spirits.

About the author

Abby Day is a professor of race, faith, and culture in the Department of Sociology, Goldsmiths, University of London, where her teaching, research, writing, and supervision cover sociology of religion, media and religion, and critical criminology. Her recent research interests focus on gender, generations, and the cross-cultural/religious meaning of "belief."

Suggestions for further reading

In this book
See also chapters 54 (belief), 57 (ritual), and 58 (spiritual).

Elsewhere
Aagedal, Olaf. *Deconstructing Death—Changing Cultures of Death, Dying, Bereavement and Care in the Nordic Countries*. Odense: University Press of Southern Denmark, 2013.

Beaman, Lori G., and Peter Beyer. "Betwixt and Between: A Canadian Perspective on the Challenges of Researching the Spiritual but Not Religious." In *Social Identities between the Sacred and the Secular*, edited by Abby Day, Giselle Vincett, and Christopher R. Cotter, 127–144. Abingdon: Routledge, 2013.

Day, Abby. *Believing in Belonging: Belief and Social Identity in the Modern World*. Oxford: Oxford University Press, 2011.

Demerath, N. J., III. "The Varieties of Sacred Experience: Finding the Sacred in a Secular Grove." *Journal for the Scientific Study of Religion* 39(1) (2000): 1–11.

56
Do atheists have sacred scripture?

Ethan G. Quillen

When a Christian seeks spiritual guidance, they reach for the New Testament. The Muslim reaches for the Qur'an. The Jew, the Torah. For practitioners of these "Abrahamic faiths," the idea of "sacred scripture" is pretty straightforward. But what about atheists? What does an atheist reach for? To get anywhere close to an answer here, two clarifications are needed.

First, because of the uniqueness of our subject, and the reality that it is, in fact, a much more complex ideology than is often assumed, we have to acknowledge that this question is just as complicated. As in, we can't simply pick out some text and say, "This. This is sacred to atheists." While it might be easy to claim Darwin's *On the Origin of Species* or Dawkins's *The God Delusion* as "sacred atheist texts," doing so would be rather specious. And lazy. Because, if we're to believe that there are as many types of atheisms as there are atheists, then we need to also assume that all those different atheists hold sacred just as many different texts. After all, by rejecting the "sacrality" of the New Testament, Qur'an, and Torah, has not the atheist essentially opened a void that can then be filled by just about anything? And by doing so utterly redefined what "sacred" means in the first place? Which brings us to clarification two.

What does "sacred" mean? We probably all have a good idea about what a "text" is, but a "sacred" one, that's something different altogether. The Christian, for example, holds the New Testament sacred because, for them, it is the word of God. They swear oaths on it and use it to guide their lives. It is there when they are born and baptized, when they are married, and when they die. But let's look at it through an atheist lens: while sacred to a Christian, isn't this thing nothing more than paper and ink?

OK, maybe that's not entirely fair. Because these things are indeed more than just the physical attributes that make up their existence. The New Testament is also the written form of the *idea* of Christianity: its dogma, narrative, myths, ethics, rituals, and all the other dimensions that, when combined, give meaning to the word "Christian." Which means, though just ink and paper, it has been imbued with sacrality. The New Testament has been "blessed" and transformed into something greater. Albeit from an external source. Let's not forget, it is the Christian who blesses it. A sort of cyclical chicken-and-egg scenario where the book gives meaning to the Christian, who in turn gives meaning to the book. Which also means that this process could, in theory, be conducted with just about anything.

What if, let's say, someone's life is altered by a book they read at a particularly transformative moment? Maybe someone, seeking meaning beyond their day-to-day existence, picks up a tattered version of J. R. R. Tolkien's *The Hobbit*, or C. S. Lewis's *Narnia* series. In the stories of Bilbo and the Pevensie children, they learn about themselves. They see the ethics of difficult decision-making, and they come to terms with death and loss and the differences between good and evil and right and wrong. They learn to love. They learn to empathize, to see the world through another's eyes. They turn to them at challenging times and discover new lessons from repeat readings at different stages of their life. And then, hoping to pass these lessons on, they gift them to the next generation. Which means that because of the role that these fictional tales have played in their life, for our hypothetical person here, they have the ability to become something greater, to transform and become just as "sacred" as those in the New Testament. Ink and paper given meaning.

While our example here is a decent theoretical response to the chicken-and-egg scenario referenced above, let's look at a more material one.

In the early 1960s, Elliott Welsh didn't want to fight in the Vietnam War. But as a young American man of draftable age, he had no choice. So when his draft number was called, he declined. He was arrested, tried, found guilty of refusing to submit for induction into the armed services, and sentenced to three years imprisonment.

Welsh was a unique case. While he had legally applied to be considered for conscientious objector status, a condition the US military had put in place during the Civil War, his request was rejected because he failed to cite his reasoning as based on an accepted religious creed, as the law demanded. In other words, killing for Welsh was unconscionable and immoral not because the Bible told him so but because he felt it to be true, based in part on his own personal philosophy and ethics, amassed over years of studying what we might comparatively call "secular texts."

What eventually happened to Welsh not only changed the way that the judicial branch of the US government defined American religion at that time but also offers us a unique insight into our discussion here.

In 1970, the US Supreme Court passed a ruling based on Welsh's case in which it argued that, yes, he had every right to excuse himself from military service on ethical grounds, regardless of not having an established religious reason to support it. And it did so by relying on the American theologian Paul Tillich's notion of *ultimate concern*: "And if that word [God] has not much meaning for you, translate it, and speak of the depths of your life, of the source of your being, or your ultimate concern, *of what you take seriously without any reservation*" (emphasis in original). So when it came to Welsh's request, the court declared,

> If an individual deeply and sincerely holds beliefs that are purely ethical or moral in source and content, but that nevertheless impose upon him a duty of conscience to refrain from participating in any war at any time, those beliefs certainly occupy in the life of that individual "a place parallel to that filled by . . . God" in traditionally religious persons. Because his beliefs function as a religion in his life, such an individual is as much entitled to a "religious" conscientious objector exemption under [military law] as is someone who derives his conscientious opposition to war from traditional religious convictions.

Welsh wasn't "religious" in the way a Quaker is religious, but the court viewed them as sharing the same commitment to nonviolence. Which, according to its decision, meant they were both equally permitted the right to refrain from military service on religious grounds. The Quaker basing his or her objection on ethics derived from the New Testament, and Welsh, from "secular" texts that, to him, offered him the same sort of sacred lessons. In other words, since these secular texts held for him a place parallel to the New Testament, they were sacred.

So what might be the answer to our question, "Do atheists have sacred scripture?" Based on our discussion here, an easy one looks to be, *yes*. But we also have to acknowledge that this isn't perfect. Which is perhaps the larger purpose of asking and considering it in the first place. Maybe questions like these aren't supposed to be easily answered. Maybe instead, we're meant to think on them and, rather than find an "answer," come to a greater appreciation of the fact that the subjects we discuss are sometimes more complex than easy answers might resolve.

About the author

Ethan G. Quillen holds a PhD in religious studies from the University of Edinburgh. He writes about the different ways in which atheists "live" their atheisms, from judicial battles and fictional representations to the construction of churches through parody.

Suggestions for further reading

In this book
See also chapters 12 (atheistic religions), 36 (law), and 55 (experience).

Elsewhere
Quillen, Ethan G. *Atheist Exceptionalism: Religion, Atheism, and the United States Supreme Court.* London: Routledge, 2018.

Smart, Ninian. *Dimensions of the Sacred: An Anatomy of the World's Beliefs.* Berkeley: University of California Press, 1996.

Tillich, Paul. *The Shaking of the Foundations.* New York: C. Scribner's Sons, 1948.

Welsh v. United States, 398 U.S. 333 (1970). https://supreme.justia.com/cases/federal/us/398/333/#tab-opinion-1948603.

57

Do atheists have rituals?

Richard Cimino and Christopher Smith

Merriam-Webster's Unabridged Dictionary defines a "ritual" as "the forms of conducting a devotional service especially as established by tradition or by sacerdotal prescription: the prescribed order and words of a religious ceremony." In such a definition, we can see how rituals have been historically tied to religion in various ways. This is one reason why some atheists have not only opposed the idea that atheism is religious-like but likewise opposed the very idea of atheist rituals. Nonetheless, a sociological definition of ritual could trim the overtly religious overtones of the term and broaden it to include a set of actions performed mainly for their symbolic values and meanings, which may be prescribed by the traditions of a community. Using this more expansive definition, it becomes easier to argue that there are not simply the more traditional and familiar rituals that atheists engage in (marriage, funerals, and the political ritual of voting) but also actual atheist rituals.

But as mentioned above, the celebration of rites of passage has been contentious enough in the atheist movement. It is not that atheists do not observe these rituals in their personal lives or that many atheist groups have not taken up some observances, but practicing them within secularist settings is seen by some as a distraction from the real mission of debunking theism and fighting for a secularist society. The strong intellectual bent of many atheist gatherings, more concerned with debate and discussion than strengthening communal ties, mitigates the use of rituals. Many atheist and secular communities also have their roots in "low church" and lay-led forms of religious dissent, such as Unitarianism, where there is a minimum of rituals. Besides, as several atheists told us, they did not make the effort of discarding their previous religious beliefs and practices only to have their Sunday mornings occupied again with secular services and observances. Of course, some atheist and secularist groups never ceased offering ceremonies and rituals. Those who are known as "religious humanists," defining religion in the sense of holding a secular world view and practices, include the American Humanist Association, the Ethical Culture Society, and a segment of the Unitarian Universalist Association. These groups have regular services, regularly hold weddings and funerals, and may even have quasi-Christian and Jewish practices, such as baby dedications.

The religious—even if nontheist—aspect of these groups has caused schisms in secularist ranks, such as the formation of the Council for Secular Humanism in the 1970s. But even this group, now organized under the umbrella group Center for Inquiry (CFI), has introduced a program for training and certifying "secular celebrants," individuals who lead secular groups in performing various ceremonies. The birth of Sunday Assemblies in many Western countries in 2013 showed the use of rituals and community building even further. Like an evangelical megachurch, the assemblies feature "testimonies" of atheist sentiment and experience, singing contemporary "hymns" (though taken from Beatles and other secular rock music), and preaching on atheist and humanist themes, as well as the celebration of rites of passage. The Sunday Assemblies and other similar groups have particularly appealed to younger atheists, many of them ex-evangelicals and ex-Mormons who missed the sense of community they found in their former religions.

In our research, we also found a growth in what can be called atheist rituals, rites, and practices related to building atheist identity and community. This can be seen in the commemoration of special days in the atheist calendar, such as Darwin Day in February, Blasphemy Day in September, and the winter and spring solaces as secular substitutes for Christmas and Easter. But specific practices and traditions found in everyday atheist life can become ritualized. In our research, we found that the use of humor—often ridicule of religion—was a regular and cherished part of atheist identity and had the effect of unifying and creating a sense of community among participants offline as well as online. Even the displaying and waving of a Richard Dawkins's book that we saw at atheist rallies could qualify as a ritual, signifying belonging and loyalty. Of course, our research also showed how this collective identity is grounded in a very individualist ethos, which inevitably works to undercut a strong sense of belonging. In the end, while we can definitely say that atheists do have rituals, with many atheists expressing the positive effects of rituals without the traditional trappings, there will continue to be those atheists who reject the notion of atheist rituals and see the mere mention of such as regressive in principle. Yet such a tension points to the fact that the movement is still young and active as opposed to generationally inherited and accepted.

About the authors

Richard Cimino is a visiting professor in sociology at the State University of New York at Old Westbury. He is also the editor of *Religion Watch*, a monthly publication reporting on new research and trends in contemporary religion. He is a coauthor of *Atheist Awakening: Secular Activism and Community in America* (Oxford University Press, 2014).

Christopher Smith is an independent scholar, a coauthor of *Atheist Awakening: Secular Activism and Community in America* (Oxford University Press, 2014), and the author of other articles on atheism.

Suggestions for further reading

In this book
See also chapters 40 (members), 41 (organization), 55 (experience), and 58 (spiritual).

Elsewhere
Botton, Alain de. *Religion for Atheists*. New York: Penguin Random House, 2013.

Cimino, Richard, and Christopher Smith. *Atheist Awakening: Secular Activism and Community in America*. Oxford: Oxford University Press, 2014.

Engelke, Matthew. "Humanist Ceremonies: The Case of Non-religious Funerals in England." In *The Wiley Blackwell Handbook of Humanism*, edited by Andrew Copson and A. C. Grayling, 216–233. Oxford: Blackwell, 2015.

Hagglund, Martin. *The Life: Secular Faith and Spiritual Freedom*. New York: Anchor, 2019.

Smith, Jesse. "Becoming an Atheist in America: Constructing Identity and Meaning from the Rejection of Theism." *Sociology of Religion* 72(2) (2011): 215–237.

58

Can an atheist be spiritual?

Atko Remmel

In October 2013, a long-distance swimmer, Diana Nyad, declared herself an atheist on Oprah Winfrey's talk show. Nyad then explained, "I can stand at the beach's edge with the most devout Christian, Jew, Buddhist, go on down the line, and weep with the beauty of this universe and be moved by all of humanity. . . . So to me, my definition of God is humanity and is the love of humanity." "Well, I don't call you an atheist then," Winfrey said. "I think if you believe in the awe and the wonder and the mystery, then that is what God is." After Nyad declared herself "an atheist who's in awe," Winfrey asked, "So do you consider yourself a spiritual person, even as an atheist?" Nyad replied, "I do. I don't think there's any contradiction in those terms. I think you can be an atheist who doesn't believe in an overarching being who created all of this and sees over it. But there's spirituality because we human beings, . . . we all live with something that is cherished, and we feel the treasure of it."

As this example shows, understandings of atheism and its accompanying features may differ greatly. Especially in the context of widespread prejudices against atheists, as in the United States, atheism is often understood as a lack of something substantial rather than the existence of something alternative. Given the fact that irreligiosity has historically been an exception rather than a norm and that some form of religion has long been considered essential for the fabric of society, there is an enduring tradition of mistrust toward atheists that renders atheists immoral and a danger to social cohesion. Since atheism has historically often been cognate to rationalism, empiricism, and materialism, atheists are also presumed to have certain limitations in their thinking or experiences. This is one of the main sources for the debate on the congruence of atheism and spirituality, where the issue of atheists' ability to experience awe (and wonder and mystery) has acquired a central position.

The second facet concerns the understanding of spirituality. The word derives from the Latin word *spiritus*, meaning "breath," contrasted in

Christian theology with flesh and materiality. Until the nineteenth century, the term "spirituality" carried the connotation of proper Christian behavior, devout religious life, but also matters belonging to church jurisdiction. Thus, the words "spiritual" and "religious" were (and for many still are) largely synonymous, another root of the question of whether atheists can be spiritual.

Since the nineteenth century, however, spirituality acquired a somewhat new meaning of the essence of universal religiosity. Further developments widened the meaning even further, and today spirituality is recognized as a category that describes religiosity but also life outside it, as indicated, for instance, by the label "spiritual but not religious." This has led many to talk about atheist (or secular) spirituality, as in the titles of the following books: *The Little Book of Atheist Spirituality* (2008), *Spiritual Atheism* (2010), *Going Godless: Rediscovering Spirituality in a Material World* (2010), and *Waking Up: A Guide to Spirituality without Religion* (2014).

In broad terms, atheist spirituality is understood as seeking answers to existential matters and "ultimate" questions (the meaning of life, good and evil, and the existence of god) outside the framework of institutional religions. More specifically, different authors emphasize the personal potential for well-being and individual transformation or self-transcendence; finding inner peace, awareness, mindfulness, morality, wonder, and awe; or the grand and thoughtful passions of life and a life lived in accordance with those grand thoughts and passions like love, trust, reverence, and gratitude. The core idea is that these experiences and the ability to live a fully spiritual life do not require a belief in gods or the supernatural. Instead, in the quest for finding answers to these questions, atheist spiritualities often look within the individual but also seek explanations from science and nature.

But are all atheists spiritual, from a historical and current perspective? If we understand atheist spirituality as a search for meaning and well-being within some atheist framework, then the answer is probably yes. In this case, atheist spirituality could be ascribed, for instance, to the ancient Greek philosophical school of Pyrrhonism, which promoted happiness as the main goal of human life. Pyrrhonists understood philosophy as a means for reaching *ataraxia* (tranquility) in order to get rid of the fear of gods and death, the chief obstacles to a fully joyful life.

Yet for some people, atheism is an insignificant facet of their world view, or they may not be interested in existential questions. Additionally, historical accounts of atheist spirituality could be criticized as anachronistic, since the concept of atheist spirituality has only arisen in the past decades as an accompanying feature of the new visibility of atheism in the Western world. Looking from that angle, atheist spirituality could be regarded as a "bridge-building" strategy, opposing these currents in secular thinking that starkly contrast their world view to religion. The notion of spirituality blurs the boundaries between religion and its others, emphasizes common human condition, and tries to show that atheists are normal human beings. It is just about framing personal experiences with a different ontology.

In doing so, spiritual atheism is deliberately eclectic and prone to borrowing from religious traditions. For instance, Sam Harris is explicit about his Buddhist influences, whereas the Sunday Assembly, established in 2013 and operating under the motto "Live better, help often, wonder more," is described as "all the church, minus the god." Similar examples, however, can be found in history as well. Nineteenth-century French positivist Auguste Comte founded the Religion of Humanity, which was based largely on Catholicism with its own community rituals. However, the object of worship was humanity instead of God, very much in line with Nyad's declaration at the beginning of the chapter.

In conclusion, it may be justified to talk about atheist spirituality when there is a deep interest in existential questions and atheism has an important place in shaping world views. This makes it possible to find atheist spiritualities in different places and ages. Alternatively, atheist spirituality can be regarded as a recent phenomenon or a bridge-building strategy. Finally, there are voices who consider the inclusion of the two catchwords in book titles—"atheism" and "spirituality"—simply as a marketing strategy or who dismiss "the entire line of 'spiritual' thinking as nothing more than a metaphor run amok," as Jack David Eller once noted.

About the author

Atko Remmel is an associate professor at the University of Tartu and a senior research fellow at the University of Tallinn, Estonia. He has published on antireligious policy and atheist propaganda in the Soviet Union, (non)religion and nationalism, secularization and religious change, and contemporary forms of (non)religion and spirituality. He has carried out fieldwork among nonreligious populations in Estonia and on people's relationship with nature.

Suggestions for further reading

In this book
See also chapters 55 (experience), 57 (ritual), and 62 (value in religion).

Elsewhere

Comte-Sponville, André. *The Little Book of Atheist Spirituality*. New York: Penguin, 2008.

Huss, Boaz. "Spirituality: The Emergence of a New Cultural Category and Its Challenge to the Religious and the Secular." *Journal of Contemporary Religion* 29(1) (2014): 47–60.

Remmel, Atko, and Mikko Sillfors. "Crossbreeding Atheism with Spirituality: Notes on Soviet and Western Attempts." *Secularism and Nonreligion* 7(1) (2018). https://secularismandnonreligion.org/articles/10.5334/snr.94/.

Taira, Teemu. "Atheist Spirituality: A Follow-On from New Atheism?" In *Post-secular Religious Practices*, edited by Tore Ahlbäck, 388–404. Turku: Donner Institute for Research in Religious and Cultural History, 2012. https://journal.fi/scripta/article/view/67423.

Wernick, Andrew. *Auguste Comte and the Religion of Humanity: The Post-theistic Program of French Social Theory*. Cambridge: Cambridge University Press, 2001.

59
Are atheists immoral?

Kyle Thompson

A recent Pew Research Center survey of thirty-nine countries found that "clear majorities" in twenty-two of the surveyed countries reported that "it is necessary to believe in God to be moral and have good values." Indeed, belief in God is often considered requisite for living a good, fulfilling, and moral life. When a Christian is at a crossroads between temptation and morality, she believes she is accountable to God, even if her actions are not subject to social or legal reproach. However, for an atheist at a similar junction, there is no divine check on her actions. So the story goes, atheists are apt to act immorally as long as no one is watching.

Compelling as this account might be, it is incorrect. If we look closer, we can see some flaws in its reasoning—let's have the French philosopher Pierre Bayle and his *Various Thoughts on the Occasion of a Comet* (1682) be our guide. In the seventeenth century, he made powerful observations about the connection between religious belief and moral behavior—interestingly, he wrote these controversial ideas in a series of fictional letters that cloaked his identity. Most notably, Bayle posited that a society of atheists would do just fine, thank you very much, so long as it rewarded good behavior and repulsed the bad. Bayle astutely observed that Christians sin while confidently believing in God's system of rewards and punishments; therefore, it must be that moral behavior is caused by something baser than our metaphysical beliefs. He suggested that earthly forces do the heavy lifting—namely, our natural dispositions and our passions. This explains both the immoral theist and the moral atheist: if the source of morality is something natural and social rather than theological, then atheists are at no disadvantage when acting morally.

Though philosophers debate the precise origin of morality, Bayle's general observation is difficult to dispute: the belief in God is neither a necessary nor a sufficient condition for being moral. To show this, we just have to examine contemporary sociological data to vindicate Bayle. The most striking fact is that some of the most morally healthy nations are significantly atheistic. Specifically, according to a variety of measures of societal thriving, a number of the most atheistic countries sit in the top rankings—such as Denmark and Sweden—while a number of the most theistic countries rank much worse and often wind up in the bottom rankings. In *Living the Secular Life* (2014), sociologist Phil Zuckerman notes that atheistic nations tend to do exceptionally well when it comes to women's rights and life expectancy, lower murder rates, more peace, lower corruption, higher happiness, and so on. If theism was a requirement for moral behavior, then we'd expect to find the opposite trends. We don't.

But aren't there other factors that might explain these differences? For example, wealth or a history of colonialism might explain why some nations are currently faring better than others. Sure enough, it is implausible that atheism and secularity simply *caused* Denmark and Sweden to thrive, while theism and religiosity *caused* Colombia, for example, to struggle. But this observation only emphasizes the core claim that atheists are at least as moral as their religious neighbors, friends, and citizens. To note that atheism and theism don't cause a given society to operate in morally healthy ways is just to say that morality is grounded in something more fundamental to human life than believing certain theological claims. The sociological data clearly show that widespread theism doesn't guarantee moral behavior any more than widespread atheism spells a hellscape—if anything, the *opposite* correlation has more data going for it.

But what about the atheistic regime of terror under Stalin compared to Mother Teresa's lifelong dedication to compassion? Doesn't that show that atheism leads to conflict and bloodshed, whereas theism brings peace and harmony? If that were so, then we couldn't explain warfare carried out under the banner of religion, such as the Crusades, any better than we could make sense of the success of present-day secular societies. While it is occasionally helpful to generalize about atheists as a whole, just as we do with Christians or Muslims, it is painfully inaccurate to do so in certain contexts. Christians in the United States should find it tedious to have to clarify that they aren't represented by the hateful views of the Westboro Baptist Church or by the slave-owning Americans of the past who sheltered their immorality with the Bible. The same applies to moral atheists who have every right to be irritated when it is implied that they uphold values similar to Stalin. It is quite easy to draw clear and meaningful distinctions between religiously motivated violence and the everyday adherents of a given faith; it is also easy to differentiate between tyrannical atheism and the everyday sort lived out by folks in the United Kingdom, Japan, or Nebraska. In fact, Zuckerman and other social scientists note the wildly different characteristics and effects of irreligion that is foisted upon a people, dubbed "coercive secularization," as compared to irreligion that freely develops, called "organic secularization." The first kind is forced upon people as part of an oppressive government, and the outcome is often violence and societal unrest. The second kind is a gradual and voluntary sloughing off, the kind we see in the Scandinavian countries previously highlighted, and it is compatible with moral behavior and societal well-being. As for Stalin's reign, the Crusades, or any violence supported by religious or antireligious sentiments, scholars are wont to remind us that they are rarely if ever caused by a singular theistic or atheistic belief—complex social, ideological, economic, and political factors draw out the worst in humanity.

Having looked at atheism at a global level, let's consider some more specific features of atheism and secularity in the United States. While it is generally assumed that many religious folks are theists in the United States and that many secular folks are atheists or lean away from theism, it is important to note that the empirical data don't always allow us to make clear distinctions between "religious" and "theist" on the one hand or "secular" and "atheist" on the other. With this in mind, it turns out that secular Americans morally outperform many religious folks in a number of areas. Zuckerman notes that secular folks tend to be more tolerant, less prejudiced and racist, more supportive of women's equality and gay rights, and less supportive of aggressive militarism. In other ways, religious folks morally outperform secular folks. Most notably, they tend to be more charitable in donating their money and volunteering their time for good causes. Theists often participate in organized religious communities, and these communities encourage and facilitate this behavior effectively. One challenge atheists do face is that many lack a structured "church" community that facilitates certain moral behaviors. However, those structured communities can encourage theists to hold on to negative views such as prejudice toward LGBTQ+ folks.

Despite well-documented antiatheist prejudice in various parts of the world, it turns out that atheists are just as moral as religious folks and oftentimes more moral. When we look at the empirical data or the reasoning of philosophers, the same picture emerges: most of the time, the belief in God is not the driving force behind why people do good or bad. Learning that your neighbor or coworker is an atheist says about as much as it would if they were a believer: they are probably a decent person who values compassion, community, honesty, and charity. The only difference is they might sleep in on Sundays.

About the author

Kyle Thompson is a philosopher whose research interests center on the intersection between philosophy and the social sciences. He teaches philosophy, religion, and writing as an adjunct instructor at various institutions, including Harvey Mudd College and MiraCosta College.

Suggestions for further reading

In this book
See also chapters 30 (politics), 53 (values), 44 (media), and 60 (tolerant).

Elsewhere
Bayle, Pierre. *Various Thoughts on the Occasion of a Comet.* Translated by Robert C. Bartlett. 1682. Reprint, Albany: State University of New York Press, 2000.

Pew Research Center. "Worldwide, Many See Belief in God as Essential to Morality." https://www.pewresearch.org/global/2014/03/13/worldwide -many-see-belief-in-god-as-essential-to-morality/.

Zuckerman, Phil. *Living the Secular Life: New Answers to Old Questions.* New York: Penguin, 2014.

Zuckerman, Phil, Luke W. Galen, and Frank L. Pasquale. *The Nonreligious: Understanding Secular People and Societies.* New York: Oxford University Press, 2016.

Zuckerman, Phil, and Kyle Thompson. "Secular Living as a Context for Moral Development." In *The Oxford Handbook of Moral Development: An Interdisciplinary Perspective,* edited by Lene Arnett Jensen, 613–628. Oxford: Oxford University Press, 2020.

60
Are atheists intolerant?

Filip Užarević

Are atheists in Western cultures inclusive and open-minded? Or just like the religious and members of various other political and ideological world views, might atheists be prone to prejudices of their own? Atheism in contemporary Western societies stems from the Enlightenment era, often coinciding with rationalist as well as socially liberal and progressive world views. For example, a 2016 study, authored by Ståhl, Zaal, and Skitka, suggests that being a nonbeliever tends to go hand in hand with relatively high personal importance of rationality, and in a 2015 nationally representative Pew Research Center survey, "U.S. Public Becoming Less Religious," nonbelievers in general and atheists in particular tended to have liberal attitudes toward most sociopolitical topics, such as marriage equality and abortion. Research such as this seems to portray a picture of nonbelievers as rather open-minded and tolerant people who appreciate rationality.

However, history suggests that the "rule" of atheism entailing tolerance has exceptions. Indeed, there are clear historical occurrences where the opposite was the case. A leading example is "scientific atheism" in the Soviet regime, a world view supporting a totalitarian system that prosecuted religious individuals in various ways. Although drastic instances such as this (and several others throughout history) are generally not applicable to contemporary societies, the ideas that oppose religion and rationality as incompatible are still present (e.g., in the works of Richard Dawkins) and are at times criticized as closed-minded or even fundamentalist.

The above reveals two interesting points of view on atheism and atheists. On the one hand, atheists seem to appreciate rationality and open-minded views. On the other hand, it seems that atheists, at least in some circumstances, are not immune to typical group biases, such as intolerance of the dissimilar. So are nonbelievers tolerant or intolerant? What does the psychological research say?

Before answering, an important clarification needs to be made. For the remainder of this chapter, instead of focusing strictly on atheists, I will use

236 ATHEISM IN FIVE MINUTES

the term "nonbelievers," which encompasses several related categories, including atheists in a narrow sense (people who disbelieve in God or gods), agnostics, but also those scoring relatively low on continuous scales of religiosity as well as those scoring high in scales measuring antireligious attitudes. Admittedly, simply lumping all these different categories under the same roof is suboptimal. Correspondingly to previous researchers' observations, such as Luke Galen's, I recognize that equating those who simply score low on religiosity scales with nonbelievers may obfuscate important heterogeneity. However, this decision, although imperfect, reflects the current state of the psychological research on this topic—if solely research involving atheists (in the narrow sense of the word, as defined above) were to be included in the analysis, this would reduce an already limited number of studies to consider.

Now to get to the main question: Are nonbelievers, as defined here, intolerant? Up until a few years ago, the topic of nonbelievers' (in)tolerance had been neglected in psychological literature. However, there has been plenty of research focusing on religious people's (in)tolerance. This research (e.g., two 2010 meta-analyses, one by Hall, Matz, and Wood, and the other by Whitley) suggested that religious believers, compared to nonbelievers, show a higher intolerance toward minority outgroups, such as gay persons, as well as racial/ethnic outgroups. If we were to look at this research from the alternative perspective—that is, from the perspective of what they are saying about *nonbelievers*—it seemingly suggests that nonbelievers are relatively more accepting of such outgroups. So from that perspective, nonbelievers are tolerant, at least to minority groups.

However, the research emerging during the past few years suggests that the relationship between nonbelief and intolerance is somewhat more complex, in that nonbelievers may not be equally tolerant of *all* outgroups. Indeed, nonbelievers, as people with their own world views (liberal, rationalist, and scientifically minded), have been shown to express a degree of intolerance toward groups seen as threatening such world views. For example, a study by Užarević and Saroglou found that, generally, nonbelievers—atheists and agnostics, in particular—were tolerant toward an ethnic outgroup (the Chinese) but showed a comparative degree of reservation toward mainstream religious groups (Catholics and Muslims) and a clear dislike of illiberal groups (antigay activists and religious fundamentalists). This suggests that nonbelievers might not be universally tolerant and, as most groups, that they tend to dislike outgroups that threaten their respective world views.

So nonbelievers do not seem to be universally tolerant—they are just like most other people in that they tend to distance themselves from the people they disagree with. Still, it is important to note that nonbelievers' prejudice does seem to be limited in some important ways. First, as shown in a study by Cowgill and colleagues, nonbelievers' prejudice may not appear when their reputational concerns are at stake. Second, in research by Užarević, Saroglou, and Pichon, nonbelievers were less likely to be prosocial toward a target person who was presented as religious (compared to a target person whose religiosity was not mentioned), but only when the religious target person asked for help for a *religious cause*. When the target person asked for help for something neutral (not related to religion), nonbelievers did generally not discriminate against the religious person. This suggests that nonbelievers' intolerance is limited in that it reflects primarily a rejection of value-threatening *ideas and behaviors* rather than a rejection of outgroup members *as persons*.

To sum up, the current state of research suggests that nonbelievers are tolerant of various outgroups such as sexual or racial minority members. However, nonbelievers do show a degree of intolerance toward their ideological outgroups, such as religious people and illiberals. Nevertheless, this prejudice is importantly limited, as it may reflect not a dislike of outgroup members as persons but rather an opposition to their values and behaviors.

Although this research does seem to tell a rather consistent story, its limitations should not be forgotten. Specifically, it would be very useful for future research to focus on the different types of nonbelievers, especially since there seems to be important heterogeneity among them (e.g., Silver et al. define six distinct nonbeliever subtypes). Taking into account these subtleties is necessary if the relationships between (non)religiosity and (in)tolerance are to be unraveled.

About the author

Filip Užarević is a postdoctoral researcher at the Institute of Social Sciences Ivo Pilar. He completed his MA studies at the Faculty of Humanities and Social Sciences at the University of Zagreb and obtained his PhD at Université catholique de Louvain (Belgium). His primary research interests relate to the psychology of religion.

Suggestions for further reading

In this book
See also chapters 37 (converting), 59 (morality), and 61 (attitudes toward religions).

Elsewhere

Brandt, Mark J., and Daryl R. Van Tongeren. "People Both High and Low on Religious Fundamentalism Are Prejudiced toward Dissimilar Groups." *Journal of Personality and Social Psychology* 112(1) (2017): 76–97.

Cowgill, Colleen M., Kimberly Rios, and Ain Simpson. "Generous Heathens? Reputational Concerns and Atheists' Behavior toward Christians in Economic Games." *Journal of Experimental Social Psychology* 73 (2017): 169–179.

Hall, Deborah. L., David. C. Matz, and Wendy Wood. "Why Don't We Practice What We Preach? A Meta-analytic Review of Religious Racism." *Personality and Social Psychology Review* 14(1) (2010): 126–139.

Silver, Christopher F., Thomas J. Coleman III, Ralph W. Hood Jr., and Jenny M. Holcombe. "The Six Types of Nonbelief: A Qualitative and Quantitative Study of Type and Narrative." *Mental Health, Religion & Culture* 17(10) (2014): 990–1001.

Ståhl, Tomas, Maarten P. Zaal, and Linda J. Skitka. "Moralized Rationality: Relying on Logic and Evidence in the Formation and Evaluation of Belief Can Be Seen as a Moral Issue." *PLOS One* 11 (2016): e0166332.

Užarević, Filip, and Thomas J. Coleman III. "The Psychology of Nonbelievers." *Current Opinion in Psychology* 40 (2020): 131–138.

Užarević, Filip, Vassilis Saroglou, and Isabelle Pichon. "Rejecting Opposite Ideologies without Discriminating against Ideological Opponents? Understanding Nonbelievers' Outgroup Attitudes." *Basic and Applied Social Psychology* 42(1) (2020): 62–77.

Whitley, Bernard E., Jr. "Religiosity and Attitudes toward Lesbians and Gay Men: A Meta-analysis." *International Journal for the Psychology of Religion* 19(1) (2009): 21–38.

61

Do atheists value some religions more than other religions?

Joel Thiessen and Sarah Wilkins-Laflamme

A universal answer to this question is complicated because atheists around the world have different exposures to and experiences with a variety of religions, sometimes positive, sometimes negative, and sometimes just characterized by indifference. In some nations or regions, the majority religion could be Christianity or Islam or Sikhism. In other settings, those who do not believe in God form a majority, like in Norway since 2016. In other contexts still, atheists are expressly discriminated against because they do not believe in a god or supernatural being.

For our answer, we will focus on Canada and the United States. Here, atheists are inclined to value religions that are perceived to be more "inclusive" and tolerant—most notably, Buddhism—while reserving their disdain for religions believed to be "exclusive" and intolerant, including notably Evangelical Christians, Muslims, Catholics, Mormons, and Jehovah's Witnesses. To better understand what is meant by "inclusive" and "exclusive," consider the following quotations from personal interviews with atheists in Calgary, Alberta, Canada:

> When you talk to people, especially in the **Catholic** Church . . . there was a lot of fear stuff, and I . . . could never quite believe that I needed to be afraid of something. . . . I could never quite believe the hell part. Maybe the heaven part. That sounded kind of nice, but the hell? I don't think so. There's no fire burning there. (Faye, early fifties)

> **Evangelical** organization . . . it's too bad your parents aren't Christian . . . cultish . . . blind worshipping. . . . You can believe whatever you want, but always keep your mind open, asking questions. As soon as anybody says to you, "Don't ask, just obey," that to me is a huge warning sign just to back away from that. It seemed to me that

it was a whole lot of just worship. . . . There was no critical thinking
in it. (Sandra, midfifties)

The **Muslim** can't marry outside your religion. . . . It's like, "Oh, if I
like this girl, I have to become Muslim." . . . If you're a Muslim, you
can't marry . . . like, what the hell not, like what makes me not good
enough anymore? Just because I'm not in the same religion, . . . the
Muslim is, like, not being able to marry outside your circle. . . . And
then . . . having your wife wear the shawl . . . you can see the control
on the woman. . . . Like, it's you have to follow this, and it's like, "Oh,
it's . . . her choice." . . . Yeah, it's her choice because you brainwash
her into thinking it was her choice. . . . I mean, the **Buddhist** . . . is
something that I would identify more towards . . . because they don't
have, per se, as much written, . . . and then they're not as destructive
as **Muslim** and **Catholic**. . . . Like, that one is a lot more peaceful, and
it's like inner peace. (Patrick, early thirties)

Buddhism . . . [I like] their gentleness about the world and their
beliefs that way. And a lot of the **Christian** history and the **Muslim**
history, there's a lot of violence. (Tracie, late thirties)

Since 2015, scholars in the United States and Canada have given more
attention to how those who say they have "no religion" view different
religious groups. Atheists are a subgroup within the larger "religious none"
category, and we have some survey data to further our knowledge on this
topic. In a 2017 Pew Research Center survey where respondents rated
different religious groups along a "feelings thermometer," with 0 indicating
the coldest feelings and 100 representing the warmest feelings, atheists
gave their lowest score to Evangelical Christians (35) and their highest
ranking to Buddhists (73). Interestingly, in regions where there are more
Evangelical Christians (e.g., American South), atheists scored Evangelicals
even lower.

Data of this kind in Canada is limited to religious nones on the whole
rather than atheists in particular, though the same story line is evident
there as well. When asked to give a positive (+1), neutral (0), or negative
(−1) feeling rating toward different religious groups in a 2015 Angus Reid
Institute survey, religious nones scored groups in the following way: Evangelicals (−40), Mormons (−35), Muslims (−28), Roman Catholics (−9),
Sikhs (−9), Protestants (+5), Jews (+6), Hindus (+8), and Buddhists (+38).

But why do atheists value some religions more than others? As we
intimated at the outset, social environment matters greatly, including

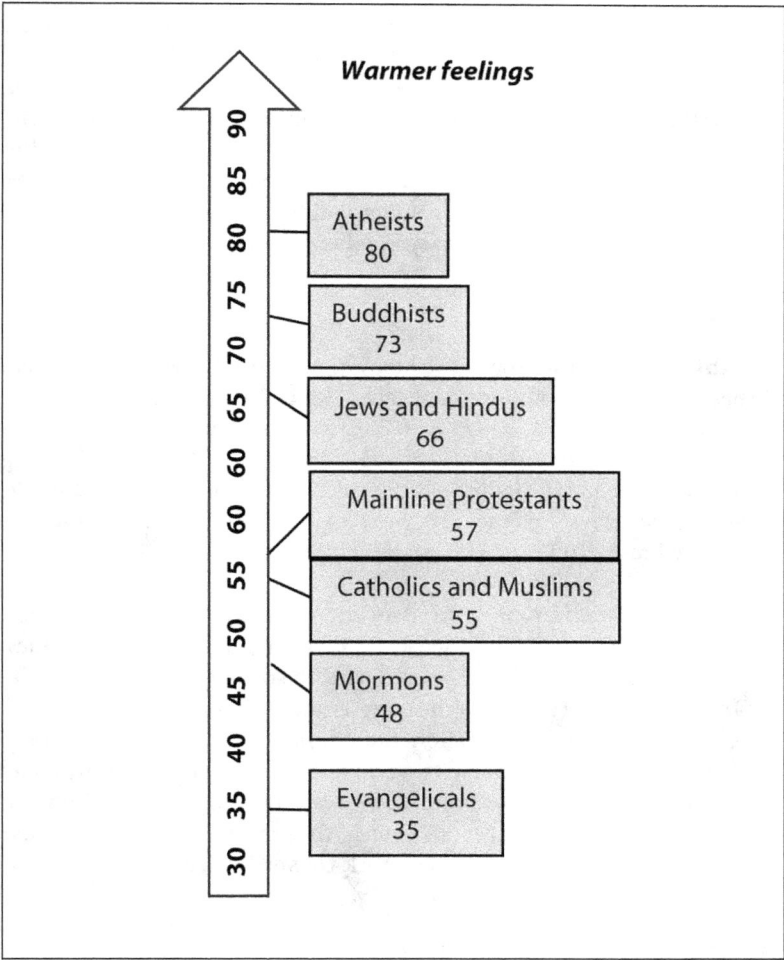

Figure 61.1. Average feeling thermometer scores among atheists, Pew American Trends Panel, January 2017, N = 553.

a nation's historical and political context, media coverage of different religions, and one's family and friends. Atheists in different regions of the world value certain religions more than others, in part, because of the dominant religion that surrounds them—and this value ascribed to a particular religion could be high or low, depending on how the dominant religion views and treats atheists specifically or nonmembers more generally. In addition, media coverage that portrays some religions more positively or negatively shapes people's perceptions of certain religions being more inclusive or exclusive. Finally, individuals tend to view other religions based on how they were raised in their families to think about those religions and, in turn, tend to choose their closest friends based on those who tend to view the world similarly. Simply put, an atheist's social environment plays a powerful role to shape their perceptions of different religions, which is why the religions that atheists value vary in different corners of the world.

About the authors

Joel Thiessen is a professor of sociology at Ambrose University (Canada). He has authored or coauthored several books, including *None of the Above: Nonreligious Identity in the US and Canada* (New York University Press, 2020), *The Millennial Mosaic: How Pluralism and Choice Are Shaping Canadian Youth and the Future of Canada* (Dundurn Press, 2019), and *The Meaning of Sunday: The Practice of Belief in a Secular Age* (McGill-Queen's University Press, 2015).

Sarah Wilkins-Laflamme is an associate professor in the Department of Sociology and Legal Studies at the University of Waterloo (Canada). She completed her DPhil (PhD equivalent) in sociology at the University of Oxford in 2015. Her research interests include quantitative methods, sociology of religion, immigration and ethnicity, and political sociology. She has authored or coauthored two books, including *Religion, Spirituality and Secularity among Millennials: The Generation Shaping American and Canadian Trends* (Routledge, 2022) and *None of the Above: Nonreligious Identity in the US and Canada* (New York University Press, 2020).

Suggestions for further reading

In this book
See also chapters 37 (converting), 60 (tolerant), and 62 (value in religion).

Elsewhere
Angus Reid Institute. "Religion and Faith in Canada Today: Strong Belief, Ambivalence and Rejection Define Our Views." http://angusreid.org/wp -content/uploads/2016/01/2015.03.25_Faith.pdf.

Edgell, Penny, Joseph Gerteis, and Douglas Hartmann. "Atheists as 'Other': Moral Boundaries and Cultural Membership in American Society." *American Sociological Review* 71(2) (2006): 211–234.

Thiessen, Joel, and Sarah Wilkins-Laflamme. *None of the Above: Nonreligious Identity in the US and Canada.* New York: New York University Press, 2020.

Williamson, David A., and George Yancey. *There Is No God: Atheists in America.* Lanham, MD: Rowman & Littlefield, 2013.

62
What do atheists value in religion, if anything?

Teemu Taira

It is not uncommon to see atheists and liberal Christians join forces against more conservative religious groups. This applies especially to relatively secular societies where atheists do not generally feel discriminated against and focus on fighting against more extreme or restrictive views. However, at the beginning of the twenty-first century, one of the main messages of the "New Atheists" was that liberal believers are partially responsible for the success of "fundamentalism" because liberal believers maintain that it is appropriate to believe in supernatural beings without evidence. At the same time, some "New Atheists" themselves saw something valuable in religions.

Sam Harris's vitriolic criticism against monotheistic religions in his *The End of Faith* (2004) contained very positive views about spirituality and the wisdom of the East. Harris had traveled to India and Nepal after college and studied with Hindu and Buddhist teachers, and he wrote about the value of spiritual and mystical experiences that are rare, significant, and personally transformative. He called spiritual practices genuinely desirable, yet at the same time, he insisted that they are deeply rational and universal, something that binds people together, whereas religious irrationality divides people.

Harris was not alone in this. Victor Stenger, an emeritus professor of physics and astronomy, called himself the fifth New Atheist (after four others: Dawkins, Dennett, Harris, and Hitchens) and suggested that Buddhist and other Eastern teachings are still applicable today. He continued that meditation and other practices have the same positive effect, even when stripped of any supernatural baggage. A similar message was delivered by other commentators (e.g., Steve Antinoff in his *Spiritual Atheism*, 2009) about the compatibility of atheism and spirituality, especially meditation practices. Ten years after his first book, Harris published another about the importance of spirituality, entitled *Waking Up: A Guide to Spirituality without Religion* (2014).

A common trope among the mentioned authors is that spirituality without supernatural elements is valuable but religion is not. However, other self-identifying atheists have argued that established religious institutions and communities have a certain value, even for those who do not believe in the existence of God. For instance, French philosopher André Comte-Sponville writes in *The Little Book of Atheist Spirituality* (2007) about the relevance of spirituality for atheists but also suggests that even monotheistic religions may provide useful resources for them. The need for rituals at key moments in life persists even for atheists, and because atheistic rituals have not developed satisfactorily enough, existing ritual structures may prove to be significant for both atheists and religious people. Writing about French Catholicism, he agrees that their rituals are part of the tradition of marking important passages of life and binding people together. This approach is common in several parts of Europe, especially in the Nordic countries, where people are relatively happy to be members of the majority church, even when they do not believe in its doctrines. People are passive in participation, but they value the work churches do—upholding traditions, maintaining public discussions on a good life and the common good, and providing services for those who need them. This is what sociologists of religion have variously called "vicarious religion" or "cultural religion," implying that religious institutions can be appreciated even by atheists because of their social functions.

In the public debate on atheism, perhaps the most substantial recent atheistic defense of the value of religious institutions has been presented by the Swiss-born philosopher Alain de Botton in his *Religion for Atheists: A Non-believer's Guide to the Uses of Religion* (2012). He highlights how religious art and architecture have had a significant effect in increasing our imaginative powers and reflection and how "secular" art and architecture might learn from them. He also notes the value that religious traditions place on education, learning, morality, kindness, and tenderness. Most crucial, however, is the atheists' need to learn to cope better with mental and bodily suffering and the challenges of community. Regarding the latter, de Botton clarifies how inspiration from communal meals by religious communities, other means of strengthening bonds of affection, and welcoming of strangers might improve everyone's life independently of the presence or absence of belief in God. Overall, de Botton does not argue that these aspects can only be maintained within a religious context; he suggests that atheists should value these things that religious institutions underline and learn from them.

It has been typical in the recent decades for people to speculate and debate about what value religious institutions may have for atheists, if anything. It is much less common to find examples in which the presented ideas are enacted in practice. However, there has been one major attempt in the 2010s. The Sunday Assembly, founded in Britain in 2013, has spread to several parts of the (mainly Anglophone) world in the succeeding years. The organizing idea around the "atheist church" or "godless congregation" is that a communal celebration of life is a significant part of our existence. In practice, the Sunday Assembly has focused on meetings that include singing together, taking time for reflection, listening to talks, and just spending time together. The movement gained a lot of media interest and expanded for a couple of years, but more recently, it seems to have dried up.

What is left out of these discussions but present elsewhere is the possible historical value that religious traditions and institutions may have for our present-day societies. Several theologians suggest that without Christianity, there would not be universal human rights, democracy, or other values, which many of us take for granted. While the historical emergence of values is a relevant object of study, the debate often takes a strongly normative twist in defending religious institutions. The questions that are rarely raised are in what sense the debated values in religions are values that would be there without the particular religious history and whether a particular religion can claim ownership of such values.

On this basis, it could be answered that some atheists see the relevance in meditation practices and community building. Others value the ability of religious institutions to offer support for life passages, provide services that other societal institutions do not offer, and participate in public discussions about the common good. Yet others appreciate the historical contribution religious traditions may have made to present-day societies. Critics maintain that all the benefits are attainable without religious traditions and institutions.

About the author

Teemu Taira is a senior lecturer in the study of religion at the University of Helsinki.

Suggestions for further reading

In this book
See also chapters 40 (members), 57 (ritual), 58 (spiritual), and 61 (attitudes toward religions).

Elsewhere

Botton, Alain de. *Religion for Atheists: A Non-believer's Guide to the Uses of Religion*. London: Hamilton, 2012.

Mortimer, Tim, and Mel Prideaux. "Exploring Identities between the Religious and the Secular through the Attendees of an Ostensibly 'Atheist Church.'" *Religion* 48(1) (2018): 64–82.

Smith, Jesse. "Communal Secularity: Congregational Work at the Sunday Assembly." In *Organized Secularism in the United States*, edited by Ryan T. Cragun, Christel Manning, and Lori L. Fazzino, 151–170. Berlin: De Gruyter, 2017.

Taira, Teemu. "Atheist Spirituality: A Follow-On from New Atheism?" In *Post-secular Religious Practices*, edited by Tore Ahlbäck, 388–404. Turku: Donner Institute for Research in Religious and Cultural History, 2012. https://journal.fi/scripta/article/view/67423.

63

Is atheism good for your health?

Kevin McCaffree and Anondah Saide

This is an interesting question, but first, we must consider why atheism and health might be related in the first place. Atheism is a quite simple concept: it is simply the *absence of belief in deities*. An atheist can be a healthy person or an unhealthy person. Asking "Is atheism good for your health?" is a little bit like asking "Is individualism good for your health?" It might be, but it might not be. It depends on the person and how the belief impacts other aspects of their life.

A fruitful way to think about this question is to consider it from a more nuanced perspective: "Under what conditions might atheism be associated with good health, be associated with poor health, or be unrelated to health?"

A substantial amount of prior research on this topic has found that being religious is associated with positive outcomes, such as improved mental (e.g., reduced anxiety and depression), physical (e.g., lower rates of disease), and behavioral (e.g., lower risk-taking) health. In fact, studies so consistently find such linkages that researchers often take these relationships as a given. However, in the last two decades, researchers have come to understand that they were overlooking an important hidden explanation for the link between religiosity and improved health: social connection. For the most part, strong believers in god tend to be frequent attenders of church, and by attending church frequently, they form social bonds and engage in reciprocal, supportive interactions with other like-minded believers. It turns out that *this* is what seems to have been driving the association between religiosity and health—integration into a supportive social community.

Think about it. A person who attends church frequently has consistent access to others who can be relied on for advice, monetary assistance, and other forms of support during challenging and uncertain times. Frequent church attenders can ask other church members for help watching their children, finding a job, or mending a marriage teetering on divorce.

Churches in the United States and elsewhere have been, first and foremost, community hubs facilitating the social integration of people into mainstream society. Thus, the belief in God may not *cause* healthiness. Rather, perceiving social support from others may lead to feeling confident in one's ability to adapt to the uncertainty and challenges of life and to regulate their emotions, all of which can facilitate healthy coping and healthy decision-making.

Having said this, we can now consider in a bit more detail when atheism might be bad for your health, when it might be unrelated to your health, and when it might be good for your health. First, let's consider when atheism might be bad for your health. Though the research evidence suggests that traditional religiosity is declining all over the world today, this was not always the case. And in many parts of many countries, traditional religiosity remains dominant. Imagine being an atheist in a community where everyone (or most everyone) else is fervently religious. Consider how lonely and isolating this might feel.

And what if the atheist speaks out about how they feel? What if they express their lack of belief in a god or gods? In a highly religious social environment, such expressions might lead to stigma, discrimination, or, worse, outright hostility and violence. In a highly religious social environment, being an atheist is synonymous with being a deviant outcast. The research clearly shows that, under these circumstances, being an atheist is likely not very good for your physical health or psychological well-being. Even if one keeps their atheism to themselves, self-doubt or self-criticism for being different from others might also lead to poor health or social isolation. For example, a study conducted in 2015 by Heather Kugelmass and Alfredo Garcia found that nonreligious adolescents with religious parents were twice as likely as religious adolescents with religious parents to suffer from mental disorders. The authors suggest that this effect may be due to conflict with parents over religious participation.

However, in other circumstances, atheism might be neutral with regard to health. Some researchers have suggested that many atheists are, really, apatheists, or "apathetic atheists." This includes people who take for granted that gods do not exist or simply don't care about the topic. As a result, atheism might not be particularly central to their sense of self-identity. People like this may prefer to think about topics other than religions, gods, or the lack thereof; perhaps they'd prefer to think about politics or their hobbies or forming new friendships. Indeed, a growing body of research suggests that those with a strong atheist self-identity are responding to highly religious contexts. On the other hand, if most everyone around you is either an atheist or indifferent to the question of the existence of god(s), it makes little sense to proudly proclaim, or identify closely with, your atheism. In these circumstances, atheism tends to be unrelated to health. And indeed, many studies reveal no significant relationship between atheism and health.

Finally, there are, of course, circumstances where researchers would expect atheism to be related to improved health. If someone has a strong interest in the philosophy or history of atheism or if they're just seeking to meet other atheists like themselves, they might join a club or social group and effectively integrate themselves into a social community. For the same reason that religiosity can be related to positive health outcomes, so too can an interest in atheism be a precursor for building supportive social contacts with others sharing similar interests.

Once integrated into such a community, when the vicissitudes of life inevitably cause suffering—be it divorce, illness, joblessness, or some other difficulty—those in the community can be relied on for support. In a community, people look out for one another, offer to help one another, and willingly sacrifice time and money to provide aid when it is needed. Just the same, social groups of all kinds (not just churches) have rituals and habits associated with group membership, which can confer a sense of predictability and order to life. In these circumstances, we would expect atheism to be positively related to physical health and psychological well-being.

In conclusion, we want to reiterate the importance of thinking flexibly and with nuance when it comes to associating any ideology or outlook with health. It is unlikely that ideologies or outlooks directly cause changes in health absent a consideration of circumstances or context. Perhaps there are exceptions—a (bizarre) belief that fast food is the healthiest food might cause unhealthiness, but even here, how much fast food the person eats, which type of fast food, and whether they exist in a network of people who exercise will all be mitigating factors. Remember, no matter what, context matters.

About the authors

Kevin McCaffree is an associate professor at the University of North Texas in the Department of Sociology.

Anondah Saide is an assistant professor at the University of North Texas in the Department of Educational Psychology.

Suggestions for further reading

In this book
See also chapters 38 (discrimination), 40 (members), and 52 (mortality).

Elsewhere
Kugelmass, Heather, and Alfredo Garcia. "Mental Disorder among Nonreligious Adolescents." *Mental Health, Religion & Culture* 18(5) (2015): 368–379.

McCaffree, Kevin. "Atheism, Social Networks and Health: A Review and Theoretical Model." *Secularism and Nonreligion* 8 (2019). https://secularismandnonreligion.org/articles/10.5334/snr.101/.

Future

64
What is the future of atheism?

Teemu Taira

In 2015, the Pew Research Center published a report in which the future landscape of religion was sketched out. Data from the early 2000s was used to project what the situation would be in 2050. Despite all the recent stories and studies about the rise of the "nones," the report suggested that the relative amount of nonreligious people (including atheists) is likely to decrease from 16.4 percent in 2010 to 13.2 percent in 2050. How can this be the case?

The demographic projection was based on two key factors, current age structures and fertility rates, but it also took expected conversion rates and migration into account. The median age of the unaffiliated (who are not the same as atheists) was thirty-four, whereas the global median age was twenty-eight. Of the religious identities included in the study, only Jews (thirty-six) were older than the unaffiliated (Buddhists were also thirty-four); on the younger end, the median age of Muslims was twenty-three. Furthermore, religious people tend to have higher fertility rates. This applies especially to Muslims, who are projected to increase their percentage from 23.2 to 29.7. This is not simply an issue of developed countries with low fertility rates and developing countries with high fertility rates. Even on the same continent, religious people tend to have a higher fertility rate than the unaffiliated.

Due to migration and religious switching, it is projected that the share of the unaffiliated is growing everywhere except in Asia. In Europe and North America, the unaffiliated are at a disadvantage because of the migration, but switching from religious status to unaffiliated is so common that the overall share of the latter is projected to grow from 12.4 to 13.2 percent in Europe and from 5.2 to 9 percent in the United States. The share of unaffiliated is projected to grow especially in France, the United Kingdom, the United States, and Japan, for example.

Although the Pew report's projection is plausible, suggesting that religiosity will increase in the long run because the most secular areas and secular individuals will not meet the replacement rate (usually considered 2.1 children per woman), there are reasons to nuance the picture. Namely, the predictive models are based on what we know and can measure. If something unexpected happens, it can affect the measured object or the measures used—for instance, it is not hard to imagine a global catastrophe in a particular area that would change the age structure of a particular religion or a highly contagious virus drastically decreasing the fertility among people living in a certain area. Even in a "normal" situation, fertility rates can go up and down in a short time period.

The fertility rates are low in most secular societies, but they have dropped dramatically in some more religious areas too, such as in Asia, Latin America, and some Muslim-majority countries. An example of the latter is Iran, where the total fertility rate (TFR) was around 6.5 children per woman in 1982 and today stands below 1.7—lower than in many European countries. Although the connection between fertility and religion is complex, it is largely agreed that decreasing TFR tends to correspond to declining religious commitment. In other words, some traditionally very religious areas are expected to secularize if the fertility rate continues as at present. This does not apply to the whole world—the TFR is 5–6 in several African countries—but it suggests that the contrasting picture of an ever-secularizing Europe and North America and the rest of the world as fervently religious is way too simplistic.

Despite the demographic disadvantage, the trend has been toward increasing secularity. This is because people have increasingly abandoned religion, and the retention rate of nonreligious people has become greater. As Joseph Baker and Buster Smith argue, it is partly for these reasons that the number of "nones" has tripled in a short time in the United States. It remains to be seen how these matters will develop in the future, but in the United States, for example, the popularity of atheism is expected to stabilize, unless the apostasy rate continues to rise for some currently unknown reason. Even so, Baker and Smith predict that there will be about 27 percent of "nones" in the United States in 2050—a much higher estimation than in the Pew report, mainly because their analysis was based on later data. Only some will be atheists, but the comparison of different predictions of the unaffiliated suggests that atheism will continue to be a significant minority position in the future, both in the United States and globally.

A further aspect is that even if religious people keep outnumbering nonreligious ones, the overall impact will depend on who will fill powerful leading positions in society. If the influencers and decision-makers are atheists, an increase in the social significance of religion would still not follow from a possibly decreasing percentage of the nonreligious. Societies are not automatically organized on the basis of the majority's preferences.

The general theories predicting the future should be complemented with a detailed understanding of national and regional histories, assuming that it is in our interest to detect nuances in the "big picture." For instance, the fertility rate in Poland fell below the replacement level already in the 1980s, and the country's economy has boomed, but the country's religious development has not echoed other Catholic nations in Europe. Instead, Poland remains one of the most religious nations in Europe. Poland is an exception, and it may be a case of delayed decline in religion, but the current situation shows that more contextualized knowledge is needed to understand the present in the same way that it is needed to anticipate the future in particular countries. Furthermore, we should not discount the possibility that forthcoming political events, societal movements, and even individual intellectuals may strongly contribute to the short-term future of atheism at least.

Moreover, when the future of atheism is measured, it varies a lot depending on what is being talked about. Religious practices have been in decline for decades in many societies, as have membership rates in religious institutions. Religious beliefs connected to a particular institution or tradition have been declining too, particularly in Europe, but that does not mean that all supernatural or counterintuitive beliefs are going to go away. Religious identification has declined steeply in some countries, whereas it remains high especially when such identification is or has been strongly tied to national identity. However, none of this automatically makes atheist identification markedly more popular. People may technically be atheists without finding atheist identification to be relevant. Especially in regions that are already highly secular, the term "atheism" may lose its relevance as an identity. In very religious areas, atheist identification is a statement about one's minority position, and sometimes it can be socially costly or even dangerous. All these analytically distinct issues may go hand in hand in some contexts and be separate in others. This makes the anticipation of the future of atheism incredibly complicated.

In addition, many predictions have turned out to be wrong, mainly because unexpected changes have happened. This applies to any area of life, religion and atheism included. The social scientists of the 1950s did not predict the swift secularization of the 1960s. Neither did the social scientists of the 1990s anticipate the rise of the "nones" in the 2000s and 2010s—for instance, a study predicted in 2010 that the percentage of the "nones" would stay under 18 in the United States between 2003 and 2043, whereas soon after the study was published, it stood at over 25 percent.

One can better rely on the current predictive models if one considers that nothing will surprise us in the forthcoming years, yet writing this in the middle of the COVID-19 pandemic makes it even more difficult to think that the future does not have any surprises for us.

Whatever one thinks about the utility of predictive models concerning the future of atheism, it is wise to be skeptical of their certainty. If the models are not as reliable as they are claimed to be, it is a healthy attitude to ask what functions the predictive models have. Do they function as strategic arguments in favor of some policies rather than detached and neutral calculations about the future? In any case, it can be asked why some predictions are considered relevant at the present moment and for what purpose. What sorts of polity decisions are proposed on their basis? This is not to deny the informative dimension of reflections on the future of atheism. Rather, it is to argue that the predictive models are not as innocuous as some policy makers—or even scholars—would like us to believe.

About the author

Teemu Taira is a senior lecturer in the study of religion at the University of Helsinki.

Suggestions for further reading

In this book
See also chapters 22 (most atheistic societies), 23 (why are societies atheistic), and 26 (young people).

Elsewhere
Baker, Joseph O., and Buster G. Smith. *American Secularism: Cultural Contours of Nonreligious Belief Systems*. New York: New York University Press, 2015.

Inglehart, Ronald F. *Religion's Sudden Decline: What's Causing It, and What Comes Next?* Oxford: Oxford University Press, 2021.

Jenkins, Philip. *Fertility and Faith: The Demographic Revolution and the Transformation of World Religions*. Waco: Baylor University Press, 2020.

Pew Research Center. "The Future of World Religions: Population Growth Projections, 2010–2050." 2015. https://assets.pewresearch.org/wp-content/uploads/sites/11/2015/03/PF_15.04.02_ProjectionsFullReport.pdf.

Index

www.ingramcontent.com/pod-product-compliance
Lightning Source LLC
Chambersburg PA
CBHW070757270326
41927CB00010B/2178